Targets
for Research
in Library Education

Also edited by
HAROLD BORKO

Computer Applications in the Behavioral Sciences (1962)
Automated Language Processing (1967)
Computers and the Problems of Society,
  with Harold Sackman (1972)

Targets
for Research
in Library Education

Harold Borko
Editor

American Library Association
Chicago 1973

The research reported herein was performed pursuant to a contract with the Office of Education, U.S. Department of Health, Education, and Welfare. Contractors undertaking such projects under government sponsorship are encouraged to express freely their professional judgment in the conduct of the project. Points of view or opinions stated do not, therefore, necessarily represent official Office of Education position or policy.

Library of Congress Cataloging in Publication Data

Borko, Harold.
    Targets for research in library education.

    Includes bibliographies.
    1. Library education.   2. Library science—
Research. I. Title.
Z668.B722   020'.72   72-9923
ISBN 0-8389-0098-4

International Standard Book Number 0–8389–0098–4 (1973)
Library of Congress Catalog Card Number 72–9923

                          Printed in the United States of America

Contents

Frank L. Schick   vii   Preface: Library-Related Research

    xiii   Acknowledgments

Harold Borko   1   Introduction

Part One: Identifying Needed Research

Jesse H. Shera   9   The Aims and Content of Graduate Library Education

James Krikelas and Margaret E. Monroe   31   General vs. Specialized Library Education

Gerald Jahoda   49   The Integration of Information Science and Library Automation into the Library School Educational Program

Irving Lieberman   65   Relating Instructional Methodology to Teaching in Library Schools

Robert B. Downs   86   Library School Administration

Lucille Whalen   100   Library School Faculty and Students

Agnes L. Reagan   116   The Relationships of Professional Associations to Library Schools and Libraries

Page Ackerman   130   The Library School and Requirements
                                 for Staffing Libraries

James J. Kortendick, S.S. 145   Continuing Education for Librarians

Leon Carnovsky   173   Research Needs Relating to the Role
                                 of the Library in the Community

Part Two: Determining Research Priorities

Kevin D. Reilly   187   The Delphi Technique: Fundamentals
                                 and Applications

Harold Borko   201   Predicting Research Needs in Library
                                 and Information Science Education

                          229   Subject Index

                          235   Index of Names

Frank L. Schick

Preface: Library-Related Research

Few librarians and library educators who criticize research relating to their fields realize in 1972 how far research has progressed during the last decade and a half. The criticism usually relates to the recognition that librarianship is more of a service and less of a fact-finding field of endeavor and that librarians are primarily trained to assist in the research activities of others rather than to conduct their own. One can add here that the average librarian who spends about forty hours a week on his job not always has the stamina to spend his free time on original research or the writing of proposals, which either are not adequately funded or are not published with the prominence hoped for. If the librarian-researcher commits his findings to writing, he is occasionally criticized for writing poorly or for having dwelled on topics of limited interest to the reviewer. Or he finds that while many praise his work there are no funds, possibilities, or opportunities to translate his conclusions into action.

However, during the 1950s, the climate for library-related research underwent definite but subtle changes due to the influence of the doctoral library programs, particularly among the faculty and students at the University of Chicago and Columbia University. From these two centers, the concern for research spread to other library schools. Of particular relevance here is the establishment of library research centers, which were started at Case Western Reserve in 1955 and were developed in 1961 at the University of Illinois, in 1962 at the University of Pittsburgh, in 1963 at the University of California, and reached other universities such as Maryland before the end of the 1960s.

Through these activities, based in library schools, faculty members from other disciplines were drawn to library research. Among the first projects were the studies headed by Robert D. Leigh, sponsored by the Committee on Freedom of the Press and the Public Library Inquiry, which introduced several new factors.

Funds were made available by private foundations which made possible the freeing of competent researchers temporarily from other activities. Team research partially replaced individual efforts and resulted in speedier investigations of wider scope. Funds for publishing could be obtained more easily. Practitioners in the library profession started to combine with nonlibrarian specialists to produce significant results. The leadership role of the Library of Congress was brought to bear on many of these problems when, in 1956, Verner Clapp was appointed President of the Council on Library Resources, Inc. Clapp initiated the first major approach to funded library research, which was expanded by the U.S. Office of Education beginning around 1959, and which has continued to the present.

Information about library-related research, however, had no recognized outlet, and research in progress as well as the findings of completed studies were scattered among many journals, with the exception of doctoral dissertations, which were regularly listed in *The Library Quarterly*. Usually, the most up-to-date information about research was carried in the heads or notebooks of library school faculty members. This fact was demonstrated at a meeting of the Detroit Area Librarians in the late 1950s. Dr. Maurice F. Tauber of Columbia's School of Library Service had been invited to talk for about an hour on library research. The audience refused to let him leave for more than twice the stipulated time—a tribute not only to the speaker, his knowledge, and presentation, but an indication of intense general interest in the subject and its relationship to day-to-day operations.

The coordination of library research reporting
   (from LiRiP to LIST)

When joining the Library Services Branch of the U.S. Office of Education in 1958 with the primary responsibility of coordinating U.S. library research and statistics, I prepared a proposal, which, in the following year, resulted in the publication *Library Research in Progress (LiRiP)*, released irregularly in fourteen issues from 1959 to 1964.

After five years of the LiRiP operation, which covered about 85 to 90 percent of the country's library-related research effort, we concluded from the 902 projects studied that the research output represented an investment of nearly $8¾ million, half of which (51.2 percent) was funded by various government agencies, one-third (31.8 percent) by the Council on Library Resources, Inc., and the remaining 15 percent by various agencies and foundations.

From the same data base, it was obvious that two-thirds of the projects were conducted by employees of academic institutions. Degree candidates contributed 42 percent, library school faculty members 10 percent, other faculty members 8 percent, and college and university librarians 7 percent. Of all projects reported only 8 percent dealt directly with library personnel and training. After LiRiP was phased out, the American Library Association tried to continue to collect the same information about library research in progress but never published it. The trend to report ongoing research with emphasis on information science was continued with a different slant in the National Science Foundation's *Current Research and Development in Scientific Information,* which ceased in 1968.

At present there are various reporting systems in existence. Wasserman (1970) points out that:

> The *Yearbook* of the Library Association of Great Britain inventories research in progress in British librarianship, restricting its scope to that one nation. The *Journal of Education for Librarianship* incorporates information about dissertations in progress at American library schools. . . . The Science Information Exchange offers a retrieval program for research in the sciences, natural and physical, as well as social and behavioral, although the data in the files are not issued in published form. . . . The Committee on Scientific and Technical Information (COSATI) has, from time to time, commissioned research inventories in the broad field of information science under the direction of its more important committees, but this data tends to be of limited types of effort and has not been available for general use. . . . The ERIC Center in Librarianship and Information Science . . . more recently, functioning under the aegis of the American Society for Information Science, is an ongoing program dedicated to gathering information about efforts in the field, relying particularly upon documentation, rather than work in progress as the basis for its reporting. The principal abstracting and indexing services of the field, *Library and Information Abstracts, Information Science Abstracts,* and *Library Literature,* also inventory publications in the broad field, but do not go beyond the literature.

Wasserman concludes with justification that:

> In spite of the fact that there have been and are in existence a very wide range of resources operative informally attempting to bring intelligence about research and innovation in the field into focus, none was intended to cover fully the field of librarianship and information

science and to provide access to information about unpublished efforts across the broad spectrum with any regular frequency.

To fill the existing information gap with emphasis on research in progress, Wasserman (1971) started "LIST," which continues with minor variations where LiRiP left off in 1965.

During the last fifteen years, there has been significant expansion and intensification of all phases of library research, including the library education component. It is then possible to relate *Targets for Research in Library Education* with its antecedents. The *Library Trends* issue of October 1957, entitled "Research in Librarianship," edited by Maurice F. Tauber, summarized in Tauber's introduction the salient points of the issue. Three of these relate to library education:

> Basic examinations are needed of all aspects of library education—programs, curricula, instructional methods, relations between performance on the job and library school training, and the place of the library school in the structure of higher education.

> Library school faculties, particularly those associated with institutions having advanced or doctoral programs, have a special responsibility for the development of integrated programs of research.

> Financial support is necessary for qualified students who need to be free from day-to-day work responsibilities if they are to complete investigations which would be useful to the profession.

The first of these statements could have motivated the development of the present publication. The second and third are as relevant today as when written. The same journal issue contained a paper by Lowell Martin (1957) on "Research in Education of Librarianship," which contains a paragraph which Tauber says served as the theme for the issue.

> *Research Produces Knowledge.* Knowledge is needed for understanding. Understanding combined with skill leads to effective action. It is hardly necessary to add that this neat progression from inquiry to decision is not the natural law of life. On the contrary, the process often works in reverse. Aristotle did not say that the rational life is prevalent; he simply said that it is best.

Martin provides some additional insights which deserve to be cited:

> The man of action starts with decision and not with inquiry, and he may display limited understanding and actually scorn research. The intellectual lives in the sphere of understanding, gained through background and insight; he expects action to correspond with understanding (and because it does not, he is often at odds with life around him),

and he expects research to confirm his previous insight (and because of this is often not a good research man). Confronted with a job that needs doing, the practical man acts, the intellectual reflects, only the research man investigates. This is an oversimplification, for in practice the several levels do and indeed should run together.

But this formulation reminds us that conduct based on inquiry is neither typical nor natural, but takes special effort and discipline. These distinctions provide a framework within which to place research in education for librarianship. And they serve to warn us that library education will be unusual if research has played a major role in its development.

Robert D. Leigh combined the characteristics of the practical, intellectual, and research-minded educator. He recognized the lack of available information and in 1959 formed a Library School's Committee for Research on Inter-Library Cooperation in the public library field. Representing schools with a doctoral program in librarianship and the Library Services Branch of the U.S. Office of Education, the committee set as its objective the coordination of public library research of faculty members and doctoral candidates to ensure the most effective employment of the limited resources and trained personnel.

To assist the committee in this effort, the Council on Library Resources made a small grant which defrayed the expenses of holding meetings and having reports processed for the members.

Due to the retirement of Leigh and his untimely death in 1961, the committee's work was not completed. However, bibliographic essays by various committee members had been prepared in draft form. These essays indicated which of the research topics were sufficiently covered by the literature and what gaps and omissions existed in the area of public library cooperative activities, which would be corrected through research. The literature surveys covering the years 1955 through 1959 were undertaken by committee members Lester Asheim, Leon Carnovsky, Mary Duncan Isbell, Helen N. Focke, Harold Lancour, Robert D. Leigh, Frank L. Schick, and Ed Wight. In connection with assignments of the University of Illinois Graduate School of Library Science and the Library Services Branch, papers were also prepared by Mary Lee Bundy, Herbert A. Carl, and Evelyn Day Mullen.

John G. Lorenz, as director of the Library Services Branch, maintained a list of research projects. Lists for all types of libraries were compiled as well as in library education and personnel and manpower.

The section on library education was based on a variety of observations and sources including the 1962 Library Manpower Conference at Albany, New York, the Conference on Training Science Information

Specialists at Georgia Institute of Technology, Atlanta, and the Institute on the Future of Library Education at Western Reserve University, Cleveland (*Journal* 1962). As a result of this combined effort, a paper describing research needs on librarianship was published (Schick 1963).

This review indicates the long road on which research efforts have moved to reach the level of sophistication shown and the conclusions presented in the following pages of this volume. If the present publication does not exert a recognizable impact on library science education in the 1970s, it will not be the fault of those who designed and executed this project.*

References

Journal of Education for Librarianship 3:3–80 (Summer 1962).

Martin, Lowell. "Research in Education for Librarianship." *Library Trends* 6:207–18 (Oct. 1957).

Schick, Frank L.; Frantz, John C.; et al. "Library Science Research Needs," *Journal of Education for Librarianship*, 3:280–91 (Spring 1963).

Tauber, Maurice F. "Introduction," *Library Trends* 6:108 (Oct. 1957).

Wasserman, Paul, and Daniel, Evelyn. "The Birth of LIST," *Library Journal* 95:38, 79–83 (15 Nov. 1970).

———, ed. *LIST 1971* (Library and Information Science Today). New York: Science Associates, International, Inc., 1971.

*Publisher's note: Availability of federal funds is important in determining the extent of research pursued in librarianship and library science education, as in other enterprises having a public benefit. The following list indicates federal government appropriations from fiscal years 1967 through 1973.

1967	$3,550,000
1968	$3,550,000
1969	$3,000,000
1970	$2,171,000
1971	$2,171,000
1972	$2,750,000
1973	$1,785,000 (est.)

Acknowledgments

More than most, this study owes whatever virtues it has to a group of devoted individuals who constituted an advisory committee. They are: Rev. James J. Kortendick, Chairman, Catholic University of America; Jack Dalton, Columbia University; Guy Garrison, Drexel Institute of Technology; Irving Klempner, State University of New York at Albany; Patricia Knapp, Wayne State University; Alan M. Rees, Case Western Reserve University; Vladimir Slamecka, Georgia Institute of Technology.

It is with a great deal of gratitude that I acknowledge this debt. However, the advisors are not to be held accountable for any inaccuracies in the report, for the execution of the study was the responsibility of the investigator and his staff.

In addition to the advisory committee, the people who really did the major task of identifying needs in library and information science education are the consultants who wrote the chapters. Without them, there would have been no study. Their work speaks for itself, and I can only add personal thanks for their efforts and cooperation.

A third group of contributors to the success of the study were the many colleagues who responded to not one but two questionnaires. An 80 percent return was achieved—an almost phenomenal rate and a clear indication of the interest our profession has in improving educational practices. To these colleagues, I again say thanks and hope that their efforts bear fruit.

The study was administered through the University of California at Los Angeles Institute of Library Research. The project received strong support from Andrew H. Horn, Dean of the School of Library Service; Robert M. Hayes, director of the Institute of Library Research; Kevin D. Reilly, who served as associate project head; Nancy Brault, librarian and research assistant; and the secretaries, Patricia Honley, Mary King, and Joyce Graves.

Perhaps my most important debt is owed to the U.S. Office of Education, particularly to Kurt Cylke and his successor, Lawrence Papier, at the Library and Information Sciences Research Branch, for their financial support and sponsorship.

The task of carrying out the research has been a very stimulating one, but the real value of the study will be seen in the new research suggested by this project and in the application of the results to library science education.

HAROLD BORKO, Editor
University of California at Los Angeles

Harold Borko

Introduction

Library and information science education is striving to meet the needs for training individuals in what has been called the "information industry." In the process of expanding, the library schools are looking inward as they seek to improve their own administrative procedures, to revise and upgrade their curricula, and to modernize their teaching methods. They wish to change and improve, but what needs to be changed and in what direction? Efforts to create improvements are being hampered by the lack of a comprehensive and integrated body of knowledge which would identify current educational needs and the most effective methods for their achievement. In essence, the research to support innovative educational decision-making is lacking. At a time when the library schools are expanding and searching for a more effective teaching program, the U.S. Office of Education, the Council on Library Resources, and other government and private agencies are receiving requests to support projects in the areas of library and information science. These organizations recognize the need for research and development and are anxious to support appropriate efforts. However, they too are hampered by the lack of a comprehensive plan which would identify the needs and priorities for educational research. Without such a plan, the results obtained from the expenditure of critical intellectual and financial resources would lack direction, and the impact of the studies would be reduced.

The need to improve and enhance the relevance of library and information science education was recognized almost simultaneously by a number of key individuals and organizations. In November 1968, a

1

conference was called to discuss constructive action that should be taken toward solution of the problem. The conveners of this conference were the Reverend James J. Kortendick, the President-Elect of the Association of American Library Schools; Kurt Cylke, acting Chief of the Library and Information Sciences Research Branch of U.S.O.E.; and Foster Mohrhardt of the Council of Library Resources. The conference was held on November 10–11, 1968, at the Villa Cortona in Bethesda, Maryland, under the chairmanship of Father Kortendick, and it was attended by a dozen individuals representing organizations interested and involved in library and information science education.

The discussions that took place at this meeting have been recorded and transcribed and are a matter of record. A number of important decisions were made, among them: (1) The American Association of Library Schools should sponsor and submit a proposal to the Library and Information Sciences Research Branch, U.S. Office of Education, requesting support for a study which would identify needed research in library and information science education; (2) the broad objectives of the study were stated, discussed, and approved; and (3) an advisory committee and ten consultants and a principal investigator were appointed to guide and participate in the study.

Although somewhat more broadly conceived originally, the present study deals with the research needs for education in library science and indicates the data and the research that would be required to fulfill these needs. Educational administrators are aware that they must plan and modify their existing curricula to provide relevant education for the purpose of meeting future needs. The problems those administrators face are: (1) how to determine future requirements, (2) how to identify the areas in which change is needed, (3) how to gather the information on which to base their decisions, and (4) how to implement the desired improvements. In essence, the task is to identify the kinds of research that need to be done to provide information on which to base an innovative educational program. To accomplish this objective, ten recognized leaders in library and information science education were asked to discuss research needs in specified areas. These individuals were asked to write papers:

1. That would identify the problems inherent in the topic under discussion
2. That would specify the information needed in order to answer the questions being asked, to solve the problems that need to be solved, and to provide a basis for choosing between alternative courses of action
3. That would identify the kinds of research that should be undertaken to provide the needed information

4. That would speculate on the effects these research programs could have and how the accumulated data could be utilized to improve the effectiveness of library school educational programs.

These ten papers comprise Part One of this work. In preparing them, the authors were *not* asked to provide solutions. They were asked only to identify the problems, the needed research, and the possible applications of research results to library education. An effort was made to achieve a certain similarity in their organization and structure, although rigid conformity to an arbitrary format was not required. Each author has his own style, and individual forms of expression are preserved in their writing.

Following preparation of the papers, some eighty suggestions for research were gathered by the editor. These were then compared so that duplicate proposals could be either eliminated, combined, or reworked. The resulting number of proposed projects was thirty-six. The research proposals were then evaluated for their importance. In order to establish priorities, the Delphi Technique was used. Part Two contains a general description and explanation of the Delphi Technique. The methods employed, resulting tabulations, and the priorities are described there, but a summary may be stated here.

The priorities were obtained by identifying five broad areas from the ratings derived through use of the questionnaire:

Priority group I—Projects of very great importance: Improving and updating the skills of professional librarians

Priority group II—Projects of great importance: Library school educational planning and relevance

Priority group III—Projects of moderate importance: Administration of the library school and library with regard to specific courses, skills, and programs

Priority group IV—Projects of lesser importance: Forms of instruction and supportive facilities for maintaining instruction

Priority group V—Projects of least importance: The role of professional associations and communication among librarians.

The suggestions for research made in this study are obviously related to the methods used for gathering the original list of research ideas. Other methods could have been used. For example, a search could have been made through the published literature and particularly through theses and dissertations which generally conclude with suggestions for follow-on research. Even using other consultants might have provided a different list. This may be true, but no matter how the list is devised, it could still be open to criticism. The method used in the present study did result in a reasonably comprehensive list of research topics. It is an initial list of research suggestions made at a particular point in time by a selected sample of people in the field of librarianship. There is room for disagreement, and other topics could be suggested, but the opinions of those who suggested these research topics deserve study and consideration. As for the priority ratings, there is strong evidence that Delphi predictions are more accurate than other methods of gathering opinions of ratings. The editor believes that these Delphi ratings provide the most meaningful list of research suggestions that has been compiled for library education to date. One can argue about the exact rank of certain needs, but, overall, this is a statistically reliable listing.

Librarianship and information science constitute an evolving, dynamic field. There is much that needs to be accomplished, and there is healthy controversy on what should be done first and on how it should be done. The proposals of any one person will be unacceptable by equally qualified colleagues. Our field has no supreme authorities; each man stands on feet of clay. The authors of these chapters recognize this fact. They are not writing as oracles, nor are they presenting a final solution. They are presenting thoughtful opinions and making reasonable suggestions. But others—faculty and students—may disagree, and herein lies the value of this book and its usefulness as a text in seminars.

In reviewing the technical report on which this book was based, a number of individuals commented on the overlap of content between some chapters and the apparent inconsistencies between the views of some contributing authors. Some reviewers found these differences disturbing, while others thought them provocative. This is as it should be, for each individual chapter provides an approach and a springboard for discussion. As the students evaluate the proposed research topics and try to formulate these into testable hypotheses—and even more so, as they try to prepare appropriate experimental designs for testing these hypotheses—they will become steeped in the methodology of research. These chapters should stimulate discussion and provide ideas for research.

It may be of interest to explore the use of this book in the classroom. In planning a course of study and preparing a syllabus for a seminar on research methodology in library schools, the editor used *Targets for Research in Library Education* as a text. As an example, it might be helpful to outline some of the ideas on which this course is based.

Students completing the two-year MLS degree at UCLA are required to prepare a research paper of a quality acceptable for publication in one of the standard library journals. The objectives of the seminar in research methodology are to help the student select a problem for study and to help him plan an acceptable research design. This course is usually taken during the second year; thus a participating student has some knowledge of librarianship and its needs.

The seminar begins with the instructor posing the question of how one can study the needs for research in library and information science education. The project on which the textbook is based is discussed and the methodology explained. Each student is asked to choose a topic in library education practice that is of particular interest to him. Generally, these topics coincide closely with one of the chapters in the present volume, e.g., research needs relating to instructional methodology or to library school administration.

The student's assignment is to read the pertinent chapter and the relevant reference material and be prepared to discuss the research needs in that area. A designated topic is assigned for each week. All students read the related chapter, and one or two students are assigned to lead the discussion. The class discussion generally centers on two themes: (1) What are the testable hypotheses? (2) What research design can be formulated to test these hypotheses? Class participation and interest is normally quite high. The discussions concerning methodology usually involve procedures for gathering data, questionnaires, case studies, problems of statistical sampling, techniques of data analysis, etc. Elaborations are often requested on the Delphi Technique.

All students in the course are required to write a term paper which includes the following topics:

1. The selected research topic, its relations to librarianship, and its importance
2. The hypotheses to be tested
3. The sample to be used and its method of selection
4. The methods of analysis to be employed and a justification of their appropriateness
5. The possible results that might be obtained and how these results would be used to improve library education or the practice of librarianship
6. A selected annotated bibliography.

As progress is made in preparing the paper, the problems encountered are discussed and suggestions for improvement are made by the entire class. In another course, such as directed individual study, the student may follow up on the implementation of his design, or, indeed, he may choose an entirely different topic. Perhaps at a later date, as an educator or librarian, the former student will be in a position to organize and support efforts to solve the problems of library education and practice. Certainly, research and planning efforts along the lines

Part One

Identifying Needed Research

Jesse H. Shera

The Aims and Content of Graduate Library Education

Definition and scope of the problem

Understanding the nature of the research needed in the objectives and content of graduate library education requires an initial agreement respecting the meaning of research, a recognition of what graduate library education is, and what the objectives of such education are. Research may be defined as the systematic attempt to discover new facts or new relationships among facts by means of the formulation of a preliminary explanation, or hypothesis, which is subjected to an appropriate, objective investigation for verification or disproof in terms that can be expressed in a general way (Shera 1964). The aim of graduate education in librarianship, which must define the content of the program of study, is to provide graduate students with the appropriate knowledge and skills that will enable them to perform in a satisfactory way as professional librarians. The term "professional librarianship" is understood to include practitioners, teachers of library education, and research investigators of problems in librarianship. Thus, one can say with considerable validity, that the ultimate aims of graduate library education are those of librarianship itself. Expressed more simply, the goals are to prepare students to do what librarianship does. Hence, the task of research in library education is to discover the best way to prepare students for their professional careers by providing evidence which will prove that such ways are optimal, given the existing state of knowledge in higher education and librarianship.

Neither higher education nor librarianship has been particularly disposed to engage in research about itself. Higher education, it may be observed, has studied almost everything except higher education; librarianship has never been research-oriented. Indeed, it would be quite difficult to demonstrate that librarians, by and large, have assumed any true responsibility for the clarification of specific professional issues confronting them, as distinguished from a vague, abstract concept of "service." Ralph A. Beals (1942, p. 165–67) set forth a classification of library literature more than a quarter of a century ago that is still applicable today. Writings about librarianship, he told an audience at the University of Chicago in 1942, fall into three major categories: "Glad tidings" are of two kinds—"speculative essays of what might, could, would, or should be true . . . and announcements, more or less unvarnished, on something about to be done or very recently undertaken. Like the 'apostle's faith,' they are the essence of things hoped for—the substances of things unseen." "Testimony" was used by Beals, not in the legal sense, but "in the sense commonly associated with religious sects, retrospective accounts of something done or benefits conferred . . . often, although not always, cast in the first person plural." "Research" has no relation to the presence or absence of statistics but includes, said Beals, "any study in which a problem is defined and analyzed into its constituent parts in which valid data are collected and related to relevant factors, in which hypothesis are formed and, through testing, rejected, amended, or proved . . . offers acceptable credentials as research." Regrettably, in both education and librarianship, the credentials that research has attempted to offer are not very impressive. In attempting to lay the foundation for inquiry into the aims and curricula of the library school, one is, in a sense, going counter to a well-established historical trend.

Very much in the Beals tradition, Philip Ennis (1967) has charged that today's library research, such as it is, is noncumulative, fragmentary, weak, and oriented to immediate practical ends. As remedial measures, Ennis proposes that there be a real commitment to the research enterprise by library educators and administrators. Such a commitment would imply important changes in the relationship between the knowledge base and the service orientation, the strengthening of the research sensitivity or school libraries and public libraries, and the building of library schools of research-oriented faculties. Ennis suggests three areas that are especially in need of investigation: the measurement of library performance, the analysis of the uses of print, and the theory of the organization of knowledge. However, Ennis does not mention inquiry into library education itself as a remedial measure.

Historical review

At a time when library education was represented only by apprentice training in the public libraries—and even in the first library schools—there was scant opportunity and little need for inquiry into the effectiveness of technical preparation for staff appointment. The goal, then, was simple: to train librarians in the elementary skills needed to perform their largely routine duties. The only real test of the value of the instructional program was whether the "graduate" could do his work when he assumed the responsibilities of a job. Standards of performance in those days were simple, objective, and largely idiosyncratic. Sarah Vann (1961), in her history of professional library education before 1923, describes sporadic attempts at the beginning of the 20th century to inquire into the condition of the few existing library schools. She even attempted to apply some educational standards. However, the earliest significant attempt to examine the state of library education was embodied in a report prepared in 1916 by Alvin S. Johnson for the Carnegie Corporation of New York. That report sought to provide a policy for the corporation's donations to free public libraries. Johnson examined the thirteen library schools then in existence. He regarded only about half of them as being of much importance. He deplored the excessive emphasis on technical training, superimposed as it was on nothing more than a high school education. Although one can scarcely characterize the Johnson report as a major research undertaking in library education, it is important because it drew the attention of the Carnegie Corporation to the need for a serious, major investigation of library education. It thus paved the way for the famous Williamson report seven years later (1923), which still remains, despite the passage of time, the single existing best study of library education. The Williamson report is so well-known, so widely summarized and discussed in the literature of library education that it is sufficient here to point out that it was a serious, extensive inquiry, buttressed by a substantial amount of statistical evidence, into the condition of library education in the 1920s. The research methods, however, were directed entirely toward the status quo. The report's recommendations, sound and intelligent as they are, were highly personalized. Williamson took a hard look at library education. Then he drew his own conclusions on what should be done about it. Moreover, the method of inquiry itself was relatively simple and unsophisticated, but so was library education in the 1920s.

What might be regarded as the first major attempt to apply the findings of research to library education programs is the job analysis study inaugurated in 1925 (Charters 1927). Briefly stated, the objective of the investigation was to conduct an intensive study of what librarians do in various library operations—the tasks they perform, the knowledge needed to perform such duties, and the personal attributes needed for success. From this massive collection of data, and with the assistance of a substantial number of advisory practitioners, a series of texts for teaching in library schools was prepared by appropriate authorities in the several fields of librarianship. The first text to be prepared in this fashion was Jennie M. Flexner's volume on circulation work in public libraries which appeared in 1927. But probably the best known today are the texts on cataloging by Margaret Mann and on the school library by Lucille Fargo. As one might expect, these texts were hardly inspiring. However, they were heavily oriented to operations as they were practiced at the time of the study; in no way did their authors seek to identify future trends. Nevertheless, some of the texts, notably Mann, went through more than one edition and dominated much of library school instruction until the close of the second world war. Indeed, Mann and Fargo still appear on supplementary course reading lists.

The event that may properly be characterized as the most important and influential single development in library education since the publication of the Williamson report, if indeed not the most important event in the entire recent history of library education, was the establishment in 1926 of the Graduate Library School at the University of Chicago through a grant from the Carnegie Corporation. However, the school arose out of no basic research into the character of librarianship, much less library education, or even of any survey of needs. It came into being largely because of a hunch, a subjective conviction, on the part of Carl Milam and other influential librarians in the Chicago area, that library education needed a program of advanced study, especially one that terminated in the doctorate, and it needed such a program to maintain academic and professional respectability.

The founding of the school, which, after lengthy negotiation, was accepted with reluctance by the administration of the University of Chicago, touched off a controversy—which lasted for a decade or more —over the nature of advanced study in the library world. The program as envisaged by its first dean, George A. Works, who came to the new post from the Department of Education of the University of Chicago, was represented by an almost completely unstructured curriculum in which a limited number of carefully selected and experienced students worked privately with the faculty on problems of major importance in librarianship. The question immediately arose of the nature of the thesis problem. The answer, at first, seemed to lie in the humanities, particularly the history of books, printing, and libraries.

The arrival in 1932 of Louis Round Wilson as dean brought the school to its position of pre-eminence and influence (Tauber 1967). Wilson, again without benefit of research, but richly endowed with experience as librarian of the University of North Carolina, saw librarianship as a part of the communication processes in society. Therefore, one must look, he believed, to the social sciences rather than the humanities for the intellectual foundations of librarianship and for guidance in curriculum development. As a result, more than a score of books poured from the University of Chicago Press, representing both faculty and student research on the social effects of reading, communication, library government and administration, the geography of reading, library service to the underprivileged, the history of libraries sociologically interpreted, and the philosophy of librarianship.

This is not the place to present in detail the history of the school that came to be known affectionately by its alumni as "The GLS." It is important to point out as emphatically as possible that the great growth and influence of the school—unparalleled in the history of library education—came not because of research in the theory of professional education in librarianship, but because a small group of intelligent men intuitively knew what needed to be done and set themselves and their students to burrowing like rabbits all over the library terrain. To describe the situation another way, the school did not grow out of any formalized statement of objectives based on inquiry; the objectives grew, quite literally, out of the school. In higher education as in everything else, there is no substitute for wisdom, and the best research in the world cannot compensate for its absence. One should, of course, warn against the danger of arguing from a special case. But, in the history of higher education, the Wilson achievements are not a special case; philosophically, they are one with Harvard under Eliot, Cornell under White, Chicago under Hutchins, and many other such "special cases." One might call this "the Great Man theory" of educational reform.

Ernest J. Reece of the Columbia University faculty performed a monumental chore in bringing together a mass of material dealing with the curricula in library schools in the 1930s (Reece 1936). Reece's volume is rich in flashes of insight. But the author did not evolve a model curriculum, or even present in any systematic way the real meaning of his findings or the ways in which they might be implemented for the improvement of library education. Reece was on the right track, and he set about his task in the right way. That was to collect the information that would be essential to decision-making in library education. But, perhaps because the book does not give up its wisdom readily, and the reader must thread his tortuous way through a labyrinth of detail, one finds little evidence that it had any real impact or initiated an educational revolution, as it should have done. Five years after the publication of his study, Reece complained that there had been relatively little change in the substance of library education programs in the fifty years of their history, that inexcusable weaknesses still existed in the organization of curricula, and, most important of all, that modifications were mandatory in the light of changing practices in the field. He therefore set forth certain avenues of development that might profitably be followed in curricular revision (Reece 1943). Again, however, one must report that, although both studies were widely quoted in subsequent writings about library education, it is difficult to discover any tangible results in library school practice.

In reviewing the research in library education published between 1957–63, Reece (1965) found only a slight numerical increase in such publication over that of previous decades and added cautiously, "At that, there may be enough to offset the predominance of unsupported opinion and conviction common previously." Nevertheless, one finds it difficult to escape the belief that he is trying to make the best of a sorry picture.

In 1941, at the request of Carl M. White, then director of the University of Illinois library school, a team of three investigators—John Dale Russell of the Department of Education at the University of Chicago, Keyes D. Metcalf, director of the Harvard University library, and Andrew D. Osborn, chief of the Catalog Department of the same university—initiated an intensive study of the Urbana school as seen against a backdrop of ideals and standards in library education as they then existed (Metcalf 1943). Despite the influence of the ALA Board of Education for Librarianship and the progress reported by Ralph Munn (1936), Louis Round Wilson (1937), and Helen F. Pierce (1941), the investigators were disposed to agree with Wilhelm Munthe (1939) that the instructional program was still far behind advances in other areas of librarianship. As a result of their study, they found serious deficiencies in the training and qualifications of the instructors; too much of the school's program was elementary. Moreover, the absence of a philosophy of librarianship deprived the program of depth and focus. The objectives of library education, Metcalf and his associates believed, were threefold: to make clear the principles according to which libraries function, to impart the techniques and skills used in libraries, and "to promote professional understanding and standards." Fulfillment of the first objective must necessarily wait upon the development of a philosophy of librarianship. The third is the responsibility of courses in library administration and history, which suffer from an excess of the inspirational and the sentimental. It is in the second objective that the greatest degree of success has been achieved.

By the close of the second world war, the literature of education for librarianship began to increase rapidly in volume, but there was little improvement in depth. Leigh's survey of library education for the *Public Library Inquiry* is noted below and, in 1948, the Graduate Library School at Chicago sponsored a conference on the implications of the *Public Library Inquiry* for library education. But the proceedings were little more than a collection of personal reactions of varying degrees of perception, none of which could qualify as being the results of research (Berelson 1949).

By the late 1940s, practically all of the library schools had converted the original bachelor of library science degree (which had been a fifth-year degree conferred as a graduate degree) to the master of library science degree. But the change was largely one of nomenclature rather than substance. It was a practical response to the growing criticism among library school graduates that they were being penalized in competition with those who had received the master's degree for study in a subject field. Certainly, the change was not the result of serious inquiry into its rationale, or even an attempt—except here and there in the form of a sporadic addition of a course in research methods—to enrich the instructional program in ways that would make it more truly graduate in character. Indeed, not many years were to pass before the master's thesis, or paper, was either dropped entirely or given optional status. Again, the decision was based solely upon expediency and the very practical necessity, forced by rising enrollments, to maintain teaching loads at a reasonable level.

Louis Round Wilson retired from the deanship at Chicago in 1942. The school entered a slow but steady decline from which it has never recovered. Unfortunately for library education (though in the 1950s and 1960s, other schools began to institute doctoral programs of highly varying degrees of excellence), the leadership from Chicago was gone, and there was nothing to take its place. Joseph L. Wheeler (1946), in his survey of library education prepared for the Carnegie Corporation, viewed with some concern the changes at Chicago and expressed the hope that it would eventually return to its original position of influence. Wheeler's study, which was impressionistic rather than statistical, did little more than reiterate the Williamson criticisms: Curricula are overburdened with detail, teaching is elementary, and the schools generally are unresponsive to the needs of the profession. He even went so far as to recommend that certain of the weaker schools be discontinued and that the strong ones be given increased support. But the librarian from Baltimore revealed his essential conservatism when he concluded his study with:

> There is no quick answer to education for librarianship. The old-fashioned idea of discipline and hard work is valid still.   In 1946, just as in the past, we need a sincere conviction that books, reading, study, and thinking are the foundations of progress; that knowledge and love of books make the keystone to librarianship. If librarians are so persuaded, then libraries will be better prepared to serve their function in society.

One could scarcely find a statement that better illustrates the weaknesses in library education from the days of Melvil Dewey's first school to the present.

The *Public Library Inquiry,* which was supported by the Carnegie Corporation and attracted widespread interest in the library world during the late 1940s, devoted a substantial amount of attention to library education. Robert D. Leigh, who was the director of the *Inquiry,* also conducted the investigation into the state of the library schools, their objectives, course offerings, faculty, students, and financial support. His report (Leigh 1952, p. 299–451) opened with a concise review of the history of education for librarianship in the United States. The review was followed by an intensive statistical investigation of the accredited library schools that compares favorably with that of Williamson, although it never received the widespread acclaim accorded the latter. Leigh found a great diversity among the schools in almost all aspects of library education despite the growing efforts of the ALA Board of Education for Librarianship and the schools themselves to establish and maintain standards. Yet, he concluded that, when viewed historically, the trend in instructional resources "is distinctly favorable," by which he, at least, implied that considerable progress had been made since the days of Williamson. "As for the actual curriculum," he wrote, "in the newer library school programs, the prevailing pattern of courses seems to be aimed at educating librarians to meet the personnel needs defined by the official objectives." He also noted a significant decline in emphasis upon specific details and techniques, especially in the teaching of cataloging and bibliography, while the earlier courses in book selection were tending toward courses in "book knowledge" organized around the major fields of the physical sciences, the social sciences, and the humanities. However, Leigh's presentation, like that of Williamson before him, is largely restricted to a detailed presentation of the existing state of library education to which he added some subjective opinions respecting trends. Leigh gave no indication of any need for research into education for librarianship, much less a suggestion of the problems that might need investigating.

One curricular experiment at the University of Chicago should be reported for the light it throws on attempts to alter basically the instructional program. By 1946, there had been considerable speculation about the four so-called core courses required of all first-year students: book selection, reference materials, cataloging and classification, and library administration. Ralph A. Beals, then dean of the school, with the present writer began to consider the possibility of bringing the first three elements of this four-course sequence into a coherent, unified, and coordinated whole. Fundamental to this new approach to the curriculum was the belief that, in every situation involving books and people, the librarian must bring to bear a body of knowledge, a point of view, and a set of skills which, taken together, are his peculiar professional possession. They encompass the tools with which he must work, regardless of the level of the clientele with whom he must operate. Such a program, then, must center on the substantive content of library materials and the critical estimate of their intrinsic worth. But it must also familiarize the student with the totality of the equipment, both physical and intellectual, that the librarian must have to expedite the transfer of recorded knowledge to those who use it, or should use it. Accordingly, in 1948, a sequence of courses was inaugurated that approached the "core" curriculum, not from the point of view of what the librarian does, as had been done by Charters, but from the substantive areas of knowledge grouped under the three categories of the physical sciences, the social sciences, and the humanities. However, by the time the program was ready for implementation, Beals had left Chicago to become director of the New York Public Library. The real architect of the program was Margaret E. Egan, and, subsequently, under the deanship of Bernard R. Berelson and with support from the Carnegie Corporation, a series of texts was prepared (Shera 1953, Asheim 1957, and Hoselitz 1960) for the fields of history, the humanities, and the social sciences. (The text for the physical sciences was never completed.) The program was never adopted outside of Chicago, although it persists there in an abbreviated form. Actually, it has never had a fair trial, because those who believed in it most strongly and who were mainly responsible for its planning left the Midwest before progress had reached a point at which results could be adequately evaluated. Moreover, the program, for all its merits—and the present writer *is* convinced that it could have been richly rewarding—demanded great skill in coordination. In addition, it virtually made it mandatory that the student devote two years to the acquisition of this first professional degree.

In the meantime, acceptance of the conventional "core," to which were grafted traditional advanced and specialized courses, continued to receive support. In 1953, the Chicago school under the deanship of Lester Asheim sponsored a conference on the core curriculum. However, it accomplished nothing except to bring together a substantial amount of untested opinion (Asheim 1954).

In an attempt to streamline the core, Case Western Reserve University in 1966 inaugurated its so-called Foundations Course (Focke 1968). This intensive course is divided into five areas, or groups: people and communication, materials, tools, institutionalization, and services. The course has several objectives: to provide the entering student with a generalized overview of librarianship in a way that will make clear the interrelationships and interdependencies of the various forms and specializations of the field; to present a theoretical structure of librarianship that will make these relationships clear; to provide some understanding of the historical development of the library in a way that will relate it to the communication process in society and the emergence of the library as a social instrumentality; to give a reasonable certainty that all students have a common background of understanding of the field prior to their entry upon a library specialty; to relieve the subsequent courses of much of their technical detail, terminology, and standard procedures that must be mastered by the recruit before he can progress very far in his quest for competence; and to provide those students who have not at the time of matriculation decided on a specific area of library activity with the basis for making a rational choice in harmony with their competencies and interests. This course was an outgrowth of the general philosophy of library education set forth by Focke, Egan, and the present writer at a conference held in Cleveland in 1955 (Egan 1956, p. 197–209).

In 1962, the H. W. Wilson Foundation made a grant to the American Library Association for the development of a national plan for library education. Also, prior to the 1963 Midwinter Meeting of the Association in Chicago, an invitational meeting of those primarily concerned with the subject was held (Shera 1963). The undertaking, however, was a complete failure (*Report* 1963), and eventually was abandoned due, at least in part, to unrealistic planning and false goals (Shera 1964). The foundation, however, undaunted by this initial failure, provided the ALA with funds for the establishment of an Office of Library Education at ALA Headquarters, which is still too new to permit of evaluation.

During this period, a fair amount of experimentation was taking place in some of the schools. At Simmons College, Kenneth Shaffer and Thomas Galvin were investigating the utility of the case study methods in teaching such subjects as library administration and reference work (Shaffer 1959; 1960; 1961; 1963; Galvin 1965). At the University of

Maryland, Paul Wasserman introduced a curriculum that strongly emphasized administration and management. Walter J. Stuart (1965, p. 131–32) of the U. S. Office of Education has made some progress exploring the implications of the systems concept in teaching of information science. Also, Manfred Kochen (1965, p. 98–99) has been experimenting with a course, offered at the University of Michigan, on information-retrieval theory. Quite obviously, at certain strategic points, the new concepts of librarianship are beginning to have some influence. Doctoral programs, some of them well-organized and developed, began to proliferate at an accelerated, even alarming, rate which was not always to the advantage of the field. Increasingly, too, library schools began to address themselves seriously to the need for a sixth-year program that would provide advanced study but not be oriented toward research, as the doctoral program was supposed to be.

Following remotely the trails blazed by Charters and Leigh, Anna Hall (1968) of the Carnegie Library at Pittsburgh analyzed data from thirteen large public libraries and twelve library schools to determine the relationship, if any, between the knowledge and skills needed to perform professional activities and the extent to which library school curricula fulfill those needs. Thus Hall was able to formulate a taxonomy of educational objectives against which curricular content could be aligned. She found that practicing librarians placed high priority upon the mastery of complex skills and abilities as well as acquaintance with subject matter related to, but not necessarily unique to librarianship. Hall concluded that most of the necessary factual information was adequately taught but that the higher intellectual abilities and skills above the factual competence were neglected. In short, she was really proving the thesis espoused by Williamson almost a half-century earlier. In contrast to Hall's findings, six recent library school graduates on the staff of the Enoch Pratt Free Library complained that library schools generally devoted an excessive amount of attention to the theoretical, to the neglect of the practical ("What's Wrong . . ." 1966).

The doctoral and other advanced programs

Ever since 1861, when Yale University awarded the first Ph.D. in the United States, the degree has been regarded as symbolizing competence and achievement in research. It is therefore not surprising that (librarianship having long been regarded as a service occupation), for virtually a quarter of a century the Graduate Library School of the University of Chicago stood as the only entity of its kind in the library world. It was the academic librarians, quite naturally because of the high prestige value of the doctorate in the halls of academe, that first felt the need for the advanced degree. Indeed, Munn (1936) spoke for most public librarians when he wrote of the educational requirements for professional positions at the Carnegie Library at Pittsburgh: "I believe that the Pittsburgh staff does not need more bibliographical and technical training than is now given in one-year library schools."

J. Periam Danton (1959), who was himself among the first to complete the pioneer doctoral program at the Graduate Library School of the University of Chicago, summarized the objectives of doctoral study as "(1) To furnish mature librarians, having scholarly ability and interests, with opportunity for advanced study and research in the library field; (2) To develop in the student (a) subject mastery and (b) competence in research and investigation; (3) To organize, conduct, and publish studies which will extend the bounds of knowledge in fields pertinent to the theory and practice of librarianship; and through these means, (4) To provide for the profession qualified researchers and personnel for teaching and higher administrative positions." Danton quite properly pointed out that the objectives of the doctorate in library science were virtually identical with those of advanced graduate study in the subject disciplines, especially among the professional fields. The only difference was that in librarianship the emphasis tended to be, in part at least, more oriented toward the practical than is true for programs in the purely "academic" disciplines. His study, although its statistics are now seriously out-of-date, still stands as something of a landmark for its analysis of the programs, subjects of dissertations, qualifications of faculty and students, factors which were preventing the schools from attaining fully their objectives, and the contribution the doctorate has made to the profession. There exists a real need to bring his careful investigation up-to-date, a need that is not met by Davis' tabulation (1968) of master's and doctoral theses from 1950 to 1967, or Walker's (1963) analysis of thesis content for the years 1949–58.

The introduction of doctoral programs into library school curricula should, and in many cases did, make possible the enrichment of the student's educational experience through coordination with graduate courses in the parent university. In a number of instances, the doctoral programs are truly interdisciplinary and require that the student be examined in a subject field as well as in librarianship. But as Neal Harlow (1968) warns, some of these coordinate subjects can be intellectually and psychologically more rewarding than others, and, therefore, the real purpose for the librarian in acquiring the degree should be kept constantly before the student and his advisor. Harlow's warning would seem to be rather obvious. But, on the other hand, both Harrison (1968, p. 329–36) and Osborn (1967) have seriously questioned the academic standards and the value of the results of many of the doctoral programs and whether they really achieve their objectives. The question of who needs the doctorate in librarianship and what is done with it—in terms of its worth to the recipient—are areas in which serious and objective study is needed. Not only in education for librarianship but throughout higher education generally, there is a serious need for a comprehensive study of the deterioration of degree structure, especially as it relates to a kind of "academic Gresham's law," in which cheap degrees drive out those which have true substance.

The quite obvious lack of need of most librarians for the doctorate, combined with an awareness that formal professional education beyond the master's degree is, or should be, of substantial importance to most librarians, has given rise to a growing belief that an advanced, but nonresearch-oriented program, would be desirable. Ray Swank (1965, p. 20–27) saw four important roles for such an intermediate curriculum: a sixth-year specialized curriculum, an internship, an opportunity for continuing education, and an alternative curriculum in information science. So-called post-master's programs now exist in a number of the schools accredited by the ALA. Floyd N. Fryden (1969), a graduate student at the University of Chicago, has surveyed these offerings at eleven schools. Three objectives were identified: (1) to prepare teachers in undergraduate or graduate library school curricula, (2) to prepare practicing librarians to advance into administrative or specialized positions, and (3) to provide additional knowledge and training that would permit practicing librarians to improve their performance in their existing positions. In most of the schools, the degree is terminal, although in three it was the first step toward the doctorate. Requirements, curricula, and relation to substantive courses in other parts of the university varied widely, although perhaps the most interesting and significant fact is their heavy dependence for financial support upon Title IIB of the federal *Higher Education Act* of 1965. Only three of the programs were formally begun prior to the autum of 1966, and only two have received no aid from the act. In one of these two instances, however, substantial assistance was received from state aid. In the remaining eight schools, there was a close correlation between the number of fellowships received and the number of students enrolled. Thus the question inevitably arises about the relation between available money and real need in promoting these educational ventures. Quite obviously, the present method of support takes basic decisions concerning the character and effectiveness of these programs out of the hands of the schools themselves and places them under the control of an extramural agency. More information is needed, too, about the experience of other professional groups in providing education beyond the first degree. The work begun by Fryden should be carried forward in greater intensity and depth than was possible for him.

Two additional studies of library education, neither of which is as yet completed, should be mentioned. The first is that section of the University of Maryland *Manpower Study* which deals with library education. (The study is under the direction of Rodney White of Cornell University.) This investigation makes use of a battery of questionnaires, sent to both students and faculty of library schools, and protracted visits to the schools themselves in a concerted effort to determine the present state of library education and the reaction of students and faculty to it. White's background, it should be pointed out, is in business management and administration, and his two major investigators are graduate students in Cornell's program of hospital management.

The second study, financed by the Carnegie Corporation of New York, which is also nearing completion, is a highly subjective inquiry into the sociological foundations of library education: it is being prepared by the present writer. In making the grant, the corporation specified that it was to be "a distillation of" the author's own "thinking about library education." Also, the Office of Library Education of the ALA, together with its committee of advisors, has been considering the possibility of "another Williamson report," to be prepared by a social scientist, although it would seem that any such undertaking should wait for the results of the two investigations mentioned above.

Research needs of education for librarianship

"The big question about graduate education," wrote Bernard Berelson (1960, p. 202) in his study of the subject for the Carnegie Corporation, "is the one on which it is most difficult to get solid evidence: How good is it? The ultimate answer to that question must be found in one of two directions. . . . One is an inquiry into the content of the programs. . . . The other is an objective investigation into the quality of the product; that is an extremely large and complicated matter in itself. Either of these, or both together, would give a more nearly final answer to the persistent question of quality." Thus Berelson settles for an inquiry into "how good people *think*" graduate education is, and we return to the questionnnaire with all its faults and its paucity of virtues.

Oliver Carmichael's (1961) somewhat strident critique of graduate education gives no hint that its author believes that the objectives and curricula of the modern graduate school, although it seriously needs reform, is a proper subject to be "researched." Similarly, Jencks and Riesman (1968), in their monumental inquiry into the academic revolution, give no hint that the salvation of higher education, or even its efficiency, is to be sought in any intensive research program that will lay bare faults and evaluate reform.

With respect to library education itself, Conrad Rawski (1968, p. 93) touched the root of the problem when he wrote about the amount of subject knowledge required by the practicing librarian: "Now, what kind of subject knowledge is appropriate to a professional librarian? The answer to the question depends on a host of variables among which our own assumptions may be the most distinct and the most ignored. I do not think that we could reach a consensus on what should be taught. But, instead of prolonged debate in experiential terms, we might view the question of appropriateness as a problem situation and attempt to inquire into what *might* be taught under certain stated conditions. It is the uncertainty of these conditions, or rather our failure to recognize and address ourselves to this uncertainty, which has beclouded the program of subject literature since the days of curricular debate at Chicago's Graduate Library School."

Yet, despite the evidence that educators generally have been distrustful of research directed toward the improvement of the house of intellect, librarians persist in babbling about the need for research into library education as a guide to change. Thus Schick (1963) and Reagan (1962) have posed such topics for research as: a study to determine the feasibility of a coordinated research program for the accredited library schools; a study to determine the optimum number of library schools for the nation; a study to determine the quality of administrative performance in the management of library schools; and a survey of the needs of library schools for larger faculties, better quarters, research funds, and other facilities. Other topics suggested at one time or another include: a study of the optimal amount of curricular flexibility; the recommended or elective courses that should be included in the master's program, the identification of courses outside the library school customarily taken by the student and their importance or relevance to the program of study; the sources of dissatisfaction with the current curricula; and the relation of laboratory and field work to the library school program.

One has but to list such topics to recognize the naive conception of research they imply and, even were they carried out, the very limited value they would have in contributing to the enrichment of the student's educational experience. "I do want to point out," Abraham Kaplan (1964) told a University of Chicago conference on the intellectual foundations of library education, "that the term 'research,' which is certainly one of the 'O.K. words' of our time, is very widely used to mean nothing other than literally a re-search—that is to say, not an extension of the domain of knowledge, but the making available to particular people some things that were already known but not specifically known to them at that time." He went on to say, "I find often operative—very widely, for instance, in the conduct of the behavioral sciences—a very human and very understandable tendency (but no less objectionable for being understood) to do the things that we already know how to do. We tend to formulate our problems in such a way as to make it seem that the solutions to those problems demand precisely what we already happen to have at hand. With respect to the conduct of inquiry and especially in behavioral science, I label this effect 'the law of the instrument.' " Certainly one would be hard-pressed to find an area that better exemplifies Kaplan's law than the so-called research in education for librarianship.

The apparent lack of success in devising a research program directed toward the solution of problems in library education is to be found in the essential incompatibility of the research process and the nature of education as a human phenomenon. Research, as the present writer (Shera 1964) told the Allerton Park Conference on research in librarianship, is an intellectual act that begins with an awareness of one's ignorance and progresses through the critical examination of evidence that is both reliable and relevant to the revelation of truth which is generalizable and universal. It is finally a search for an explanation of phenomena, not primarily a guide to action, although the guidance of action may be a consequence of its findings. However, the real difficulty in applying research to the educational process, and especially to the process of educating librarians, is that we are groping in the dark for hard "facts." And we do not know what the "hard" facts are. We do not know what learning and librarianship are or how either influences conduct or behavior. At the present time, we know learning only at the most elementary, behavioristic level, and such knowledge is of little help in understanding the intellectual processes involved in higher education. We may watch the behavior patterns of mice in a maze and, from them, make the leap from mouse to man, but the extrapolation is not necessarily valid. Because of the empirical character of much of educational research and its excessive dependence upon local observation and limited and incomplete data, more often than not, it is parochial and provincial rather than general in its applicability. And, always it is in jeopardy from emotional coloration. The educator means to do good, and, by dint of hard work and self-sacrifice, he does what he means to do. And, therefore, what he does is good, right, and proper.

But the true scholar will not always accept the educator's premises, and the fine educational model comes fluttering down like the house of cards that it all too often is. As for librarianship, there is no structure, no frame of reference, no real agreement about what librarianship *is* and what the librarian's professional responsibilities are against which the librarian's educational program can be measured. Certainly, it is not our intention to discredit valid and relevant knowledge about either higher education or librarianship. But that knowledge must be valid and relevant.

The uncharted road

"Wohin der Weg?" was the cosmic outcry of a Faust who had wearied of metaphysical research. And Mephistopheles' response has much symbolic meaning for research in higher education today—*"Kein Weg! Ins Unbetretene."* The way of research is, indeed, uncharted. David Riesman (Jencks and Riesman 1968) has stated the problem somewhat more explicitly: "Educational reform depends on the local landscape, the local resources that student and faculty presently bring with them; indeed, change must be incremental and must build on what is already available." "In scientific work," wrote Marion J. Levy (1966, p. 7), "it is more important to be fruitful for further work than to be right." We must stop trying to deceive ourselves that it is in the mystique of research that the key to the solution of all the problems of library education and the cure for all our ills must be sought. We would not discredit research, but it is important to remember that much of the research that is vital to the improvement of library education will come from *without* rather than from *within* the library profession. The library educator would do well, therefore, to study seriously such important contributions to educational theory as Ralph Tyler's *Basic Principles of Curriculum and Instruction* (1950); Hilda Taba's *Curriculum Development: Theory and Practice* (1962); the two volumes on the *Taxonomy of Educational Objectives* by Bloom and Krathwell (1956, 1964); Virgil Herrick's *Strategies of Curriculum Development* (1965); the two volumes on learning theory by Mowrer (1960); *A Study of Thinking* by Jerome Bruner and associates (Bruner 1956); and those two delightful little books by Bruner alone, *The Process of Education* (1960) and *Toward a Theory of Instruction* (1966).

The library educator can also derive much benefit from thoughtful and frequent rereading of a literature that, in general, does not fit the stereotype of research *qua* research—the philosophical and autobiographical writings of the great "names" in the field of scholarship—

names such as Cardinal Newman, John Dewey, Charles W. Eliot, Alfred North Whitehead, Robert M. Hutchins, Ortega y Gasset, Henry M. Wriston, Clark Kerr, and a host of others like those listed in the present writer's "Twelve Apostles . . ." (Shera 1969). Experience is the source of all wisdom, and such writers are rich in experience and can speak with authority.

What, then, must library education have to refine its goals and make its curriculum more relevant to the needs of today and tomorrow? First, there must be maintained an effective dialogue between library educators and those engaged in scholarly work in other and related academic disciplines. For only through enrichment from without can library education avoid sophistry and the stifling vortex of that centripetal force which is parochialism. Any procedure that contributes to the interdisciplinarity of librarianship is to be welcomed. Riesman (Jencks and Riesman 1968) speaks with enthusiasm of the program at Sarah Lawrence College, "where there are virtually no curricular requirements, but where the adviser or don carefully counsels a student in imaginative ways, opening new possibilities, suggesting paths through the available courses . . . where she can be persuaded although not compelled to abandon self-protectiveness in exploring the curriculum." Again, Riesman points to the work at the State University of New York at Buffalo where President Martin Meyerson has begun tentatively "to link each graduate professional school to the relevant area in the arts and science faculties," and the work at the new college in Old Westbury, New York, which is attempting to build undergraduate programs in medicine, law, and perhaps theology into the curriculum. Such programs would perhaps give new direction and vitality, not only to the library school, but to the liberal arts program and save it, if properly designed and controlled, from a premature vocationalism.

Quite obviously, library education can never achieve its goals or provide a sound program of study unless it enlists a faculty composed of the best minds in the profession—people who are dedicated to the art of teaching, equipped with sound scholarship, and skilled in communication. To such a faculty must be attracted highly motivated and intelligent students, for, without them, no educational program—however well designed and "researched"—can be a success. And this faculty and these students must be brought together in an atmosphere hospitable to exploration. "One thing above all else must remain strong on our campuses," wrote Tishler (1969) in a recent issue of *Science*, "if the universities are to serve society beneficially. This is the freedom to speak one's mind and the freedom to participate in responsible dissent. This is the basis of the long, hard battle for tenure fought by university professors which allows them to behave as scholars and critics without fear for their jobs." Freedom to experiment and the resources with which to do it, the right to challenge and to disagree, the bringing together in a fruitful and understanding relationship the best library school faculties and scholars in other disciplines—these are the great needs of library education today. Then can we say with Stephan Machlup (1967), "Let's give up striving for complete coverage of some body of knowledge. Let's give up the aim of a structured curriculum through which all students are to attain that minimum without which . . . (end of sentence, *ad lib*). Let's give up trying to tell our colleagues what their courses should contain. Let's give up trying to avoid overlap and duplication. Let's instead provide students with an enormous choice of educational materials—yes, lectures, of course, and libraries, but also games and toys (you don't have to call it research), films, tea and beer parties, trips, long-distance telephone conversations, and other electronic aids to data retrieval. All of these can be tightly or loosely 'programmed,' linear or branched. And let's make sure there's a constant lively dialogue, with the faculty doing its share of the listening, not just about our subject, but also about how successfully it is getting across." When library education has achieved Machlup's goal, it will, indeed, have attained maturity and won't need to apologize to anyone in the ivy-covered walls of academe.

References

Asheim, Lester. *The Core of Education for Librarianship.* Chicago: American Library Association, 1954.

———. *The Humanities and the Library.* Chicago: American Library Association, 1957.

Beals, Ralph A. "Implications of Communication Research for the Public Library." In *Print, Radio, and Film in a Democracy,* edited by Douglas Waples. Chicago: University of Chicago Press, 1942.

Berelson, Bernard R., ed. *Education for Librarianship.* Chicago: American Library Association, 1949.

———. *Graduate Education in the United States.* New York: McGraw-Hill, 1960.

Bloom, Benjamin S., ed. *Taxonomy of Educational Objectives,* vol. 1. New York: McKay, 1956.

Bruner, Jerome S. *The Process of Education.* Cambridge, Mass.: Harvard University Press, 1960.

———. *Toward a Theory of Instruction.* Cambridge, Mass.: Harvard University Press, 1966.

———, et al. *A Study of Thinking.* New York: Wiley, 1956.

Carmichael, Oliver C. *Graduate Education: A Critique and a Proposal.* New York: Harper, 1961.

Charters, W. W. "Job Analysis in Education for Librarianship." *Libraries* 32:7 (June 1927).

Danton, J. Periam. "Doctoral Studies in Librarianship in the United States." *College and Research Libraries* 20:435–53; 458 (Nov. 1959).

Davis, Richard A. "Theses and Dissertations Accepted by Graduate Library Schools, 1966 through December 1967." *The Library Quarterly* 38:442–52. (Oct. 1968).

Egan, Margaret E. "Education for Librarianship." In *Documentation in Action,* edited by Jesse Shera, et al. New York: Reinhold, 1956.

Ennis, Philip H. "Commitment to Research." *Wilson Library Bulletin* 41:899–901 (May 1967).

Focke, Helen M. "Foundations of Library Science." *Journal of Education for Librarianship.* 8:241–50 (Spring 1968).

Fryden, Floyd N. "Post-Master's Degree Programs in the Accredited United States Library Schools." *The Library Quarterly* 39:233–44 (July 1969).

Galvin, Thomas J. *Problems in Reference Service; Case Studies in Method and Policy.* New York: Bowker, 1965.

Hall, Anna C. *An Analysis of Certain Professional Occupations in Relation to Formal Education Objectives.* Pittsburgh: Carnegie Library, 1968. ERIC microfiche ED 021 606.

Harlow, Neal. "Doctoral Study—Key to What?" *College and Research Libraries* 29:483–85 (Nov. 1968).

Harrison, J. Clement. "Graduate Study, a Mid-Atlantic Point of View." In *Library Education, An International Survey,* edited by Larry E. Bone. Urbana, Ill.: University of Illinois Graduate School of Library Science, 1968.

Herrick, Virgil E. *Strategies of Curriculum Development.* Columbus, Ohio: Merrill, 1965.

Hoselitz, Berthold F., ed. *A Reader's Guide to the Social Sciences.* Glencoe, Ill.: Free Press, 1960.

Jencks, Christopher, and Riesman, David. *The Academic Revolution.* Garden City, N.Y.: Doubleday, 1968.

Kaplan, Abraham. "The Age of the Symbol—A Philosophy of Library Education." *The Library Quarterly* 34:295–304 (Oct. 1964).

Kochen, Manfred. "A University Course in Information Retrieval." In *Proceedings of a Symposium on Education for Information Science,* edited by L. B. Heilprin, et al. Washington, D.C.: Spartan Books, 1965.

Krathwell, David R., et al. *Taxonomy of Educational Objectives,* vol. 2. New York: McKay, 1964.

Leigh, Robert D. "The Education of Librarians." In *The Public Librarian,* edited by Alice I. Bryan. New York: Columbia Press, 1952.

Levy, Marion J., Jr. *Modernization and the Structure of Society.* Princeton, N.J.: Princeton University Press, 1966.

Machlup, Stephan. "In Defense of Diversity." *AAUP Bulletin* (American Association of University Professors) 53:337–38 (Sept. 1967).

Metcalf, Keyes D.; Russell, John Dale; and Osborn, Andrew D. *The Program of Instruction in Library Schools.* Urbana, Ill.: University of Illinois Press, 1943.

Mowrer, O. Hobart. *Learning Theory and the Symbolic Process.* New York: Wiley, 1960.

———. *Learning Theory and Behavior.* New York: Wiley, 1960.

Munn, Ralph. *Conditions and Trends in Education for Librarianship.* New York: Carnegie Corporation, 1936.

Munthe, Wilhelm. *American Librarianship from a European Angle.* Chicago: American Library Association, 1939.

Osborn, Andrew D. "The Doctorate." *Drexel Library Quarterly* 3:658–63 (Apr. 1967).

Pierce, Helen F. *Graduate Study in Librarianship in the United States.* Chicago: American Library Association, 1941.

Rawski, Conrad H. "Subject Literatures and Librarianship." In *Library School Teaching Methods,* edited by Larry E. Bone. Urbana, Ill.: University of Illinois Graduate School of Library Science, 1968.

Reagan, Agnes L. "Needed Research in Education for Librarianship." *ALA Bulletin* 56:333–34 (Apr. 1962).

Reece, Ernest J. *The Curriculum in Library Schools.* New York: Columbia University Press, 1936.

———. *Programs for Library Schools.* New York: Columbia University Press, 1943.

———. "Research in Education for Librarianship, 1957–1963." *Newsletter* no. 53. Chicago: American Library Association Library Education Division, p. 10–20 (Mar. 1965).

"A Report from the Commission on a National Plan for Libraries." *ALA Bulletin* 61:419–22 (Apr. 1963).

Schick, Frank L. "Library Science Research Needs." *Journal of Education for Librarianship* 23:280–91 (Spring 1963).

Shaffer, Kenneth R. *Twenty-five Short Cases in Library Personnel Administration.* Hamden, Conn.: Shoe String Press, 1959.

———. *Twenty-five Cases in Executive-Trustee Relationships.* Hamden, Conn.: Shoe String Press, 1960.

———. *The Book Collection; Policy Case Studies in Public and Academic Libraries.* Hamden, Conn.: Shoe String Press, 1961.

———. *Library Personnel Administration and Supervision.* Hamden, Conn.: Shoe String Press, 1963.

Shera, Jesse H. *Historians, Books, and Libraries.* Cleveland, Ohio: Western Reserve University Press, 1953.

———. "Toward a New Dimension for Library Education." *ALA Bulletin* 57:213–17 (Apr. 1963).

———. "Darwin, Bacon, and Research in Librarianship." *Library Trends* 13:144 (July 1964).

———. "In Defense of Diversity." *Journal of Library Education* 4:137–42 (Winter 1964).

———. "Twelve Apostles and a Few Heretics." *Journal of Education for Librarianship* 10:3–10 (Summer 1969).

Stuart, Walter J. "Curricular Aspects of the Systems Concept." In *Proceedings of a Symposium on Education for Information Science*, edited by L. B. Heilprin, et al. Washington, D.C.: Spartan Books, 1965.

Swank, Raynard C. "The Graduate Library School Curriculum. In *Institute on Problems of Library Schools Administration,* edited by Sarah R. Reed. Washington, D.C.: U.S. Office of Education, 1965.

Taba, Hilda. *Curriculum Development: Theory and Practice.* New York: Harcourt, 1962.

Tauber, Maurice F. *Louis Round Wilson: Librarian and Administrator.* New York: Columbia University Press, 1967.

Tishler, Max. "The Siege of the House of Reason." *Science* 166:192–94 (Oct. 10, 1969).

Tyler, Ralph W. *Basic Principles of Curriculum and Instruction.* Chicago: University of Chicago Press, 1950.

Vann, Sarah K. *Training for Librarianship Before 1923.* Chicago: American Library Association, 1961.

Walker, Richard D. "The Quantity and Content of Master's Theses Accepted at Library Schools Offering the Doctor's Degree, 1949–1958." *Journal of Education for Librarianship* 3:264–79 (Spring 1963).

"What's Wrong with our Library Schools?" *Library Journal* 91:1773–75 (Apr. 1, 1966).

Wheeler, Joseph L. *Programs and Problems in Education for Librarianship.* New York: Carnegie Corporation of New York, 1946.

Williamson, Charles C. *Training for Library Service.* New York: Carnegie Corporation of New York, 1923.

Wilson, Louis Round. "The American Library School Today." *The Library Quarterly* 7:211–45 (Apr. 1937).

James Krikelas and
Margaret E. Monroe

General vs. Specialized Library Education

When knowledge was comparatively limited in scope, all students could pursue essentially the same curriculum.[1]

Specialization makes manageable the human effort to advance man's knowledge. . . . (There) is the intellectual obligation to make a serious effort first to see the relationships of all our specialties to each other and second, to see the relevance of both our specialties and their interrelationships to (the whole).[2]

Definition of the problem

Any inquiry into the question of general as opposed to specialized library education will be more profitable if it is removed from the context of alternatives and is rephrased as a question of the roles of general and specialized education in preparation for librarianship. It is clear that the concept of "core courses" is rooted in "general" library education and that sequences of courses designed to prepare librarians for expertise in narrow fields fall into the area of "specialized" education. There are, however, a variety of other approaches to specialization, and the realities of the situation force the question to be not one of *whether*, but rather of *how* and *when*.

[1]Hollis Casswell, "The Generalist, His Unique Contributions," *Education Leadership* 24 (Dec. 1966):213.

[2]Henry Winthrop, "Specialization and Intellectual Integration in Library Education," *Educational Theory* 217 (Jan. 1967):26.

31

As the practice of librarianship becomes more elaborate and the work of librarians increasingly differentiated, specializations are a most obvious feature of the professional landscape. Professional commitment to the generalizable body of knowledge that applies to all librarianship is being re-examined in the light of three pressures: to make efficient and economical the course of professional education; to allow the specialty to shape the pattern of professional education for those who will work in that specialty; and to enable persons of a wide variety of special competencies to enter professional study.

The impetus toward a totally specialized education, however, is being resisted at this juncture by two major forces: the loss to librarianship of an identity across and above specialties, and wasteful duplication of the teaching of basic principles in each of their many contexts (Jackson and Rothstein 1962, White 1949, p. 225–31). The fields of information science and school librarianship present the greatest challenge to "general" library education. Single-purpose programs to prepare for these two fields are well established in some universities. At other institutions, special curricula in the two fields are separately identified within the more general library education programs. Unique requirements for admission, graduation, and certification are often made in these two fields.

For guidance in the evolution of library education, both in its broad structure and its curriculum development, there must be a resolution of the question of the roles of general and specialized library education.

Historical review

In a paper presented at a 1965 institute for library school administrators, Raynard C. Swank, dean of the School of Librarianship at the University of California, Berkeley, indicated that a number of changes in library practice held important implications for the education of librarians (Swank 1965, p. 20–27). One of the four trends identified by Swank was "the emergence of additional, exacting specialization in librarianship, especially in the area of information science, including operations research, systems analysis, and mechanization." The importance of this single factor was underscored by the fact that the major part of his remarks dealt with the problem of the place and content of specialized education in the library school curriculum.

Swank proposed that library schools have a number of choices they could make concerning this problem, including the decision to minimize the core curriculum to allow more time for specialization, as against the preservation of the core at the expense of special education. A third choice, which Swank acknowledged was being tried at a number of schools, was the development of a post-master's (nondoctorate) program for specialists. In this program, individuals would undertake academic preparation for their specialty after completion of the master's degree. A number of recent reports and studies support the development of specialist programs, while acknowledging their areas of initial weakness (Danton 1969, Fryden 1969, Lowrie 1964, Vainstein 1968, p. 83–95).

The fourth option, as developed at California, is a fifth-year program in a designated specialty that parallels the more traditional library science curriculum. Other possible solutions to the problem of specialization are on-the-job training and, as Shera suggested, letting "the specialists be trained in other schools with the essentials of librarianship added to their program in capsule form" (Shera 1964).

Concern about specialization in education has been evident almost from the beginning of formal library education. Ernest J. Reece (1936), in his excellent analysis of the evolution of the library school curriculum, traces the early introduction of "specialized" courses in various library schools. He notes, however, that, in some cases, this introduction resulted in the building of the basic curriculum, "not in anticipation of library work as a whole, as has been the design generally, but with reference to service in a specific kind of library."

Prior to Reece's study, Charles C. Williamson (1923) had pronounced that specialization appeared to be desirable, since it produced "a reasonable degree of efficiency in library service." He went on to note, however, that:

> The opinion is very widely held . . . that while the first year of study should be general and basic, the second year should be definitely and even minutely specialized in the field in which the student is to take up his work.

In addition, Williamson envisioned that this specialization would take place after the first general course had been completed and a year of experience in a library had been gained. Six areas of special study that Williamson acknowledged were: school librarianship, special reference and research work in academic libraries, work with children, cataloging and classification, administration, and work in business libraries.

Numerous meetings and institutes have been held to discuss the problems of education for librarianship, with typical inclusion of the subject of specialization. An extensive body of literature has been devoted to librarians' calls for more precise specialization in the curriculum to prepare for the variety of specializations developed in library practice. Some librarians, however, feel that certain specialties can be learned on the job. Ralph Munn (1949, p. 117–29), for example, expressed his belief that, for some activities, "an aptitude, an interest, and a willingness to sit up nights with some of the library's own books are the only real requirement." A review of much of the pertinent literature reveals a number of trends.

First, the number of specialties covered by library schools seems to grow daily and has increased to include almost every conceivable activity, type of library, subject area, or type of clientele served. To Williamson's rather modest list have been added such areas as medical, law, and science librarianship; county, regional, and systems library administration; subject and "area" bibliography; media and audiovisual services; public relations and personnel management; and information service and information science. Typically, the library school curriculum has expanded by the addition of one or more courses as electives in each area of specialty, crowding the traditional library school program to obscure the core course areas (Winger 1965, Leigh 1954, L. Cohen and Craven 1960).

A second trend is the relatively common acknowledgment that a basic core exists, but that specialization is an extension beyond this core. The discussion, then, is not a matter of general *versus* specialization but rather a concern for identifying the point at which specialization should take place. Such concern has led to frequent criticism of the curriculum in the preparation of special (Jackson 1967), school (Darling 1967), and academic librarians (Muller 1967). Others have expressed interest in ensuring the proper balance between "core" and specialization in the educational preparation of adult education specialists (Asheim 1955, Monroe 1959), young adult librarians (Hatch 1968), law librarians (M. Cohen 1962), and various aspects of health science librarianship (Lieberman 1968).

As the stress on the unique content of the specialization grows under the pressure of demand from the practitioners, library education has begun to develop specialized programs to replace the general program of library education. School librarianship (Henne 1964, p. 53–60, Janke 1964, p. 63–68) and information science programs (Heilprin 1965; International Conference on Education for Scientific Information Work 1967, Taylor 1964, p. 31–37; 1967) have been developed as independent programs, paralleling the traditional library science track but focused on the single specialization. The establishment of such independent programs, however, does not solve the problem of content or balance between core and specialization.

Opinions and the experience of various librarians and educators, rather than research, have formed the basis for much of the discussion of specialization in the curriculum. Martin (1957) and Reece (1965) have prepared comprehensive surveys of the research done in education for librarianship. A review of both papers, as well as of the work completed since Reece's report, indicates that few empirical studies have been undertaken which explicitly address themselves to the problem of general and specialized education and its relationship to professional proficiency. The studies that are pertinent to the question under consideration have been grouped, for convenience, into five general categories, which represent different research approaches.

The first group consists of the omnibus type of survey of the general condition of library education. The most noteworthy are those by Williamson (1923), Reece (1936), and Leigh (1952, p. 299–425). These three reports have had a direct impact on the structure and content of library school programs, and further research of this type should incorporate study of general and specialized education.

A second group of research efforts consists of the studies undertaken to develop library school curricula on the basis of job analysis. In this group are the works of Charters (1927), Reece (1949), and Ryan (1950). A recent effort by Liesener (1967) to validate the core concept using job analysis is of particular interest; it is discussed more fully in the next section.

A third, although somewhat smaller, group of studies has taken as its focus the evaluation of job performance by library school graduates in comparison with individuals lacking such preparation. Although not directly aimed at the central problem of this paper, the studies by McCrossan (1967) and Bunge (1967) represent this type of evaluative approach and also offer some general evidence of the validity of a part of the core in professional education.

The fourth group of studies is aimed at determining the attitude of librarians toward their professional preparation in terms of their job requirements. The studies by Nichol (1942) and Wight (1945) were limited to graduates of two specific schools and were intended to be used in the evaluation of their curricula. The survey by Long (1965), on the other hand, covers a specific type of librarian (the state library consultant) and contains data which reflect on the adequacy of a number of library school programs. The conclusions of this study, as they pertain to the educational preparation of librarians, is also included in the section following.

The study by Hall (1968), also discussed below, is the single representative of a fifth category. This study analyzes the substantive knowledge needed to perform specific public services through content analysis of reports of service experts as observers. This research technique has been found to be useful in other disciplines; it has been applied here for the first time to librarianship.

Three recent studies

Long's *The State Library Consultant at Work* (1965) represents one attempt to explore the work of a special type of librarian. The survey describes the state library consultant in terms of educational preparation, duties, and attitudes. The report also includes a list of subject fields the consultants found helpful in their work and a list of courses they felt would be useful in increasing effectiveness. Although elements of library science were ranked high on each list, it was also evident that administration, social studies, and communications skills were considered important. Long's conclusion is, in many ways, an indictment of the educational preparation of this group of consultants, suggesting the need for a second year of study in the chosen professional specialization.

> Since they considered consulting late, often some time after completing their formal education, consultants generally lack special preparation for consulting work. Indeed, there is some reason to believe that their formal education was in many ways inappropriate for the special work they later chose; while courses in the social sciences were most often mentioned by consultants as helpful in their work, most of them majored in the humanities. Neither had consultants had any special training in consulting methods.

A second study of particular interest is Liesener's *An Empirical Test of the Validity of the Core Concept in Preparation of University Librarians* (1967). In this study, Liesener compares the specific subject matter recommended for the essential core curriculum at the 1953 Chicago Conference (Asheim 1954) with the subject matter based on job descriptions made for one academic library. Although some of the core concepts were found to be valid, this study raised some serious doubts about the relevancy of much of the subject matter included in the core. Liesener also finds the method of job description somewhat wanting as a means to determine the "knowledge base" of various professional university library positions.

> Certain problems regarding the use of job analysis as a method for verifying the need for knowledge of the core were revealed during the process of the investigation. A thorough job analysis can reveal the tasks performed in very detailed fashion but frequently a great deal of subjective judgment is required to determine precisely the knowledge specifications needed to perform the tasks. The need for a more objective and precise method for determining job specifications for librarians was felt very keenly in this investigation and strongly suggests itself as a worthy area for further research.

Liesener's reservations are reminiscent of the concern expressed by Leon Carnovsky (1960, p. 178–219) seven years earlier:

> The trouble with the activity analysis approach is that it may be regarded in a much too literal and superficial way. Many activities, altogether indispensable in the smooth functioning of libraries, are readily—indeed better—learned on the job. If routines, charging systems, and superficial administrative procedures are codified at all, they belong properly in a library's staff manual and not in the curriculum of a library school in a university. This is not to condemn activity analysis as a basis for curriculum construction; it is merely to imply that activities should be truly *analyzed,* not merely *described;* and in such analysis the elements that call for judgment and background should be identified and incorporated in the curriculum.

While neither goal has been achieved—job description based on knowledge needs or curriculum construction based on knowledge required—one effort to determine the appropriateness of present library school education to professional activities has been reported by Hall (1968). The specific objectives of the study were to determine what knowledge was necessary to perform a few selected public service activities, to structure this knowledge into a taxonomy of educational objectives, and to measure the degree to which library education has accomplished these needs. While the research does not cover every aspect of librarianship (as the author acknowledged), the method, conclusions, and recommendations deserve consideration from anyone attempting further research in this area. By design, Hall's research was limited to education in library schools, but the analysis of job performance indicated knowledge acquired in other disciplines. Her final conclusions are critical of graduate library education as well as the unstructured nature of undergraduate programs.

Summary and evaluation of the historical review

The foregoing brief review of the relative interest in reaching a desirable balance between the general (core) and specialized components of the librarian's professional education has revealed a number of trends and shortcomings. In the early history of library education, concern over the adequacy of the program led to a number of landmark studies. Efforts were made to relate the content of the curriculum to the practice of librarianship, although the methods used may not have been very sophisticated. In the period following World War II, there was a greater concern with formalizing the level at which the specialized program was undertaken, while less attention was paid to the content. Conference proceedings and written reports outweighed the much smaller amount of empirical evidence that was being secured. The few formal studies carried out tended to indicate weaknesses in achieving proficiency in either general or specialized areas of education.

Part of the problem may have been that once certain specialties were identified—usually by type of library or type of clientele—the needed attention to development and elaboration of curriculum was slighted. Further levels or degrees of specialization within these categories were not delineated. No study seems to have been undertaken, for example, that would compare the type of knowledge necessary to perform reference functions in large academic libraries to that required in large public libraries.

The ambitious research program of school and children's librarians described by Ersted (1949), on the other hand, envisioned a whole series of questions to be studied. Among the "major hypotheses" proposed for investigation were those which focused on determining the content of professional education, on determining the location of such education in the curriculum, and comparative analysis of the educational preparations necessary for school librarians and for those working with children in the public library setting. Many of these questions were partially answered in three master's theses completed at the University of Chicago in the early 1950s. Ersted (1951) looked at the education of school librarians; Fenwick (1951) studied the education of children's librarians; and Butler (1953) looked at state certification requirements for both types of librarians. Development in the 1960s of specialist programs at advanced levels of professional study appear now to provide a potential solution to the longstanding problem of special education.

Also evident from a review of the literature is the growing realization that curriculum construction must be based on an understanding of the knowledge required for professional proficiency and cannot be limited to an evaluation of technical skills alone. This calls for the development of new approaches for evaluating professional activities; simple job descriptions will not suffice.

Another problem area is the ever-present question about the desirable undergraduate subject concentration in preparation for librarianship. Traditionally, it has been assumed that a liberal arts education is required. Although this may be true, the variety of disciplines within the "liberal arts" is so great that the term has lost most of its meaning. There is a manifest trend towards emphasis on mathematics, the natural sciences, and the social sciences, but an analysis of the appropriateness of this emphasis has never been made.

Tentative solutions and areas for research

Need for definition of terms

Discussing the problem in the context of the purpose of a particular library education program, "general" library education is represented by the multi-purpose programs, and specialized library education is represented by the single-purpose programs. Within the graduate multi-purpose program schools, the master's program typically represents "general" library education, while advanced study programs (specialist and/or doctoral) represent "specialized" library education. In the context of the typical master's program, the assumption has been made that the "core courses" represent general library education and that electives supply the "specialization" (Asheim 1954). A fourth context for definition may lie in the course programs of individual students and in the "general" vs. "specialized" impact of their course sequences. The question may be whether the "specialist" is the product of "specialized" library education. Differentiation among the various meanings of "specialized" education will hasten communication and solution of the problem.

Further definition is needed of "specialties," the areas around which library education might structure specialized programs. How stable are the specializations in the field of practice? To what extent do they guide library education? Does a specialty refer to the special context of use and special groups of users, or to the special subject matters and collections, or to the unique library functions, operations, and techniques? Are there specializations at the advanced level of "core" areas, such as reference or cataloging? Does specialization represent a unique function or simply a level of excellence in practice? Clarification of these concepts will reveal a variety of aspects of the problem, which can then be dealt with more effectively.

The structure of specialized library education vis-a-vis general library education

Specializations in different aspects of librarianship have developed different educational patterns; whether these are due to historical accident or to inherent necessity needs exploration. "General" library education beyond the concept of "core courses" needs description and analysis. An analysis should be made of the extent to which typical programs—with both "general" and "specialized" approaches—avail themselves of the emphases, courses, or materials of alternative approaches. Greater concreteness will strengthen the basis for choice of educational approach.

Undergraduate library education has been examined in the past primarily for purposes of discovering its economic necessity for society and for the student. School librarianship is the prime focus at this level of professional education. For this reason, the undergraduate program in this field should be compared with master's programs—both general and specialized—and also with specialist programs at the intermediate degree level. The orientation toward skills and techniques of most early specialization seems outmoded today for most librarians, who must be flexible in function and perspective in a rapidly changing society (Truman 1964). Stabilization and articulation of the various levels of preparation for school librarianship should be the result.

The rationale for single-purpose graduate library education programs has not been developed. Neither the accrediting agency nor developing programs have put single-purpose professional education to the test. Examination of a group of single-purpose graduate programs—whether in school librarianship or information science—should be undertaken. The lack of standards for single-purpose programs is a serious limitation; once a rationale is articulated, standards can be developed. The question as to whether standards for single-purpose programs can be generalized to cover all types of programs should be explored. Consideration should be given to creating a pattern of specialized education at advanced levels, which would be usefully related to a multi-purpose master's library education program.

The structure of specialization within the framework of "general" library education programs at the master's level needs study. The wide range among schools in the proportion of required (presumably "core") vs. elective courses can only be estimated. How students avail themselves of electives (for smorgasbord or specialization reasons) has never been analyzed; nor has the effectiveness of this student-determined approach to specialization been studied. Analysis here of the differences that may exist between curriculum structure and student experience of the curriculum may assist in planning.

The development of some relatively new master's-level programs with exclusive focus on "general" library education merits not only a fresh delineation of the rationale for such programs but also an evaluation of competence of their graduates on the job as compared with those functioning in similar positions with a specialized library education background.

The recent studies by Fryden (1969) and Danton (1969) of specialist (intermediate degree) programs provide us with a broad picture of these programs which are designed specifically to build on traditional library education at the master's level by an additional year of study which supports and strengthens the professional specialty of the student. The data from these two studies describe the range of policies and programs but do not isolate programs of excellence from programs with particular weaknesses. Furthermore, these data do not permit one to associate programs of varying effectiveness with different rationales or substance. Lowrie's study (1964, p. 69–72; 1966) of a single-purpose program suggests an area for comparative analysis. Such further study and evaluation are needed for development of standards and guidance for these new programs.

The case for development of specialization at the doctoral level is emerging against the traditional background of a general library education at the doctoral level (Carnovsky 1967, Swank 1967). Perhaps at the doctoral level, the rephrasing of the question from stark alternatives to matters of degree in emphasis is not relevant. The questions of specialization are intimately tied to questions regarding the purpose of the doctoral program; the kind and degree of specialization will vary with the program goals of research, teaching, or professional practice. Elucidation of the choice of specialization or general programs in relation to these goals is essential.

Another element in the structure of specialized library education that needs study is the articulation of the levels of specialization. Is there a definable sequence of general-to-specialized education? Experience has shown the difficulty of moving students with a specialized undergraduate education into general library education. Does early specialization presuppose an early conclusion of professional education? What is the role of continuing education? The profession has done no planning for the sequence of library education, and the question of specialization is an important concern in such planning.

Since specialization grows out of the combination of knowledge and talent of individuals, specialized library education rests, in large part, on the background its students bring to the study of librarianship. Study of the academic and professional fields related to particular areas of specialization is needed. The Allerton Park Conference report on "Training Needs of Librarians Doing Adult Education Work" (Asheim 1955) is illustrative of one approach to this area of educational planning. A decade ago, special librarianship posed the problem in terms of alternatives: subject background vs. library education, and concluded on the whole that both were needed. School librarianship is guided by state certification laws on this matter. Firmer analysis and evaluation of this question are necessary for career counseling and standards development. Research is also needed to answer the question: How much does the librarian need to know about the subject of the specialty (e.g., physicians and hospital practice)? From such information, it may be possible to outline the appropriate mixture of study in library schools and study in related fields.

The role of library education as the nexus for interdisciplinary study at the master's and advanced levels (in information science, in management and administration, in education services, etc.) needs investigation.

These specialties, while needed in library service, have not been fully incorporated into library education. To what extent have their concepts, bodies of knowledge, and techniques been incorporated? What is the desirable role of library education in respect to preparation in these specialties?

Curriculum and methodology

The conceptualization of curriculum as a cluster of courses rather than as a program sequence is especially troublesome in the area of specialized education. Typically, school librarianship has gone farthest in education, with the new field of information science establishing comparable levels of precision. The factors that work against early specialization in the field of practice (need for personal geographic mobility, late maturing of professional interests, etc.) make strict requirements in course sequence a difficulty. The traditional concept that the able student with general library education (or the able student with any kind of "accreditable" library education) can teach himself the specialties as his need arises is now being challenged. Studies of optimum program sequence in particular areas of specialization are needed.

Specialized library education, far more than general library education, traditionally has a field work or internship component. Library education in the last generation has tended to drop this program element, but now is exploring its reinstitution. Analysis of the relative effectiveness of the practice experience at different levels of study and at varying levels of responsibility are needed for particular fields of specialized education. Examination of the practicum in related professional disciplines for the structure of the experience and for the elements of effectiveness is needed immediately.

Analysis of the elements of general library education in the "core" courses as proposed and as actually taught would help to measure the gap between the concept of general library education and its actuality in practice. Exploration of the body of professional knowledge, which is presented in terms of "general librarianship" will provide an assessment of the resources upon which such general library education can be built. "General librarianship: myth or reality" must be concretely investigated.

The relationship of general to specialized courses in the master's program may be usefully elucidated. Case studies, for example, may begin to create a picture of current practice in articulation of these two aspects of the master's program.

The relation of general and specialized library education to the field of practice

The delineation of need for specialist education in library practice is a first step in which associations representing all types of libraries have engaged for current manpower studies. The precise task descriptions which incorporate the new concepts, technologies, and service relationships remain to be developed. Once the positions of library clerk, library technical assistant, and library assistant of the Asheim manpower structure have been realized, the revision of the specialties in librarianship—and their effect on library education—can become precise. It seems likely that all aspects of library service will have their professional functions. Both general and specialized library education must be restructured for education of what is generally referred to as "the new breed" of librarian.

If specialized library education is to be designed to meet the needs of the field of practice, evaluation must be made of the effectiveness of such programs in meeting those needs. The influence of such factors as mobility and change in professional interest must be measured. Similarly, the specialized work of graduates of general library education programs must be compared with that of graduates of specialized programs in meeting the needs of those in the field.

Any study of the sources of leadership in the professional specialties must evaluate the general and specialized library education programs from which the leaders come. The quality of leadership from the different programs might be analyzed for its relationship to specific elements in the relevant program.

Research approaches

Ideally, it would be desirable to distinguish the kinds of background knowledge needed by all librarians (the basic educational preparation) and the types of knowledge required by the various specialists to perform library services and operations in an efficient and effective manner. As an example, a group of librarians representing a variety of specialities could be studied to determine what knowledge is needed for performance of their work. The elements of knowledge common to all groups would represent the "core" of general educational needs, and those types of knowledge unique to each specialty would identify the specialized education necessary.

This approach, however, contains three specific problems which must be considered. First, various personal characteristics must be analyzed to determine the relationship between knowledge and performance. This could be accomplished by employing a number of tests which measure aptitude, intelligence, personality, etc. The second problem entails the establishment of a method to identify and categorize the components of the knowledge base. One method, the critical incident approach, has been employed by Hall (1968). Although job analysis has been found wanting, the limitation may have been imposed by the level of analysis (frequently, a task description) rather than the technique itself. The question is not what the cataloger does. Rather, it is what knowledge does the cataloger need for performing his work? The same question can be asked of the science bibliographer or the children's librarian. Once this is known, the question can be asked: How can this knowledge be provided most efficiently to the future librarian? Finally, it would be necessary to develop methods for obtaining objective measures of "professional proficiency." Surprisingly little research has been done in this area, and further studies are imperative if library education is to be solidly based.

It seems evident that, in the process of growth and development, all professions reach a point where the question of balance between general and specialized education is debated. The literature of some of these professions should be reviewed in depth to determine the techniques and procedures followed and their applicability to the problems of librarianship. It is suggested that one specific area that might be studied is the work of the American Society for Engineering Education (ASEE). A number of studies by this organization have been identified by Armsby (1955). The major curriculum study in social work completed by Boehm (1959) for the Council on Social Work Education offers another source for comparative study. Education, medicine, theology, law, among many others, may prove rich resources for further refinement in the conceptualization of "specialization."

Research in areas outlined here will often be dependent upon background in curriculum construction, learning psychology, and a variety of research methods. Team efforts by librarians and other experts, therefore, are anticipated. Research strategies may be sought in the studies of related professions, not only expediting sound inquiry on tested approaches, but also developing bases for comparisons with, and insights from, other fields.

References

American Library Association. "Standards and Guide for Undergraduate Programs in Librarianship." *ALA Bulletin* 52:695–700 (Oct. 1958).

Armsby, Henry H. "Engineering Education." In *Education for the Professions,* edited by Lloyd E. Blough. Washington, D.C.: U.S. Department of Health, Education, and Welfare, Office of Education, 1955.

Asheim, Lester, ed. *The Core of Education for Librarianship.* Chicago: American Library Association, 1954.

————. *Training Needs of Librarians Doing Adult Education Work; A Report of the Allerton Park Conference, November 14–16, 1954.* Chicago: American Library Association, 1955.

Boehm, Werner W. *Objectives of the Social Work Curriculum of the Future.* The Comprehensive Report of the Curriculum Study, vol. 1. New York: Council on Social Work Education, 1959.

Bunge, Charles A. *Professional Education and Reference Efficiency.* Research Series no. 11. Springfield, Ill.: Illinois State Library, 1967.

Butler, George E. "State Certification Requirements for Librarians Working with Children and Young People in Schools and Public Libraries." Master's thesis, University of Chicago, 1953.

Carnovsky, Leon. "Changing Patterns in Librarianship: Implications for Library Education." *Wilson Library Bulletin* 41:484–91 (Jan. 1967).

————. "Education for Librarianship." In *Libraries and Librarians of the Pacific Northwest,* edited by Norton Kroll. Seattle: University of Washington Press, 1960.

Charters, W. W. "Job Analysis in Education for Librarianship." *Libraries* 32:7–10 (Jan. 1927).

Cohen, Leonard, and Craven, Kenneth. *Science Information Personnel: The New Profession of Information Combining Science, Librarianship and Foreign Language.* New York: Modern Language Association of America, 1960.

Cohen, Morris L. "Educating Law Librarians: A Symposium." *Law Library Journal* 55:190–240 (Aug. 1962).

Danton, J. Periam. *Between M. L. S. and Ph.D.: A Study of Sixth-Year Specialist Programs in Accredited Library Schools.* Chicago: American Library Association, 1970.

Darling, Richard. "Curriculum: School Library Education." *Drexel Library Quarterly* 3:104–107 (Jan. 1967).

Ersted, Ruth. "Education for Library Service to Children and Youth." In *Education for Librarianship: Papers Presented at the Library Conference, University of Chicago, August 16–21, 1948,* edited by Bernard Berelson. Chicago: American Library Association, 1949.

————. "The Education of School Librarians." Master's thesis, University of Chicago, 1951.

Fenwick, Sara I. "The Education of Librarians Working with Children in Public Libraries." Master's thesis, University of Chicago, 1951.

Fryden, Floyd N. "Post Master's Degree Programs in the Accredited U.S. Library Schools." *Library Quarterly* 39:233–44 (July 1969).

Hall, Anna C. *Selected Educational Objectives for Public Service Librarians: A Taxonomic Approach.* Pittsburgh: University of Pittsburgh, 1968.

Hatch, Lucile. "Training the Young Adult Librarian." *Library Trends* 17: 150–65 (Oct. 1968).

Heilprin, Laurence B., et al. *Proceedings of the Symposium on Education for Information Science, Warrenton, Virginia, September 7–10, 1965.* Washington, D.C.: Spartan Books, 1965.

Henne, Frances. "Structuring Library Education Curriculums for Preparing Librarians of Material Centers." In *The School Library as a Materials Center: Educational Needs of Librarians and Teachers in its Administration and Use,* edited by Mary Helen Mahar. Washington, D.C.: U.S. Department of Health, Education, and Welfare, Office of Education, 1964.

International Conference on Education for Scientific Information Work: Queen Elizabeth College, London, 3rd to 7th April, 1967. The Hague: Federation Internationale de Documentation, 1967.

Jackson, Eugene. "Critique on Special Library Education." *Drexel Library Quarterly* 3:211–15 (Apr. 1967).

———, and Rothstein, Samuel. "Should Library Schools Produce Specialists or Generalists?" *ALA Bulletin* 56:320–23 (Apr. 1962).

Janke, Leslie H. "The Library Education Program of San Jose State College." In *The School Library as a Materials Center: Educational Needs of Librarians and Teachers in its Administration and Use,* edited by Mary Helen Mahar. Washington, D.C.: U.S. Department of Health, Education, and Welfare, Office of Education, 1964.

Leigh, Robert D. "The Education of Librarians." In *The Public Librarian,* edited by Alice I. Bryan. New York: Columbia University Press, 1952.

———, ed. *Major Problems in the Education of Librarians.* New York: Columbia University Press, 1954.

Lieberman, I., ed. *Education for Health Sciences Librarianship: Proceedings of an Invitational Conference, September 10–12, 1967.* Seattle: University of Washington School of Librarianship, 1968.

Liesener, James Will. "An Empirical Test of the Validity of the Core Concept in the Preparation of University Librarians." Ph.D. dissertation, University of Michigan, 1967.

Long, Marie Ann. *The State Library Consultant at Work.* Research Series No. 6. Springfield, Ill.: Illinois State Library, 1965.

Lowrie, Jean E. "Education and Training of School Librarians." *Bulletin of the National Association of Secondary School Principals* 50:64–69 (Jan. 1966).

———. "The Western Michigan University Program for the Instructional Materials Center Specialist." In *The School Library as a Materials Center: Educational Needs of Librarians and Teachers in its Administration and*

Use, edited by Mary Helen Mahar. Washington, D.C.: U.S. Department of Health, Education, and Welfare, Office of Education, 1964.

McCrossan, John A. *Library Science Education and its Relationship to Competence in Adult Book Selection in Public Libraries.* Research Series No. 9. Springfield, Ill.: Illinois State Library, 1967.

Martin, Lowell A. "Research in Education for Librarianship." *Library Trends* 6:207–208 (Oct. 1957).

Monroe, Margaret E. "Educating Librarians for the Work of Library Adult Education." *Library Trends* 8:91–107 (July 1959).

Muller, Robert. "Critique on University Library Education." *Drexel Library Quarterly* 3:204–10 (Apr. 1967).

Munn, Ralph. "Education for Public Librarianship." In *Education for Librarianship: Papers Presented at the Chicago Conference, University of Chicago, August 16–21, 1948,* edited by Bernard Berelson. Chicago: American Library Association, 1949.

Nichol, Isabel. "A Study of the Curriculum of the University of Denver School of Librarianship." *Library Journal* 67:65–68 (15 Jan. 1946).

Reece, Ernest J. *The Curriculum in Library Schools.* New York: Columbia University Press, 1936.

———. "Research in Education for Librarianship, 1957–63." American Library Association, Education Division *Newsletter* 53:10–20 (Mar. 1965).

———. *The Task and Training of Librarians.* New York: King's Crown Press, 1949.

Ryan, Dorothy E. "The Place of Elective Courses in Public, College, School and Special Library Work in the Basic Year of Professional Library Training." Master's thesis, Columbia University, School of Library Service, 1950.

Shera, Jesse H. "Dimensions of the Master's Program." *ALA Bulletin* 58:519–22 (June 1964).

Swank, Raynard C. "The Graduate Library School Curriculum." In *Problems of Library School Administration: Report of an Institute, April 14–15, 1965,* edited by Sarah R. Reed. Washington, D.C.: U.S. Department of Health, Education, and Welfare, Office of Education, 1965.

———. "Sixth Year Curricula and the Education of Library School Faculties." *Journal of Educational Leadership* 8:14–19 (Summer 1967).

Taylor, Robert S. "Curriculum Development in Documentation and the Information Sciences." In *Proceedings of the American Documentation Institite, vol. 1: Parameters of Information Science.* Washington, D.C.: American Documentation Institute, 1964.

———. *Curriculum for the Information Sciences: Final Report on Curriculum Development in the Information Sciences: Recommended Courses and Curricula.* Bethlehem, Pa.: Lehigh University Center for the Information Sciences, 1967.

Truman, David B. "The Changing Character of Undergraduate Education." *School and Society* 92:380–83 (Dec. 1964).

Vainstein, Rose. "What the Library Schools Can Do in the Training and Upgrading of State Library Consultants." In *The Changing Role of State Library Consultants,* edited by Guy G. Garrison. Urbana, Ill.: University of Illinois Graduate School of Library Science, 1968.

White, Carl M. "Discussion (of Advanced Study and Research in Librarianship)." In *Education for Librarianship: Papers Presented at the Library Conference, University of Chicago, August 16–21, 1948,* edited by Bernard Berelson. Chicago: American Library Association, 1949.

Wight, Edward A. *Evaluation and Revision of the Library School Curriculum.* Nashville, Tenn.: Peabody Press, 1945.

Williamson, Charles C. *Training for Library Service.* New York: Carnegie Corporation of New York, 1923.

Winger, Howard W. "Education for Area-Studies Librarianship." *Library Quarterly* 35:361-72 (Oct. 1965).

Gerald Jahoda

The Integration of Information Science and Library Automation into the Library School Educational Program

Definition of the problem

In reviewing the literature in the framework of my topic, I have dealt primarily with the questions of what to teach and with what desired objectives, in what context this teaching should be done, and what should be the background of the teacher and the student. The context in which the teaching is to be done is the master's-level library school curriculum, either as presently constituted or in revised form. This is the fifth-year program in the U.S. for librarians-to-be, who seek employment as beginning librarians in academic, public, school, or special libraries. Library automation is defined as the use of data processing and related equipment in libraries. The following definition (American Society for Information Science 1968) of information science is used for purposes of this report:

> As a discipline, Information Science investigates the properties and behavior of information, the forces that govern the transfer process, and the technology required to process information for optimum accessibility and use. Its interests include information representations in both natural and artificial systems; the use of codes for efficient message transmission, storage, and recall; and the study of information processing devices and techniques such as computers and their programming systems.
>
> It is an interdisciplinary field derived from and related to mathematics, logic, linguistics, psychology, computer technology, operations re-

search, librarianship, the graphic arts, communications, management, and similar fields.

Information Science has both a pure science component, which inquires into the subject without regard to application, and an applied science component, which develops services and products.

It is not surprising that the other nine topics being discussed in this book are directly or indirectly related to my assigned topic. I have chosen either to ignore or to avoid detailed treatment of topics that are covered extensively in the other reports. For this reason, little is said about general vs. specialized education. I have chosen as my primary concern the fifth-year program for generalists. Instructional methodology, library school faculty, and students are not given detailed attention, although these are, of course, important aspects of my topic. What could not be disregarded and, in fact, loomed large in the background is the function of the librarian and the library school program at the master's level, both today and in the future, near and distant. My own opinions on these subjects are well summarized in the following quotations from a recent report by Lester Asheim:

> . . . the term "librarian" (is used) to designate those who are qualified by background and training to go beyond the level of application of established rules and techniques to the analysis of library problems and the formulation of original and creative solutions for them (Asheim 1968, p. 1096).

> The objectives (of the new master's programs) should be to prepare people, not simply to keep libraries operating at their present levels, but to anticipate and engineer the changes and improvement required to move the profession forward (Asheim 1968, p. 1102).

Historical record

The literature on teaching library automation and information science was reviewed to answer the following questions (which also serve as subdivisions of this part of the report):

1. What to teach and with what desired effect?
2. Where in the program should these topics be taught?
3. How to teach these topics?
4. Who should be taught and who should teach these topics?

What to teach and with what desired effect?

Asheim (1968, p. 1104) makes the following comments on this subject:

> The introduction of electronic computers and other mechanized equipment and devices does not alter basic aims of library service, however much they may affect the storage and retrieval of data, the reproduction of materials, the efficient performance of certain routines and procedures, and the possibility of new and expanded services. The new machines represent new tools which may (or in some cases may not) prove useful in meeting those aims. Nevertheless, the potentialities of the machine and the new approaches to library and information service that they make possible represent an area of understanding essential to those who wish to perform effectively in the libraries of today or design the libraries of tomorrow. For that reason, a great deal of the traditional content of library school courses will have to be revised to accommodate changes that are already here or are soon to come.

Taylor (1967), who developed an information science program outside of a library school, characterizes areas of interaction between librarianship and information science on one hand and engineering on the other, as being the areas of systems analysis; environmental context; information channels; the naming, labeling, and classification processes; and man-systems interaction. He believes that information science offers a much broader view of librarianship and foresees an entirely new library school curriculum with course groupings based on the five areas listed above rather than by types of libraries.

In 1964, Robert Hayes recorded his personal belief that information science will become an integral part of the librarian's profession and operational responsibility, and that it represents the theoretical, if not scientific, foundation of librarianship. He argues that the defining concern of information science is with understanding of the processes in handling and communicating recorded information. This, Hayes states, is best achieved by concentration on the development of methodologies for systems design, using the terms in the broadest sense. Methodologies listed by Hayes are: user study, vocabulary development, analysis of technical detail of internal system processes, file organization, intellectual decision-making of relevance and screening of material, component and system evaluation, and analysis of organizational relationships, as, for example, between library and management (Hayes 1964).

In 1967, Hayes described a course that includes some of these subjects. It is required at the University of California (Los Angeles) library school of all master of library science graduates. The course, according to Hayes, is a relatively elementary introduction to the principles of systems analysis and data processing, with emphasis on those judgmental issues in evaluation with which the librarian should be concerned. The purpose of the course is to introduce the library school student to the technology of computing in such a way that he will see it in the total context of library purposes and goals. The emphasis of the course is, therefore, on the systems approach. Hayes comments that library school students generally lack the technical background for data processing work as such; yet, as library school graduates, they will find themselves in a world where that technology will play an increasingly important role. As students, they must be given sufficient orientation to be able to fit data processing into the context of library objectives. The intent of the introductory course on this subject is to bridge the gap between students' existing background and their future work (Hayes 1967). The University of Toronto School of Library Science's position on this matter is stated by Kurmey (1966). He writes that his school recognizes its responsibility to familiarize librarians with systems analysis and related disciplines utilized in library systems planning and to acquaint librarians with the powerful capabilities of the computer in libraries.

What do library schools teach in the way of library automation and information science? In a questionnaire survey of library school programs conducted by Schick, one question asked whether the school offers a separate course or courses on library automation and/or information science. Thirty-two out of forty-two of the reporting ALA accredited library schools in the United States and Canada responded that, in the academic year 1966–67, they offered separate courses dealing with these topics. Fifteen non-accredited library schools also offered such courses (Schick 1968). This survey will be updated for the 1968–69 academic year, according to a recent announcement by the U.S. Office of Education (1969). Hayes (1967) lists course offerings in these areas by library schools as well as other schools under the following headings:

1. Methods analysis for librarians, including library systems analysis.
2. Information retrieval, with emphasis on mechanization and data processing in the library.
3. Information systems analysis, with emphasis on systems methodology directed to various information problems.
4. Information science research emphasis.

Rees (1969) categorizes courses in library automation and information science into the following three areas:

Area I: Library automation (systems analysis, computer and allied hardware, theory and application of automation to library processes and procedures such as acquisition, serials, circulation control or catalog production).

Area II: Documentation and information storage and retrieval systems (design of retrieval systems, subject analysis, abstracting and indexing, structure of index language, file organization, question analysis, search strategy, dissemination, translation, testing, and evaluation).

Area III: Information science research methodology (basic principles and tools of mathematics, logic, linguistics, statistics, psychology, and other disciplines, and their application to the investigation of library-based and communication-related phenomena).

There are difficulties in conducting surveys of course offerings in library automation and information science, as is pointed out by Rees (1969). He states that it is difficult to relate course titles to course content. This is caused by the lack of agreement as to the definition of documentation, information retrieval, information science, and library automation. Rees concludes that the major response of library education to the communication revolution has been to add courses in library automation and information retrieval. The educational emphasis decidedly has been upon the applied aspect of information science. A concerted effort has been and continues to be made in the provision of educational offerings designed to give students a knowledge of computers and allied hardware and their applications to library procedures. At the same time, an attempt is made to teach the structure of retrieval systems and their relevance to librarianship.

Where in the program should these topics be taught?

There seems to be agreement that library automation and information science should be integrated into the library school curriculum. Swank (1967) reflects this view but points out that the new, integrated program cannot be completed in one year of graduate study. His guess is that one would have to plan for two full years of graduate study. Hines (1967) suggests that the entire curriculum be broadened so that almost every course is to include modern retrieval methods, science, and technology. This is also Asheim's opinion (1968). He states that a great deal of the traditional content of the library school courses will have to be revised to accommodate changes that are already here or are soon to come. It is not enough for a library school to add a course in documentation or information science to its existing program. Asheim believes that the role of the new devices, the impact of new approaches upon traditional methods, and the implications for new services or better performance of current functions should be assimilated into the entire curriculum, enriching every course where pertinent.

How to teach these topics?

Gull (1965) wrote that during the preceding five years there had been considerable experimentation and changes in librarianship, but the effect of them had not yet been widespread enough to produce a settled body of practice and knowledge which the faculty could use as the foundation for its teaching. There were no textbooks suitable for courses in the field. There were almost no comprehensive articles or good reviews. Rees and Saracevic (1965) also point to the absence of texts as one of the problems of teaching in this field. However, there are a number of films that may be used as teaching aids (Slavens 1968).

Demonstrations, exercises, and hands-on experience with information systems have been used or suggested by several writers. Western Reserve University's Comparative Systems Laboratory was used in connection with a course in information storage and retrieval systems. The students' response was very favorable, partly because they were brought to the frontier of knowledge and partly because they were given the opportunity to participate in research (Saracevic 1968). Batty (1967) suggests the use of a model of an indexing system to simulate real-life experience. The model, which was not yet ready for use at the time of publication of the article, is to be employed for demonstrations to elementary and large classes and for manipulation by advanced classes. The LEEP (Library Education Experimental Project) at Syracuse University provides a laboratory for library school students in which the Library of Congress MARC tapes are searched on the computer (LEEP 1969). O'Connor (1967) describes a series of eighteen exercises dealing primarily with indexing and abstracting that require from a few hours to a few days to execute.

Who should be taught and who should teach these topics?

Arguments presented in favor of including library automation and information science as required topics in library schools are also arguments for exposing every library school student to these topics. This presents pedagogical problems, as has been pointed out by Gull and Hayes. Gull writes that the library school students have an insufficient background in mathematics, in logic, and in science and technology. They are unacquainted with the management of large enterprises. As a result, the instructor must spend time on material with which the student should be familiar before he reaches the information science course. Hayes' comment (1967) that library school students generally lack the technical background necessary for data processing work has already been mentioned.

Who should teach library automation and information science? Gull (1965) points to a problem that existed in 1965 and does not appear to have been solved today. He states that the teacher of information science is usually either strong in librarianship but lacks background in mathematics, logic, statistics, and engineering, or he has the subject background but lacks knowledge of librarianship.

Summary and evaluation of the historical record

There seems to be agreement that all library school graduate students should be exposed to library automation and information science, and surveys indicate that most accredited library schools offer at least one such course, although it may not be required of all students. There is, however, little agreement on specific topics to be included and on testable behavioral objectives of this teaching. The topics under discussion can be divided into four parts:

1. Library automation: data processing, data transmission, reproduction, microfilming, and printing equipment in the library.
2. Systems studies: methodologies for designing and evaluating library services and procedures.
3. Information storage and retrieval systems: abstracting, indexing, and selective dissemination of information.
4. Information science research methodology: basic principles and tools of mathematics, logic, linguistics, statistics, psychology, and other disciplines, and their applications to the investigation of library-based and communication-related phenomena.

Even if we can agree that the topics should be so characterized, a number of questions and unresolved problems remain. Should information science research methodology be taught as part of the master's program for general librarians? What aspects of the topics should be taught? Should experimental work in progress be included in introductory courses? While there appears to be agreement in principle that library automation and information science should be integrated into the curriculum instead of being taught in separate courses, the practice is now to offer separate courses. If these topics are to be integrated, should they be integrated into a curriculum based on courses being offered today, or should the curriculum be reconstructed along different lines? Can a revised curriculum be offered in a calendar year, and, if not, is it realistic to lengthen the program? Academe is notoriously slow in instituting changes. Recent events on campus may provide an atmosphere more conducive to change, but research is needed both on what changes to make and how to bring them about in the most efficient and effective way. There is also the question of the articulation of the revised generalist curriculum with the information science specialist curriculum, that is, determination of which courses or sections of courses are relevant to both curricula.

Teaching methodology is, of course, closely related to what is being taught, and the latter must be specified first. Complaints expressed in 1965 about the lack of texts are still valid to a large extent. The *Annual Review of Information Science and Technology* has been helpful both as a text and as a tool for selecting readings. Little appears to have been done as yet with programmed texts or computer-aided instruction programs. There are a number of films that can be used as teaching aids. Exercises, demonstrations, and laboratories are being developed and used. And this brings me to the last two topics—the students and the teachers. Gull's comments (1965) that students do not have the necessary background for learning these topics are probably still true today. However, those comments may no longer be true in a few years when all college students are likely to be exposed to computer programming and the necessary mathematics as well as logic. The teacher who is not a specialist in library automation and information science—but who must introduce these topics into his courses—will have to be helped by training programs, teaching aids, or other means.

Alternate solutions

It is my considered opinion that, for the reasons expressed above, we are not as yet ready to present fully developed alternative solutions. I have, therefore, listed parts or components of plans or solutions. Each of these parts or components can also vary. There is another argument for dealing with parts of solutions rather than fully formed ones: The traditional research approach is to divide complex problems into their component parts and to subject these parts to a critical examination. The first three of the eight listed parts are dealt with in some detail in this section.

List of components of solution

   1. Specific subjects to be taught
   2. Approaches to teaching the subjects

3. Curriculum structure
4. Teaching methodology. What technique or combination of techniques should be used to teach the selected subjects?
5. Required educational background of entering library school students. Will we have to change or supplement the requirement that the student have an undergraduate major in the liberal arts?
6. What aspects of the subject are to be taught for academic credit, on a noncredit basis, or required before admittance into the program?
7. Length of the program. Is one calendar year sufficient, or do we need to lengthen the program?
8. Teachers of the subjects. Will we have a generation of teachers who will know both library science as well as library automation and information science? If not, how can we best retrain the present generation of teachers?

Specific subjects to be taught

Specific subjects that might be included in the curriculum are grouped under the headings library automation, systems studies techniques, information storage and retrieval systems, and information science research methodology. The selection of the topics to be included in the curriculum and the extent of coverage of the selected topics will depend upon the state of the art of both the technology and librarianship at the time the program is implemented and on the behavioral objectives of the program. Research needed to determine these factors is outlined in the next section.

1. Library automation
   a. Equipment
   Data processing equipment (unit record equipment; off-line use of computers); data transmission equipment (teletypewriters, telefacsimile equipment); microforming equipment (microfilming cameras, microform readers, and printers); reprography, including printing equipment (copying equipment; offset and letterpress printing equipment)
   b. Applications of equipment
   The use of the equipment for specific operations in libraries, e.g., acquisitions, cataloging, circulation and reference—either for single operations or combinations thereof; either by individual libraries or by or for groups of libraries
2. Systems studies techniques. Time studies, work sampling, cost studies, flowcharting, forms design and control, mathematical modeling

3. Information storage and retrieval systems. Subject analysis, abstracting, indexing, translation, structure of index language, file organization, search strategy, question analysis, testing of systems
4. Information science research methodology. Basic principles and tools of mathematics, logic, linguistics, statistics, psychology, and other disciplines, and their application to the investigation of library-based and communication-related phenomena.

Approaches to teaching the subjects

Although to a certain extent approaches become mixed in order to make teaching responsive to the interests of the student in the classroom, governing attitudes do prevail. These should be isolated in order to perceive their implications.

Graduates of the library school program are being prepared for beginning positions as reference librarians, catalogers, acquisitions librarians, or for beginning positions that call for the performance of a combination of these tasks in today's libraries. Even though libraries are expected to change, and even though library school graduates should be equipped to participate in making the changes, it is the primary responsibility of the library schools to educate students for positions in libraries of today. Since the beginning librarian will be a practitioner rather than a theoretician, little if any pure information science is to be part of his curriculum. According to this reasoning, the emphasis in teaching the topics under discussion should be on applications. Students should be taught about equipment, abstracting, indexing, and systems studies as users of such tools and techniques rather than producers thereof.

Those who oppose the applied approach will point out that practices vary among libraries. From a perspective of international librarianship, the variance is even greater. Therefore, principles should be emphasized in a graduate program. The theoretical aspects of a subject are its relatively stable elements and have the widest generality. Further, an emphasis on the "why" rather than the "how" will provide the graduate with a frame of reference both for working in today's library and for stimulating reasoned change in the field. For these reasons, pure rather than applied information science should be taught.

While proponents of the theory-only approach have sound arguments on their side, there are practical considerations which provide arguments against such an approach. There is as yet no unified theoretical framework for library automation and information science. Moreover, the library school student's ability or experience to cope with a theory-oriented curriculum is doubtful at best. An alternative solution is to expose students to directly applicable theory; for example, information retrieval system theory, as well as to applications of tools and techniques. The theoretical aspect of the program can be expanded as more relevant and digestible theory becomes available and as students become more susceptible to such treatment.

Curriculum structure

In our concern over the relation between information science and the regular program, we must dwell upon the unsettled issue of the function of the present library education framework. If this framework is useful, we can include library automation and information science within it. The position can be taken that today's curriculum structure reflects services and operations in today's libraries. Library automation and information science should, therefore, be included in established courses on materials selection, reference, technical services, administration, and other relevant courses. Library schools are ongoing operations, and changes within the existing framework are likely to be easier to accomplish and therefore more likely to be accomplished. For a short-term solution, changes within the existing framework might also be preferable, because a new structure should be based on future directions of libraries—something that might not be known for a number of years.

If the structure is found to be grossly deficient, we should consider including library automation and information science in a newly developed structure. Since the relevance of much of what is being taught in library schools has been questioned, including library automation and information science within existing courses would be a patch-up operation at best. It would be preferable to take an over-all look at the curriculum in terms of its objectives, how these objectives are now being accomplished, and what alternate ways there are for achieving specified objectives. It is not too soon, according to this position, to begin a systems analysis of the library school curriculum.

Questions to consider

To make a rational choice from among the alternatives listed in the last section, we need answers to the following questions:

1. What are the anticipated short-term developments in librarianship and related fields? Projections are also needed on technological developments and the probability of their acceptance by librarians and for anticipated financial support of libraries.

2. What are anticipated manpower needs, both in number of people and types of skills? What are the characteristics of individuals that should be attracted to librarianship? How long has the average library school graduate stayed in the profession? How long is the new graduate likely to stay in the profession?
3. What will be the job of the beginning librarian and that of the experienced librarian?
4. What background in mathematics, logic, computer programming, and other relevant subjects will the college graduate bring to library school?
5. If the function of the library school is to set the pace for the profession, what resources must be provided to the school to enable it to perform this function?
6. Is it realistic to plan a master's program that cannot be completed in a calendar year? What should be done if the answer is no?
7. How can curriculum changes best be implemented?
8. What background and experience should teachers of library automation and information science have?
9. How can teachers of library automation best be trained, retrained, and updated?
10. What are the best teaching techniques for achieving specified behavioral objectives?
11. What teaching aids can be prepared or provided to facilitate the task of the individual teacher?

Specific research project

The integration of the topic of indexing into the library school curriculum.

The objective is to prepare a plan for teaching indexing in library schools. The plan is to include subjects to be taught in specified courses, a statement of behavioral objectives and the means for testing the achievement of behavioral objectives, and a description of teaching techniques and teaching aids.

Review of the present state
of the art of indexing:

This is conceived as a review of the literature and of research in progress. The objective would be the identification of available theory, established practice, and needed research. Included in the review would be:

1. Available knowledge about types of indexes, e.g., alphabetic subject, alphabetico-classified, hierarchically classified, faceted, permuted title, citation, post-coordinate, and machine-prepared indexes
2. Index variables, e.g., depth of indexing, level of indexing, source of index entries, vocabulary construction, and amount of information per index entry
3. Search variables, e.g., desired requirements for completeness of search results, current awareness versus retrospective searching, and searching for recall vs. searching for discovery
4. Index evaluation.

The review should differentiate between historical aspects, the present state of the art, and anticipated developments in indexing. Persons with knowledge in both indexing and librarianship might be asked to prepare a state-of-the-art report. To aid in the identification of anticipated developments, the literature search might be supplemented by interviews with researchers in the field of indexing.

The present and anticipated role of
indexes and indexing in libraries:

Libraries deal with a variety of records, and each record must be organized, i.e., indexed, for purposes of being used. There are internally prepared records intended primarily for internal use, e.g., circulation records, personnel records, and financial records. There are externally prepared records intended primarily for internal use, e.g., union lists and trade bibliographies. There are internally prepared records intended primarily for public use, e.g., the card catalog and the list of serial holdings. There are externally prepared records intended primarily for public use, e.g., published abstracts, indexes, bibliographies, and other reference tools. What is the librarian's function in the preparation, use, and explanation of use of these records to the public? What additional records are likely to be introduced in view of changes in the role of libraries and those due to technology? Should there be, for example, an index to users' interest profiles, to individuals' information resources? Should the preparation of some of these records be accomplished with the aid of data-processing equipment? What new indexes and index variables might be introduced in libraries? Are some library records—for example, accession books—no longer necessary? The answers to these and other questions must await, in part, a study of the role and functions of libraries in view of the changes taking place. It is assumed that this aspect of the subject will be investigated in another research project and that the findings will be used in determining the role of indexes in libraries. For answers to questions about existing records, the preparation of an inventory of types of records in libraries is suggested. Once a list of types of records has been prepared, the function of each record should be determined along with suitable methods for its preparation and use.

The relationship of indexing and indexes
    to other topics:

Just as indexing is related to most library operations, it is also related to most subjects taught in library schools. There is a further parallel: It it difficult to specify the role of indexing in a curriculum with as yet unspecified changes. The discussion, therefore, must be limited to existing courses in library schools, with integration of indexing into a revised curriculum—should this be the chosen alternative—to be held in abeyance until we know more about the new curriculum. There is an obvious relationship between indexing and cataloging as well as reference work, one being related to the preparation of indexes and the other to the use of indexes. Also, related, though perhaps not as obviously so, are courses in selection of materials (indexes are tools used in the selection process) and courses in administration (indexes are prepared and used as aids in the decision-making process). The role of indexing in today's library school courses might be determined through examining descriptions of courses and course outlines and syllabi and through interviews with teachers.

Determining behavioral objectives:

What we want the student to know (his exit behavior) and how we can determine whether he has indeed learned what we want him to learn, are questions that need to be answered. The results of the three previous steps in this section should be used as a basis for developing testable behavioral objectives. These objectives, as well as tests for measuring the accomplishments of the objectives, should be developed in consultation with educational researchers.

Teaching techniques:

Where and how, for example, should lectures and films be used? What are the roles of texts—both conventional and programmed—and computer-aided instruction? How can demonstrations be used to illustrate specified aspects of indexing? How should practice in the preparation, searching, and evaluation of indexes be used in teaching? Should the student be asked to participate in either ongoing indexing experiments or in the preparation of published indexes and abstracts, for example, *Information Science Abstracts?* If there are alternative ways to achieve specified behavioral objectives—as is likely—controlled experiments using different teaching techniques should be carried out. Library school teachers should draw upon the experience of educational researchers in conducting such experiments.

Teaching aids:

Teaching aids will have to be developed to speed the implementation of integrated inclusion of indexing in the curriculum. It should be remembered that the teachers who are to include indexing in their courses are not likely to be experts in this field. Thus, for practical reasons, the development of teaching aids and teaching programs for teachers must be part of the research program. Teaching aids to consider (in addition to those already available) include the preparation of conventional and programmed texts and computer-aided instruction programs. Videotaped and filmed lectures and demonstrations should also be considered as well as closed-circuit television presentations for the purpose of sharing expert teachers. The preparation of a teaching collection of documents to be indexed along with subject authority lists and questions for searching the index should also be considered. Some of these teaching aids will need to be updated on a continuing basis for the purpose of reflecting the changes in the field and to correct shortcomings that will have become apparent during their use.

References

American Society for Information Science. *Description of Function and Organization.* Washington, D.C.: 1968.

Asheim, L. E. "Education and Manpower for Librarianship." *ALA Bulletin* 62:1096–1106 (Oct. 1968).

Batty, C. D. "A Documentation Training Model." *American Documentation* 18:125–30 (July 1967).

Gull, C. D. "The Challenges of Teaching the Information Sciences." *Journal of Education for Librarianship* 6:61–64 (Summer 1965).

Hayes, R. M. "The Development of a Methodology for System Design and its Role in Library Education." *Library Quarterly* 34:330–51 (Oct. 1964).

Hayes, R. M. "Data Processing in the Library School Curriculum." *ALA Bulletin* 61:662–69 (June 1967).

Hines, T. C. "Salaries and Academic Training Programs for Information Scientists." *Journal of Chemical Documentation* 7:118–20 (May 1967).

Kurmey, W. J. "Educational Developments Include Documentation and Automation." *Ontario Library Review* 50:237–39 (Dec. 1966).

LEEP (Library Education Experimental Project). Syracuse University School of Library Science. *First Thoughts about MARCS/DPS in the Classroom* 1(2) 1–2 June 1969.

O'Connor, J. "Curriculum for the Information Sciences Report #8." A manual of experiments in documentation. Bethlehem, Pa.: Lehigh University Center for Information Sciences, 1967.

Rees, A. M. "The Impact of Computer Technology on Library Education." *UNESCO Bulletin for Libraries* 23:25–29 (Jan. 1969).

————, and Saracevic, T. "Teaching Documentation at Western Reserve University." *Journal of Education for Librarianship* 6:8–13 (Summer 1965).

Saracevic, T. "Linking Research and Teaching." *American Documentation* 19:398–403 (Oct. 1968).

Schick, F. L., ed. *North American Library Education Directory and Statistics 1966–68.* Chicago: American Library Association, 1968.

Slavens, T. P. "Films for Teaching." *Journal of Education for Librarianship* 9:149–51 (Fall 1968).

Swank, R. C. "Documentation and Information Science in the Core Library School Curriculum." *Special Libraries* 58:40–44 (Jan. 1967).

Taylor, R. S. "The Interfaces between Librarianship and Information Science and Engineering." *Special Libraries* 58:45–48 (Jan. 1967).

"U. S. Office of Education awards a grant to conduct 1968/69 Library and Information Sciences program survey." *Library Journal* 94:2871 (1969).

Irving Lieberman

Relating Instructional Methodology
To Teaching in Library Schools

Definition of the problem

> Every now and then some library school graduate breaks forth with
> a bitter denunciation of the teaching he or she received at a particular
> library school. . . . These criticisms inevitably touch a responsive
> chord in most of us, whether teacher or student, for unless we
> have been extremely fortunate, we have all suffered under inept
> teaching in a library school. To be sure, if we are teachers ourselves,
> we know these complaints are not directed at us. Our teaching is
> above reproach. We suspect that the teaching of our colleagues
> needs improvement, although we have no way of really knowing, for
> probably we have never actually sat in on one of their classes, or
> collaborated with them in any significant way (Coughlin 1968).

At the outset it should be understood that the use of the newer
communications media goes far beyond previously described audiovisual materials. To comprehend the scope of our consideration, it
seems wise to include sufficient descriptive matter about the newer
media in this paper. An important aid in this regard is the volume,
New Media and College Teaching (Thornton 1968). This book consists of specific comments by the staff of the Higher Education Media
Study, funded under a contract with the Bureau of Higher Education
of the U.S. Office of Education through the cooperation of the Association for Higher Education and the Department of Audiovisual Instruction of the National Education Association. The descriptive sections in
the book include several case studies. These are followed by an insti-

tutional inventory with a brief annotation of current practice. The present writer has paraphrased and summarized the descriptive section on each of the newer media with which we will be concerned in library education.

Learning systems

In today's world it is inevitable that we be concerned with the total process of learning and we are aware that the process is achieved through a system. The system includes all of the equipment, procedures, facilities, program schedules, texts, materials, and personnel required to produce the end result. The Higher Education Media Study paid particular attention to systems (Thornton 1968):

> The economic realities in higher education today require that a proper distinction be made between the acts of *teaching* and *informing*. Two things especially seem to be needed: (1) wider understanding of the fact that simple *informing* may often be performed quite adequately through the use of materials in listening laboratories, computer-assisted instructional systems, multi-media installations, television networks, etc., and (2) a better understanding of the fact that *teaching* continues to require the in-person contributions of professors in illuminating, elaborating, questioning, and evaluating and in managing the necessary give-and-take involved in exchanging of ideas with students.

Communication media

Instructional television

When educators first thought of using television in instruction, they were often concerned with its special contributions in solving problems stemming from rising student enrollments and a relatively static supply of new holders of doctoral degrees, many of whom were being enticed into government and industrial service instead of going into college teaching. Some educators also mentioned a special potentiality of the medium for multiplying the effectiveness of especially able professors under arrangements permitting them to teach hundreds of thousands at one time, while other less-distinguished professors served as discussion leaders with smaller groups in remote locations.

The pressing problem at present is still that of developing course materials that are worth televising, rather than planning new and more complicated physical installations. In addition to the colleges now using closed-circuit television, videotape recorders, inter-institutional broadcasting, and open-circuit instruction for credit, there are fully as many institutions proceeding with plans to introduce one or more of these media as rapidly as funds and construction of the facilities will permit. Here are some of the uses of television:

1. Live presentation in a large auditorium. There is the additional option of transmitting the lecture live to any convenient number of remote receivers, or of taping it for showings at numerous times and in any number of classrooms.
2. In a large classroom equipped with monitors, or even with monitors in remote classrooms, it is possible to magnify realia (e.g., a page from the *Gutenberg Bible*) or to broadcast microscopic demonstrations so that large numbers of students may view the single visual.
3. The simple microwave transmission of televised signals to receivers at other locations, such as those in a system of colleges where it is either not possible or not economically feasible to staff a given course, or where the specific contribution of noted lecturer-demonstrator is desired.
4. Some of the most interesting uses of television are those enabling a professor to present, and the student to observe, events that would be otherwise inaccessible or unobservable, or where the presence of observers would introduce distracting or contaminative elements into the event under study.
5. A self-contained classroom television system—camera, videotape recorder, and monitor—offers exciting possibilities for teaching any type of skill. As an example, in such diverse fields as student-teaching, storytelling, or golf, a practice session allows the learner to see, to criticize, to repeat, and to improve his own performance.
6. Open-circuit television courses for college credit are a reality; students have completed work for diplomas by means of broadcast courses.

Films

The motion picture was one of the first "new media" to be used in instruction. The 16mm. silent film has had a forty-year history of utilization in classrooms in this country. Sound and color films became available for teaching almost as soon as they were introduced into theaters. Films still make important contributions to instruction, and several institutions of higher education are actively engaged in film experimentation.

A very useful innovation in film usage has direct application to independent study. This is the 8mm. cartridge-contained "single-concept" film loop. In this form, each film may run only five to ten minutes; the film can be checked out from the laboratory stockroom—or from the library—inserted by the student into the projector in a nearby carrel, and viewed as often as desired. Faculty members who are using or producing films for instructional use uniformly report that the value of both 16mm. and 8mm. films has not yet been fully realized, even after forty years; that they still can serve certain instructional functions more economically and conveniently than other newer media; and that new uses for and combining the use of film with other new media remain to be explored.

Listening laboratories and audio tapes

The listening laboratory is perhaps the most successful and widely used of the many new media now available to higher education. It seems reasonable to estimate that a majority of colleges have at least a minimal listening facility for use in language instruction. A more recent adaptation of the listening laboratory is the dial-access system. In this arrangement, the same types of recording facilities are used. However, the dial-access facility emphasizes individual study. Dial access has also made it possible to bring much instruction directly into the living quarters of students.

Programmed instruction

Programmed instruction is a technique for self-instruction which presents instructional material in small segments, each followed by a task which permits the student to demonstrate his comprehension or skill. If he performs the task correctly, he is presented with another sequence of learning-response-judgment; if he makes an error, he must either restudy the same material or "branch" to additional instruction before being allowed to proceed with further instruction. The reinforcement effect of immediate knowledge of success or failure, in such cases, is believed to be a powerful stimulus to learning.

The crucial problem of programmed instruction is that of constructing the programs themselves. The construction of a useful program for college instruction requires not only considerable scholarship on the part of the author, but a willingness to analyze the desired behavioral outcomes of instruction in the subject, to state them in hundreds of quite small increments of learning, to foresee the various misconceptions students might form at each step, to provide reteaching (branching) at each of these points, and to commit the entire program to the appropriate format, i.e., printed book, teaching machine, or computer.

Computer-assisted instruction

While the use of computers in college and university administration has now become almost commonplace, their use as actual adjuncts to instruction in higher education appears still to be quite rare and largely in an experimental stage. Thornton (1968) reports:

At the beginning of 1967, after only a very few years of experimentation with the medium, several tentative observations about the potential of true computer-assisted instruction seem to be justified:

1. It is now possible to present either complete courses or supplementary exercises to college students by means of computer dialogue. Such course material can be made available a considerable distance from the controlling central computer.

2. The records that computers can provide about the successes and difficulties of each student working through a course will be of crucial importance in improving course materials, no matter in what mode the course will later be presented.

3. Only a very few complete instructional programs for computers have been developed. Before computer-assisted instruction can be made available to large numbers of students and in most disciplines, a great deal of developmental work is needed.

4. The installation of computer-assisted instruction terminals at present is very costly, although expansion of the number of courses and of student terminals, as well as increased experience, will surely reduce the cost. Further experimentation is generally recommended, both because of the light this kind of research can throw on the nature of learning, and in order to determine whether the advantages of computer-assisted instruction balance its economic costs.

5. The available computer hardware is capable of caring for the instructional calls of 1000 or more students in several disciplines at one time, without significant delay for any student. The present lack is in the variety of software (programs), and in student consoles.

6. An outstanding advantage of computer-assisted instruction is the provision of detailed records of the progress of individual students, so that the program itself can be constantly improved and revised, examinations can be improved, and individually prescribed exercises can assist each student to learn at his own best rate.

7. Perfection of a fully flexible program of instruction along the lines under investigation at the University of Illinois and Pennsylvania State University would free instructors for much more individual and small-group instruction, and so would increase the effective amount of instruction available to each student.

8. The promise of the technique has been sufficiently demonstrated that continued experimentation in additional institutions should be encouraged. The Higher Education Media staff realize that the present cost and complexity of equipment are discouraging aspects of the medium. It is probable, however, that additional experience will reduce both cost and complexity to the point at which computer-assisted instruction might become the most economical and effective type of programmed instruction. Continued experimentation to discover the limits of this potential appear to be justified.

Multi-media facilities

The several special types of multi-media facilities that have been developed in institutions of higher learning represent efforts to solve certain problems associated with instructional uses of new media. Included in this category are the single, generously equipped classroom; the auditorium designed to accommodate large-group presentations backed with appropriate audiovisual elements; and the increasingly popular classroom building containing several multi-media classrooms served by centralized new media facilities (usually in the core of the building).

Typically, a multi-media installation will combine in a hexagonal or octagonal building a series of triangular rooms of comparatively large capacity (75 to 300 students), surrounding a projection core in which equipment is provided for projection of films, slides, videotapes, and off-the-air or closed-circuit television onto a transparent screen of large size at the front of each room. The multi-media room does enable instructors to realize the goal of quality in large-class instruction—but at a price. Effective utilization of the multi-media installations seems to require that the instructor be assisted by several technicians. In addition, appropriate use of the equipment made available in the multi-media room requires planning and rehearsal time of the instructor far in excess of that used in preparing the usual lecture.

Transparencies for overhead projection

The large overhead-projection transparency remains one of the most effective and widely used of all of the new media. The investment in overhead-projection equipment might be one of the most rewarding approaches to improving college instruction. Nearly every instructor could find a use for this technique in his classes. The key condition for effective use, to repeat, appears to be the kind and extent of institution-wide encouragement represented by providing the centrally budgeted assistance of technicians and faculty persons for the instructor who desires to improve his teaching.

Tele-lectures

Many colleges have been making excellent use of the tele-lecture technique to avail themselves of the instructional contributions of guests who cannot come to campus, but who are willing to devote time to a telephone dialogue with a remote class.

In one particular program, a medical school works with community hospitals to provide continuing education programs for medical and paramedical staffs. Charts and programs are sent to each hospital in advance of the presentation. In addition, the hospitals are encouraged to tape the lectures, so that additional physicians may hear and see the presentation at more convenient times. In this program, "live" listeners may ask questions, and all listeners in the network can hear both the questions and the answers. Tele-writer installations may also be used in such instances to provide accompanying sets of illustrative drawings (done by hand on the spot and transmitted instantaneously to the distant points of use). These and other imaginative uses of the telephone or telephone facilities suggest numerous opportunities for continuing education and for keeping up-to-date with the most recent developments.

Simulation

The technique of simulation of life situations for instructional purposes has been only rarely reported as an operational technique in colleges and universities. However, industries associated with education report experimentation with the simulation method in the education of business graduate students ("games theory"), educational administrators, and physicians. As an example, school-superintendent trainees are provided with a series of "in-basket" problems; their learning experience is to decide what additional information they need to arrive at a decision for action. It appears that simulation technique might be useful with graduate students or even in the continuing education of workers in a specialized field.

Media utilization

Newer media utilization in library education

In 1963 the graduate library schools of the United States participated in a workshop (Goldstein 1963) which was based on four premises: (1) that one of the competencies required of library school graduates is a knowledge of the new media; (2) that, in the face of present shortages of library personnel, educational television offers one means of extending our present limited library education resources to many people who would not otherwise be recruited for the library profession; (3) that media and teaching devices are now available which have implications for the teaching of library science; and (4) that, by definition, library educators must be informed about the full range of materials and methodologies which have significant implications for library education.

Three years later, Herman L. Totten (1966) began his study of the education media utilization in the teaching of library science in American accredited graduate library schools. The following questions constituted the basic frame of reference of this research: Have educational media, a dynamic force in the teaching profession, had great effect, little effect, or no effect on teaching in library schools? If educational media have affected the teaching of library science, to what extent has their influence been felt? What are the judgments of library science teachers as to how well these media are being utilized? The dissertation was an effort to answer these questions.

Among the major findings of this study were the following: (1) the basic educational media (equipment and materials) are available to teachers in accredited American graduate library schools; (2) teachers in accredited American graduate library schools feel that educational media play neither a weak nor a strong role in effective instruction; and (3) weak provisions for in-service education in the use of educational media are made in accredited American graduate library schools.

Bibliographical control of media materials

The publication of needed guides and the review of audiovisual materials have been necessary for years. Recently the problem has been compounded by the growth and development, both in size and kind, of these materials. Since 1965 there has been a strong effort by the several national professional societies and government agencies concerned with these matters to press for a solution. Progress is evident in the establishment of a national cataloging service of audiovisual media. Only with this type of effort will the extent of commercially produced newer media and materials become available. Furthermore, there is a requirement for critical evaluation of nonbook materials, not simply a listing.

Support of local use and physical facilities

The first and most important generalization that must be recognized is that there can be no permanent and lasting effect on improving instruction by the use of the newer media until there is a substantial institutional commitment to this purpose. The commitment includes the following elements: (1) administrative involvement expressed in financial support and recognition of faculty participation; (2) technical staff to assist instructors in the development of materials and the operation of technical equipment; and (3) adequate capital investment both in space and equipment required for the utilization of the newer media, so that the physical plant includes appropriate room-darkening, necessary conduit, and both built-in and free-standing items of equipment.

Teaching methodology: donkey courses and elephant classes

As mentioned at the beginning of this paper, library school students during their completion of degree requirements, as well as in retrospect after employment, have questioned the content and methodology of library education. The donkey courses, filled with their detail and memorization requirements, are both approved of and disapproved of by students and graduates. Library school faculty members are constantly examining the courses being taught to ensure effective graduate-level teaching. Perhaps the recent statement by Paul Dunkin (1968) describes the problem most accurately:

> The library school is a monster with two heads: It is a graduate school, but it is also a professional school. The graduate school will try chiefly to make the student think; the professional school will try chiefly to teach him a batch of facts, techniques, and routines. One head looks to Pegasus; the other head looks to the donkey.

An even greater difficulty is the large class size. Again, Dunkin (1968) says it particularly well:

> Elephant classes are artificial growths on the surface of librarianship.
>
> We have ourselves produced them, or without thinking we have allowed them to come. . . . We can find all sorts of reasons for elephant classes. . . . There is always the manpower shortage. . . . Librarians get somewhat larger salaries than they once did. . . . We cannot stand in the way of people who want to improve their economic status.

The most important concern with the large-size class is the loss of a direct relationship between teacher and student. We must find a way to improve and extend this relationship, without which there cannot be mutual understanding and appreciation in library education.

Historical review

Innovation in higher education is not a recent phenomenon. It can be seen in the development of the land-grant college and the many experiments that were in evidence in collegiate programs in the 1920s and 1930s. The difference today is the rapid rate of change and acceptance of innovation which may occur in the form of: (1) organizational and structural use of the college, (2) new methodologies for instruction, and (3) curricular reform, notably in more effective programs of interdisciplinary studies (Dietrich 1966, Cooper 1966). In response to these concerns, there are several discernible directions in education today.

The first direction is that of higher *quality*. Education is providing learning opportunities of greater scope and in greater depth than ever before. Schools are educating for the understanding of principles rather than facts to develop a·thinking population of people prepared to spend the rest of their lives learning. In other words, the task is to teach students *how to learn*. This objective has not been generally accepted by schools and colleges in the past, although teachers here and there have given it major attention.

The second direction is that of *efficiency*. Education is developing more efficient instructional processes enabling it to bring more education to more people in wider range and in greater depth. There are increased efforts to improve utilization of expensive facilities and human talent. A true revolution in the sciences and technology of communications and information management is in progress (Carpenter 1966). Institutions of higher learning must determine what parts of these developments are applicable to the functions and requirements of education.

The educational system has considerable inertia. Technological change must be regarded not as a revolutionary process but as an evolutionary one. One problem is the well-intentioned resistance to the introduction of technology into the educational process which stems from fear that it will dehumanize a very human process. What is often overlooked is that the human quality and the genuine personal touch are often lost even without automation (Rogers 1966). Technology will assist and support many educational functions, thus increasing the productivity of the teaching force and freeing teachers from the multitude of clerical, record-keeping chores and the elementary task of simply presenting information for student consumption. Thus, technology could help to restore the personal touch to the educational process.

The third direction is that of *individualization*. Four points will summarize the current direction of education with respect to the individual: (1) encouragement of individual initiative, responsibility, and motivation, so that learning becomes person-centered rather than people-centered; (2) development of individual interests and special abilities to allow the individual to establish his appropriate and useful role in society; (3) accommodation of differing individual capacities for learning as well as social and economic backgrounds within the total framework of formal education; (4) development of a sense of personal identification and participation in the learning process, as well as basic learning skills which may be applied in personal learning and self-education (Carter 1966).

New media in higher education

Within this framework of higher education today, let us now discuss the nonprint media. In 1963 the Association for Higher Education joined the Department of Audiovisual Instruction of the National Education Association to produce a yearbook which pointed up the contributions of the new media (Brown 1963). This volume contained a landmark survey of the nature of the uses to which the new media were being put by colleges and universities in the United States in 1961.

As a follow-up to this report, a new study (mentioned at the beginning of this paper), the Higher Education Media Study (HEMS), was made possible in 1966. The purposes of that project were:

1. To inventory some of the 1967 instructional uses of new media of communication in college and university teaching throughout the United States. This was done by the issuance of the *Media Activity Inventory-Directory* (Thornton 1968) which lists some 650 institutions of higher learning in which applications of many different kinds of new media methods were being made.
2. To provide critical descriptions of the varieties of such utilization, their accomplishments, and their problems. During the period between October 1966 and January 1967, each person whose name appeared in the directory was invited to submit a brief article describing the nature, scope, and outcomes of each innovative media use cited.
3. The final phase of the Higher Education Media Study assessed current media applications in higher education by means of personal visits to approximately sixty colleges and universities.

The report, *New Media and College Teaching* (Thornton 1968), consists of specific comments by the staff of the Higher Education Media Study of the instructional status of several varieties of new media. As already indicated, this publication is fundamental to any determination of the research needs in the area of our concern.

Perhaps no other curriculum in higher education has been as involved in the newer media as that of health sciences education. This has been true not only of preservice education but also in the vast programs of continuing education of the health sciences professions. Invaluable resources, descriptive of the most noteworthy activities, are the two reports issued by the National Medical Audiovisual Center (*Toward Improved Learning* 1967; and *Toward Improved Learning*, v. 2, 1969).

New media in library education

Another milestone was passed in 1963. In that year the graduate library schools of the country participated in a workshop under a U.S. Office of Education grant which resulted in the publication *Implications of the Teaching of Library Science* (Goldstein 1963).

Sarah H. Reed, then Library Education Specialist, Library Services Branch, U.S. Office of Education, was reporter of the workshop. She summarized certain observations which were found to recur:

> (1) When audiovisual methods are used, the spirit in which they are used is important. A teacher should not continue teaching in the same way except for the addition of the new methods. He must not only feel at ease with audiovisual devices, but he must also review and re-evaluate his course objectives and teaching methodology. Otherwise, the new techniques may detract more than they add. (2) Currently the use of audiovisual aids is made more difficult because of their rate of obsolescence and because the bulk of available materials has not been produced for library school courses but must be adapted with varying degrees of success. This is true both of materials produced by the library profession for certain purposes, such as library extension or freshman library orientation, and also of those produced commercially and geared largely to elementary or high school rather than graduate school level. (3) Even when faculty members have identified desirable visual teaching aids, many do not have ready access to production centers. For those with heavy teaching schedules, the time and effort necessary to obtain these new materials act as deterrents. (4) Although audiovisual materials can be used effectively throughout the curriculum, such aids, along with programmed instruction, were felt to be particularly appropriate at the beginning levels of library education. By these means, a springboard of competencies and knowledges could be developed with full attention to individual needs. (5) Finally, speakers and group participants agreed heartily that to substitute audiovisual aids for printed materials is a misuse of these materials. They are, rather, enrichment materials intended to expedite the learning and teaching process (Goldstein 1963).

In March 1966, Herman L. Totten began his study of the educational media utilization in the teaching of library science in American accredited graduate library schools (Totten 1966). His investigation included the role of educational media in instruction and the provisions for in-service education in their use. The following were included in the term *educational media*: educational television, teaching machines and pro-grammed learning materials, recordings, opaque materials, overhead-transparencies, slides, film strips, and motion picture film, both 16mm. and 8mm. Significantly, these are in large measure the media reported earlier in the present paper.

As a result of the major findings, the following recommendations were made: (1) that each school's institutional educational media center provide a program to cope with the evident existence of teacher inertia in the use of educational media, since such media (equipment and materials) are available for teacher use in accredited American graduate library schools; (2) that each school's institutional educational media center provide for an orientation of teachers in accredited American graduate library schools to the unique role and contribution of educational media to instruction; (3) that each school's institutional educational media center provide for in-service education in the use of educational media, including new instructional devices and materials, whereby teachers in accredited American graduate library schools may be prepared to communicate through the use of educational media.

Improving library school teaching

Before examining efforts to improve library school teaching, it seems logical to review first the development of interest in improving college teaching generally. In her paper on this subject, Violet Coughlin (1968) lists general strengths and weaknesses of college teachers:

Strengths: Well-prepared in a specialty; competent as research schol-ars; possessing high native intelligence; and generally sincerely devoted to scholarly interests.

Weaknesses: Personal traits—colorless, poor attitude toward teach-ing, no fondness for students; too narrowly trained—unable to interpret the meaning of their subject in terms of other or wider areas; interest centered in research rather than teaching; and lack of specific training for teaching—no knowledge of learning processes, place of motivation, effective techniques of presentation.

Pre-service preparation of teachers for higher education has grown considerably. Most noteworthy have been the Higher Education Act Title IIB fellowships earmarked for library school faculty development. Specialized course work in "college problems" and "improvement of college teaching" are now included in the sequence for higher educa-tion at most graduate schools. Student ratings of faculty members are a regular activity at the University of Washington as well as other institutions. In connection with doctoral programs in library education, predoctoral lectureships have become more common and provide the necessary teaching experience for future faculty members. Furthermore, the sixth-year post-master's program in librarianship has also been designated for faculty development purposes. As a particular aid in library science instruction, the *Journal of Education for Librarianship* has provided papers on "Teaching Methods" (1965). Unfortunately, these excellent presentations have been concerned more with content than with methodology.

There is substantial agreement among library school deans and directors with regard to the necessity for the in-service development of faculty. One of the more common practices is the supervision of a new faculty member by the senior subject specialist in his curriculum area. Methods of instruction as well as instructional resources are the most important basis of exchange and assistance. Frequently, the new faculty member may be assisted in his preparation through seminars, retreats, or faculty conferences. The most useful device for teaching evaluation is closed-circuit television. Since many library schools now have this equipment available, it is considered one of the strongest means for instruction improvement. Paramount, of course, is administrative support for (1) classroom space that will result in the best teaching situation, (2) the availability of appropriate graphic and other production services for instructional aids, and (3) encouragement of faculty to pursue advanced study.

Experimental instruction in library education

Many efforts concerned with computer-assisted instruction, open-circuit and closed-circuit television, and the use of tele-lecture, both separate from and combined with tele-writer instruction, have been tried and proved successful. At least two of these experiments have been reported in formal documents. Marguerite Baechtold (1968), in connection with the partial fulfillment of her educational specialist degree, explored the matter of two-way amplified telephone communication in the teaching of selected library science courses. She explored the possibility of teaching the basic reference service course on the campus at Western Michigan University and simultaneously taught an extension class some distance away. Ann M. Fox has accomplished the same experiment in the beginning course in cataloging at the Graduate School of Library Science at the University of Illinois. Both experimenters enthusiastically recommend the development of conclusive data about the nature of library science courses suited to tele-lecture teaching.

At the time of writing, the Library Education Experimental Project (LEEP) had been under way one year at the School of Library Science, Syracuse University (1969). The objective of this project, supported by a U.S. Office of Education grant, is to relate problems in cataloging to mechanized library systems. A facility with *MARC* magnetic tapes as the data base provides the library education field with first-hand knowledge of how a computer-based laboratory for library school students can be utilized.

The Institute of Library Research at the University of California, Berkeley, also under a grant from the U.S. Office of Education, has just completed the final report of Phase I of its study concerned with an Information Processing Laboratory for Education and Research in Librarianship (Maron, Humphrey, Meredith 1969). This study involves computer-assisted instruction in cataloging and reference. In addition, associative and probabilistic search strategies will be developed.

While there are few published reports on this topic readily available, there will be additional reports soon. The further testing of these experiments by the library schools of the country will ensure improved utilization of the newer media with a high probability of success in library science instruction.

Summary and evaluation of the historical record

During the last ten years, the amount of literature about programs of higher education has increased exponentially (Mayhew 1969). This period has seen an enormous growth of offices of institutional research, an evolution of centers for the study of higher education, an expansion of research budgets, and a shift from disinterest to some concern for the study of higher education by people in academic disciplines. Most of the published literature available consists of conference reports and near-print documents rather than hard-covered books.

Each spring, the Association for Higher Education, an affiliate of the National Education Association, conducts an annual conference of higher education and publishes the texts of papers under the title "Current Issues in Higher Education." All papers suggest the dynamic quality of colleges and universities during this period of intense growth (Association for Higher Education 1965).

The U.S. Office of Education, sensing the need for the practitioner of education to know about new developments and research results, has initiated a new pamphlet series under the title *New Dimensions in Higher Education.* Several of these pamphlets are not available in published form but may be secured in hard copy or microfiche from the ERIC Agencies.

Since 1959, the Center for the Study of Higher Education of the University of California at Berkeley and the Western Interstate Commission for Higher Education have sponsored summer workshops, each of which has resulted in collections of published papers. This series has brought together perhaps the freshest approach on each of the topics covered.

In 1967 the Carnegie Commission on Higher Education was established with Clark Kerr, former president of the University of California, as its chairman. Most of the financial support for the commission comes from the Carnegie Corporation of New York. The commission is concerned with eight general areas of inquiry: the functions of higher education; the structure of higher education; the governance of higher education; innovation and change; the demand for higher education; expenditures for higher education; available resources for the support of higher education; and effective use of resources. The first project completed under the commission's auspices was a comprehensive inventory of current research on higher education (Heckman 1968). The subject interest of the present paper has many references in this inventory.

Under the leadership of Samuel Baskin at Antioch College, the Union for Research and Experimentation in Higher Education has held workshop conferences to foster innovation in higher education. These have resulted in several significant mimeographed publications and may have stimulated considerable improvement in college teaching (Baskin 1967 and Workshop Conference 1966).

Advances in instructional technology were, in part, the stimulus for the authorization of the A-V Task Force survey by the American Library Association during the spring and summer of 1967. Many of the problem areas developed in this paper, as well as additional new areas of concern, have been recommended for action in the published report (*A-V Task Force Survey—Final Report* 1969). The strongest action was requested in the bibliographical control of the newer media and improvement in preparation of new librarians. The latter might be expedited with the establishment of accreditation procedures that would require the inclusion of instruction in the newer media in library education. The recommendation was made for setting up selected libraries as demonstration and display agencies, similar to those in the Knapp School Libraries Project for elementary and secondary schools. Full implementation of improvement in audiovisual instruction in library education might come from an examination of advanced "communication" courses available in library schools, schools of communication, and schools of education.

Tentative solutions

From the foregoing, it is evident that the broadest approach to the newer media must be included in both pre-service and in-service library education. More than lip service is required: In fact, actual implementation by the use of the newer media seems to be the only solution for nationwide acceptance and full utilization.

Administrative support, both financial and directional, will be essential for achieving this innovation in library education. Local production staffs with knowledge and expertise in the preparation of instructional aids will be needed if teaching methodology with the newer media is to be accomplished. Furthermore, having the necessary materials and equipment is insufficient unless the buildings in which these materials are used are also prepared for this purpose. The planning of library education space, as evidenced in the University of Toronto Library School building program, should be examined prior to development of new or rehabilitated physical plants in the nation's library schools.

While some effort has been made to list audiovisual materials useful in library instruction (Lieberman 1968), immediate updating is mandatory. Evaluation in addition to listing will ensure the best possible teaching aids. The noncommercially produced materials—which are not listed in conventional bibliographical publications—will also have to be indexed. In this way, there can be free exchange of information and even duplication of locally produced materials, which will assist in improved instruction.

To return to the increased enrollments in library education, ways and means for lowering the faculty-student ratio is of paramount importance. This may be accomplished by more selective admission. However, a more useful purpose would be served if new directions in teaching (such as the case study method at Simmons College and Indiana University and the seminar method at the University of Western Ontario) were to be duplicated in other library schools.

Finally, selected information must be disseminated to library school faculties from the published and unpublished reports of such bodies as the Association for Higher Education, the Bureau of Higher Education of the U.S. Office of Education (*New Dimensions in Higher Education Series*), the Center for the Study of Higher Education of the University of California at Berkeley, the Union for Research and Experimentation in Higher Education located at Antioch College, and the Carnegie Commission on Higher Education, Berkeley, California. This will ensure that information concerning innovative practices in higher education is readily available to library educators. At the same time, new developments in methodology among the individual library schools must also be reported regularly to the total group. Through exchange and continued experimentation, continuous progress can be achieved.

Specific proposals

A wide variety of projects in the educational use of the newer media and in distinct instructional methodologies has been conducted in several of the accredited library schools. These include laboratory work, computer-assisted instruction, closed-circuit television, and the case-study method of instruction. Unfortunately, the experiments have not been reported in sufficient detail so that they might be duplicated in different locations. This writer recommends that there be a sharing of these experiments which would result in more widespread interest, testing, and wider utilization, thus benefiting all library schools. The purpose of such testing would be to determine whether the introduction of one or another media-assisted methodology has conferred either improved learning of a traditional skill or has been effective in imparting a new skill. Conferences on a regional basis should be organized for demonstration of existing experiments with the newer media in library science curricula.

By means of appropriate support from a national level, either through grants from the federal government or from interested foundations, demonstration and display agencies at selected library schools should be created. Financial support would make possible not only local production but also the visitation of interested library school faculty and administrative officers.

In addition to publicizing and evaluating of ongoing educational projects, there is a need to disseminate to library school faculties selections from the published and unpublished reports of agencies interested in educational innovation. Such bodies are the Association for Higher Education, the Bureau of Higher Education of the U.S. Office of Education, the Center for the Study of Higher Education of the University of California at Berkeley, the Union for Research and Experimentation in Higher Education located at Antioch College, and the Carnegie Commission on Higher Education, Berkeley. Reporting of activities concerned with the organization and bibliographical control of the newer media and materials can be done through revitalization of the Education Media Council, one member of which is the American Library Association. Through this means as a beginning and through organization of subsequent conferences of faculty conferences, we will be able to design a program to cope with faculty inertia relative to the use of newer media, to orient faculty to the unique contribution and role of the new media and to provide in-service education for library school faculties on the use of the newer media.

References

American Library Association. Audiovisual Committee. *A-V Task Force Survey—Final Report.* Pittsburgh: University of Pittsburgh Libraries, June 26, 1969.

Baechtold, Marguerite. "A Study of the Feasibility of Teaching Selected Library Science Courses by Tape and Two-Way Amplified Telephone Communication." Educational Specialist's thesis, Kalamazoo, Mich.: Western Michigan University, 1968.

Baskin, Samuel. "New Developments in Higher Education." *Sociological Focus* 1:58–68 (Fall, 1967).

Brown, James W., and Thornton, James W., Jr., eds. *New Media in Higher Education.* Washington, D.C.: Association for Higher Education and the Department of Audiovisual Instruction of the National Education Association, 1963.

Carpenter, D. R. "The Use of Human and Technological Resources and the Effect on Roles of the Student." Paper read at the National Conference on Curricular and Instructional Innovation for Large Colleges and Universities, 6–11 Nov. 1966, at Michigan State University, East Lansing, Mich.

Carter, Launor F. "Personalizing Instruction in Mass Education by Innovations in the Teaching-Learning Process." Paper read at the National Conference on Curricular and Instructional Innovation for Large Colleges and Universities, 6–11 Nov. 1966, at Michigan State University, East Lansing, Mich.

Cooper, Russell M. "The Need for Educational Change." Paper read at the National Conference on Curricular and Instructional Innovation for Large Colleges and Universities, 6–11 Nov. 1966, at Michigan State University, East Lansing, Mich.

Coughlin, Violet L. "Improving Library School Teaching." In *Library Education, An International Survey,* edited by Larry E. Bone. Urbana, Ill.: University of Illinois Graduate School of Library Science, 1968.

Dietrich, John E. "National Conference on Curricular and Instructional Innovation for Large Colleges and Universities." Proposal and Summary. East Lansing, Mich.: Michigan State University, 1966.

Dunkin, Paul. "Good Teaching Methods in Library Instruction." In *Library Education, An International Survey,* edited by Larry E. Bone. Urbana, Ill.: University of Illinois Graduate School of Library Science, 1968.

Goldstein, Harold, ed. *Implications of the New Media for the Teaching of Library Science.* Monograph Series no. 1. Urbana, Ill.: University of Illinois Graduate School of Library Science, 1963.

Heckman, Dale M., and Martin, Warren Bryan. *Inventory of Current Research on Higher Education 1968.* New York: McGraw-Hill, 1968.

Library Education Experimental Project (LEEP) Newsletter, vol. 1, edited by Judith Tessier. Syracuse, N.Y.: Syracuse University School of Library Science, Mar. 1969.

Lieberman, Irving. "The Use of Non-Print in Library School Instruction." In *Library Education, An International Survey,* edited by Larry E. Bone. Urbana, Ill.: University of Illinois Graduate School of Library Science, 1968.

————. *A Working Bibliography of Commercially Available Audio-Visual Materials for the Teaching of Library Science.* Occasional paper no. 94. December, 1968. Urbana, Ill.: University of Illinois Graduate School of Library Science, 1968.

Maron, M. E.; Humphrey, A. J.; and Meredith, J. C. *An Information Processing Laboratory for Education and Research in Library Science: Phase I.* Berkeley, Calif.: University of California Institute of Library Research, 1969.

Mayhew, Lewis B. "Educational Programs—College and University." *Encyclopedia of Educational Research.* 4th ed. A project of the American Educational Research Association. New York: Macmillan, 1969.

National Education Association. Association for Higher Education. *Pressures and Priorities in Higher Education.* Proceedings of the Twentieth Annual National Conference on Higher Education, Mar. 1965, edited by F. K. Smith. Washington, D.C., 1965.

Rogers, Everett M. "The Communication of Innovations: Strategies for Change in a Complex Institution." Paper read at the National Conference on Curricular and Instructional Innovation for Large Colleges and Universities, 6–11 Nov. 1966, at Michigan State University, East Lansing, Mich.

"Teaching Methods: Part 1: Reference and Cataloging." *Journal of Education for Librarianship,* vol. 5 (Spring 1965). "Part 2: Government Publications, Education, History of Books and Libraries, Newer Media." *Journal of Education for Librarianship,* vol. 6 (Summer 1965).

Thornton, James W., Jr., and Brown, James W., eds. *New Media and College Teaching.* Washington, D.C.: National Education Association, Association for Higher Education, 1968.

Totten, Herman L. "An Analysis and Evaluation of the Use of Educational Media in the Teaching of Library Science in Accredited American Graduate Library Schools, 1966." Ph.D. dissertation, University of Oklahoma, 1966.

U.S. Public Health Service. Audiovisual Facility. *Toward Improved Learning: A Collection of Significant Reprints for the Medical Educator.* Atlanta: National Communicable Disease Center Bureau of Disease Prevention and Environmental Control, 1967.

————. *Toward Improved Learning: A Collection of Significant Reprints for the Medical Educator,* vol. 2. Atlanta: National Institutes of Health,

National Library of Medicine, National Medical Audiovisual Center, 1969.

Union for Research and Experimentation in Higher Education. *Dimensions of Change in Higher Education.* Workshop Conference to Foster Innovation in Higher Education, first conference, 19–23 May 1966, at Magnolia Manor, Mass., 1966.

Robert B. Downs

Library School Administration

Definition of problems

The present article, after a brief historical review, will consider the following aspects of library school administration and research needs relating to problem areas:

1. Administrative organization
2. Physical facilities, including location, library science libraries, special laboratories, equipment, classrooms, and offices
3. Recruitment of faculty, including questions of experience and academic preparation, and use of library staff members and nonlibrary specialists for teaching
4. Student admissions, including academic standards, interviews and standard tests; problems of foreign students, financial aid for students, and placement of graduates
5. Coordination of library school activities and programs with the university in general and the area in which the school is located
6. Financial support from state appropriations, institutional budgets, federal and foundation grants, and endowments and gifts
7. Curriculum matters, such as problems of establishing a solid core, recognition of new trends, nonlibrary science courses, participation of faculty and students in curricular planning
8. Research activities, including establishment of research centers in library schools, encouragement of faculty research, and publishing.

Historical background

Formal education for librarianship as a profession began in the United States in 1887. The pioneer institution in the field was Melvil Dewey's School of Library Economy at Columbia University. Columbia and other early library schools, following Melvil Dewey's leadership, were heavily weighted on the practical side, emphasizing perfection in technical details and preparing students to step directly into the management of library routines. In many of their aspects, the programs resembled an apprentice system.

For thirty-five years after the creation of the first school, changes in library education were gradual and far from radical. Stress continued to be placed on producing working librarians, familiar with and ready to apply in practice all the usual routines of library operation. Nevertheless, there was considerable ferment in the profession. Criticism was freely expressed of various curricular offerings: There were calls for higher standards, for going beyond technical education, for a national system of training, for better prepared faculties, and for some machinery for evaluating the schools. Three concepts that were deeply to affect American library education emerged by the end of the nineteenth century: the conviction that library schools should be affiliated with universities, that college graduation should be required for admission to a library school, and that an examining board with clearly defined authority should be established.

The Williamson report (1923), sponsored by the Carnegie Corporation, focused attention on the low quality of library education in the United States in the early 1920s and analyzed in detail the reasons for the condition. Equally as important, the study presented numerous statesmanlike recommendations for the correction of weaknesses and for creating a system of professional library education of a high order. Subsequently, the existing library schools unaffiliated with institutions of higher education suspended operations or were merged with universities; the Board of Education for Librarianship was established by the American Library Association for accreditation of library schools; and there was increased emphasis on graduate study and degrees, including doctoral programs.

A continuing topic of concern in library education is whether the schools should aim at producing specialists or generalists, and the question is raised frequently as to the practicability of the schools preparing librarians for all kinds of library work. Most library schools curricula have compromised, devoting the first period to basic general studies and afterward giving students opportunities to specialize in particular fields.

Administrative organization

For the first fifty years or more of their history, library schools were headed by library directors, i.e., the director of the university library served also as head of the library school. In recent years, the arrangement has been almost completely altered. New schools have been established with a director quite independent of the library system, and older schools, one by one, have separated the two positions. The director of the library may serve in an advisory capacity and occasionally teach a course but has no administrative control over the school. In general, the change has been beneficial to both organizations. As institutions have increased in size, curricula have become more diverse, and administration more complex—plus the fact that a library and a school have different missions and problems—the desirability, if not the necessity, of separating the positions became evident. No one individual has the time and energy to do full justice to the varying requirements of the two demanding jobs.

On the other hand, something worthwhile may have been lost in the change-over. The library is the library school student's natural laboratory, and there ought to be the closest possible coordination between library education and library service. Full integration may be more effectively achieved if there is common direction. In the case of smaller schools and libraries, unable to afford two top salaries, a combined position may attract a more outstanding individual, assuming that he is equally interested in both functions. Another consideration is that a library school director completely separated from the practical aspects of librarianship can become lost in theory and out of touch with the needs of the profession—as may other members of a library school faculty.

Since there is no probability of return to the old pattern of organization, a proper subject for research would be to investigate ways and means of retaining some of the advantages of unified direction while maintaining the school's autonomy.

Institutional organization

In the past, it was not an infrequent practice to establish the library school as a division of a larger educational unit, e.g., a college of liberal arts and sciences or a college of education. The trend, however, is strongly in the direction of a separate, more-or-less autonomous organization for the school. A recent example is at the University of Michigan, where the Department of Library Science in the College of Literature, Science, and the Arts in 1969 became the School of Library Science.

It should be noted that the founder of the Michigan school, William Warner Bishop, firmly believed that it would be advantageous for a library school to be directly associated with a general college because of the intellectual stimulus and the contacts thereby provided with scholars in other fields. Otherwise, there is a danger of the school becoming isolated, out of touch with major educational currents, and provincial in outlook. The risk is not imaginary, even though the benefits to a school in being autonomous and in control of its own destiny are obvious. Methods of obtaining close integration with the institution as a whole are an appropriate field for study through such devices as joint faculty appointments with other departments, cooperative research (for example, in the applications of technology to library operations), and utilization of pertinent curricular offerings of other divisions of the university.

Internal organization

The typical library school is headed by a dean or a director, assisted in larger institutions by an assistant or associate dean. The extent to which the faculty participates in the administration of the school varies. Large schools customarily provide for an executive committee to work with the dean, or the faculty may act as a committee of the whole in such matters as policy formulation, curricular revisions, and admissions.

Ordinarily, the size of the library school does not justify its organization by departments, as is done in colleges. If the program is sufficiently complex and diversified, however, separation into distinct units may be useful. An example is the University of Pittsburgh's Graduate School of Library and Information Science which has recently been reorganized into two departments: Department of Library Science and Department of Information and Communication Science, each with its own head.

In the current era of student activism, with vociferous demands for participation in decision-making and a direct role in educational policies and administration, library schools must recognize and make provision for student voices to be heard in their affairs. How can the most effective use be made of the students' desire to aid in educational reform and to make library school programs more relevant to their needs? Research on the problem is essential, both to avoid schismatic conflicts and for the schools to gain maximum benefits from the ideas of highly intelligent and thoughtful students.

Physical facilities

Two issues of the *Journal of Education for Librarianship,* in the summer of 1964 and the fall of 1966, are devoted to articles on library school quarters and equipment. Moreover, Keyes Metcalf's *Planning Academic and Research Library Buildings* (1965, p. 267–69) contains a section on the subject. The American Library Association's "Statement of Interpretation to Accompany the Standards for Accreditation" recommends that library school quarters be located as a unit in the main library building or in close proximity to it. A majority of library schools follow this plan, although in the recent past, several schools have broken away and moved into separate buildings. Do they thereby achieve a more definite identity?

Metcalf recommends that "a library school be placed in the library when possible. . . . If the school is in the library building, the students are close to the general library collections which serve as their laboratory." Could not this argument be offered by other departments in the university? Not all divisions use library resources as extensively or intensively as do students of library science, but certainly faculty members and students in the humanities and social sciences would be pleased to be housed adjacent to the literature of their fields. Would library science classes be any more inconvenienced than those in English, history, or political science by meeting in regular classroom buildings outside the library? Could not library school faculty members be assigned offices elsewhere, as are those in other departments?

Despite such questions, locating the library school in the central library is so obviously desirable that it scarcely needs defense. Students of library science are not studying books alone, as are students in subject disciplines. They are absorbing the atmosphere of a library and being provided with opportunities to observe and possibly to participate in the day-to-day operations that go on constantly in a large library. A process of osmosis occurs that would be lost if students were separated from the general library. The relationship is analogous to that between a medical student and a hospital.

If the principle is accepted that the library and library school should not be disassociated, the ideal procedure is to plan for the library school's requirements at the same time the library building as a whole is being programmed. It is highly desirable for the school's facilities to be concentrated in one area, preferably in a wing or other unit which may be expandable at a later date as the school grows. Flexibility in space is as necessary for the school as for the library itself.

The tradition of a separate library for a library school is of long standing. Certainly, students and faculty would waste a substantial amount of time hunting for their materials, if the latter were not conveniently segregated in a collection apart. On the other hand, it is a valuable learning experience for students to become acquainted with the total resources of a university library. Any attempt to develop a self-sufficient book collection in the library school library is probably inadvisable. The scope might be restricted to providing a strong, well-selected, up-to-date assemblage of books, journals, pamphlets, slides, and films, relegating to the general library collections of out-dated, little-used materials, such as earlier editions of books, older files of periodicals, individual library reports, and most foreign-language publications. Heavily used encyclopedias, dictionaries, bibliographies, and similar reference books should be present, but the general library should be relied upon for more specialized, less-used works. Altogether, a collection of approximately 15,000 volumes appears to be a reasonable size for a well-balanced, live, library science library.

In addition to a traditional book-form collection, a modern library school provides space for pertinent films, filmstrips, sound recordings, tapes, mounted pictures, microforms, and various types of equipment associated with audiovisual materials. Furthermore, if laboratory collections are maintained of literature for children and young people, for cataloging and classification practice, or other categories outside the field of library science proper, space must be found for them.

To accord with current trends, seating in the library school library ought to be provided for not less than 50 percent of the full-time enrollment, and 75 percent is not excessive. Individual carrel-type seating should predominate, although no attempt need be made to return to the early days of library education, when it was the style to supply individual student desks. Individual lockers are more satisfactory and less space-consuming. To take advantage of programmed learning, "wet" carrels are advisable, electronically equipped for individual instruction through tape decks, earphones, and closed-circuit television reception.

Classrooms associated with the library school will vary in size, if they are to meet satisfactorily the school's requirement for diversity. An auditorium large enough to seat the entire student body and faculty will be highly useful for convocations, lectures, colloquiums, institutes, and similar events involving the whole school. Other rooms for instructional purposes will range down in size to seminars for ten to fifteen students.

Brian Land, director of the University of Toronto School of Library Science, recommends (1966):

> All classrooms should be provided with chalkboards, bulletin boards and book shelving; motorized hidden drop screens and sound systems

for film, slide and overhead projection; rheostat control of lighting; sound outlet jacks for concurrent use with projectors or for independent public systems; telephone outlets for long-distance conference telephone circuits; and outlets for television monitors and for FM radio broadcasts.

Provision may also need to be made for specialized functions assumed by a library school. Three examples are: (1) a research center such as has been established by the Illinois, California, Pittsburgh, and Western Reserve schools, with separate staff, offices, and other facilities; (2) a publication office, if the school is active in editing and publishing; and (3) a placement division, a service to find suitable positions for new graduates and older alumni.

Not the least important of a library school's space requirements, if staff morale is to be maintained, are adequate faculty offices, particularly for senior staff members. An average of 110 square feet per person is a recommended minimum, located as near as feasible to classrooms and library facilities.

Research studies testing the validity of generally held ideas and practices concerning library school space of various types and the kinds of equipment needed to make teaching, study, and research more effective are greatly to be desired.

Faculty recruitment

When selection of faculty is considered, a variety of qualifications are sought in a single individual. Rothstein (1966) and others have pointed out that the qualifications expected of a professor of library science are almost unattainable in one individual. He must be respectable academically, meaning ordinarily the holder of a doctoral degree, either in librarianship or in a subject field. He must have a background of experience as a practicing librarian, preferably in his teaching field. Aptitude for research and scholarship must have been demonstrated by a record of publication. Furthermore, it is expected that his teaching ability will be superior, his personality attractive. He will be a good committee member, active in professional associations, and a participant in community affairs. Naturally such a paragon is virtually unprocurable; a school will have to settle for less, and selections are necessarily made on what are regarded as the most important criteria, while less-essential characteristics are overlooked.

The prime criteria for appointments to the faculty should probably be teaching ability and academic qualifications. As a component of a university, the library school cannot afford to have standards for academic appointments lower than those for the institution as a whole. A good teacher also needs a period of practical experience to avoid a too-theoretical approach in his classes; his teaching will be strengthened by an interest in writing and research; and he should be a congenial colleague who enjoys teaching and likes students.

A shortage exists of academically well-qualified candidates for teaching positions despite the increasing number of doctoral programs in graduate library schools. If the doctorate is a prerequisite for senior faculty appointments, however, it may not necessarily be in library science. For some areas, a master's degree in library science and a doctor's degree in a subject field—say, one of the sciences—may be an excellent combination. Some library school deanships, e.g., Chicago, North Carolina, and Rutgers, have been filled by nonlibrarians—specialists in automation and information sciences.

University library staffs frequently have members who are well qualified to teach and who may be drawn upon occasionally to complement the regular faculty. An illustration is the practice at Illinois of offering advanced bibliographical courses in their fields taught by departmental or divisional librarians in biological sciences, chemistry, education, engineering, law, maps, music, mathematics, and Slavic literature. The curriculum may also be enriched by listing and offering credit for relevant courses in other university divisions, within reasonable limits.

The size of a library school faculty will vary, of course, with the number and level of courses offered, the size of classes, student enrollment, and the teaching load. A well-rounded curriculum will require a minimum of ten full-time instructors, based upon actual numbers presently found in accredited library schools. In addition, a staff of teaching assistants and secretarial help will be needed to relieve the faculty of routine and clerical tasks.

These, then, appear to be the most urgent areas relating to faculty recruitment in which research is needed: the kind of preparation desirable in library school instructors, how the shortage of teachers can be met, the use of instructors from other fields, and the size of faculties.

Student admissions and placements

Only a few years ago, student recruitment was a major problem for a majority of library schools. There was considerable difficulty in attracting to librarianship the number and quality of students desired. As general university enrollments have grown and an increasing number of students go on to graduate and professional study, the problem has largely vanished. Enough applications are now received, at least by leading schools, to make possible a higher degree of selectivity in admissions.

The most reliable index for predicting success in library school is a student's undergraduate grade-point average. A mediocre undergraduate record is an almost infallible indication of an unsatisfactory career as a graduate student, and perhaps later as a librarian. For its own protection and for the good of the profession, therefore, a library school's admissions should be guided primarily by records of academic excellence, supplemented by standard tests.

Letters of reference, especially from librarians, may be useful for admission purposes. Also, interviews with the dean of the school and members of the faculty, if practicable, will shed light on such matters as attitude, appearance, and personality prior to admission.

Students from other countries, especially those whose native language is not English, present special problems. They should be required before admission to demonstrate an acceptable level of proficiency in the English language; otherwise, scholastic difficulties for them are inevitable. In any case, foreign students are likely to need more individual attention and tutoring than do other students, and admissions should be limited to the number which the library school administration and faculty can accommodate without neglecting other students.

If the most promising students are to be drawn into the library profession, financial aid is essential. In the sciences, nearly all graduate students are subsidized in one way or another, and the trend in professional schools, such as library science, is in the same direction. Among the standard forms of aid are fellowships provided by endowments or by the university itself, and by professional associations, state libraries, and federal agencies, varying in value all the way up to those which cover a student's total expenses for the period of study. More numerous are scholarships, which ordinarily cover tuition and other fees. Assistantships—on a salaried or wage basis—in the library or library school have long been popular and possess the dual advantage of providing work experience and financial support for students. Finally, student loan funds are available in nearly all institutions from endowments, government grants, and other sources.

Placement services

Traditionally, library schools provide placement services for their graduates. In some instances, a school may feel responsible only for finding an alumnus his first position, after which he is on his own. Others attempt to keep in touch with their graduates to aid in their professional advancement, to find higher-level jobs for them if merited by their records, and to be certain they are engaged in the kind of work for which they are best fitted.

Because good placement service is demanding of a school in terms of staff, time, and finances, a few schools have unloaded the entire operation on central placement agencies. The results are generally unsatisfactory from the point of view of both the employer and employee. A large university placement organization is necessarily impersonal, without direct knowledge of individuals, and largely mechanical in function. A more personal service, operated by the school and involving the faculty and administration, will win the gratitude and loyalty of alumni and the appreciation of prospective employers. Much of the work can be treated in routine fashion, of course, by the preparation of individual information folders, letters of reference, statements from past and present employers, and so forth, but supplementary comments by instructors and others well acquainted with an individual's personality, special talents, interests, and perhaps idiosyncrasies frequently are invaluable in finding the right job for the right student.

Suggested topics for research relating to students might include studies on the most desirable pre-professional background, methods of predicting probable success, problems of foreign students, varieties of financial assistance, and placement services.

Curriculum

The building of a strong curriculum is a task properly shared by the library school faculty and administration, and some consultation with students and alumni may be well advised. Unless the school wishes to depart too far from standard practices, there will be a solid core of courses dealing with such basic areas as cataloging and classification, bibliography and reference, book selection, and library administration. A good research topic would be a determination of the nature and content of a basic curriculum, a matter which demands constant review and revision, both in terms of the current needs of the profession and of sound educational philosophy.

In addition, it is desirable that each school develop one or more specialized areas in which it has particular competencies to lend distinction to its program, assuming there is a clear need for them in the profession. Examples are preparation of librarians for special types of libraries, such as law, medicine, music and fine arts, archival training, audiovisual education, and information science and systems. Sound programs, which must be judged on pragmatic and somewhat subjective grounds, will avoid, however, going overboard for passing fads, e.g., basing the curriculum on the notion that the book is obsolete and will be completely replaced by automation and the computer. A curriculum which departs too far from reality and practicality will ill-serve students and lose the profession's support.

Too much overlapping and important omissions among courses can be prevented by requiring each instructor to prepare detailed outlines and perhaps syllabi for the courses for which he is responsible. Copies supplied to other instructors and consultations among the faculty as a whole will call attention to duplication or lacunae in course content. These devices have particular value in the case of visiting professors and summer session faculty who may be unfamiliar with the school's offerings.

Research centers

Since the first library research center was established at Illinois in 1961, the idea has caught on and a number of other schools have created similar divisions. The purposes may vary. At Illinois, the focus is on applied research dealing with specific problems of public, state, and other types of libraries, operating under grants received from such sources as the U.S. Office of Education, state libraries, and institutions of higher education. At California, the emphasis has been on the special problems of the University of California libraries on their nine campuses.

The research-center concept has several distinct virtues. It helps the library profession to resolve problems on which research is needed— and it is an accepted fact that too little genuine research has been done on library matters. The center stimulates research and publication in the school where it is located and may be used to advantage in the training of doctoral candidates and other advanced students. A strong center will require its own full-time director and staff but may also draw upon faculty members and students for assistance.

A research study investigating the programs and methods of operation of existing library research centers would be of value to the profession. For example, is too much research activity being directed toward certain aspects of the field, while other important phases are neglected? What research methodologies developed in other fields may be applicable to the investigation of problems of the library profession? Are special training programs desirable for research personnel in librarianship?

Faculty research

One of the most difficult aspects of library school administration is to persuade the average faculty member to engage in research and writing. The usual plea is lack of time because of heavy loads of teaching and committee work. On the surface it would appear that a library school instructor has more time, incentive, and opportunity for making contributions to the literature of the profession than does a practicing librarian. Also, it is generally agreed that teaching and research are complementary, each strengthening the other.

If a faculty member has any interest in research or aptitude for it, he may be stimulated in any of several ways: (1) He may be given a sabbatical leave from time to time for a specific research project; (2) a lightened teaching assignment for a semester or a year may enable him to begin and perhaps to complete a study or investigation; (3) if a reduced teaching load is not practicable, more teaching assistance and clerical help may provide free time for extracurricular labors; (4) a grant from the university, a foundation, or a government agency will eliminate financial handicaps—covering the expense of such items as research assistance and travel; (5) the end usually aimed for in research is publication, and the school administration should aid in every way possible in finding a suitable medium for the results of faculty research to be issued in published form. All these points merit further study.

Publishing

Publications emanating from library schools assume a variety of forms. One of the most valuable and at the same time one of the most demanding, because of its continuing nature, is the journal, represented by such titles as the University of Chicago's *Library Quarterly* (the oldest), Illinois' *Library Trends*, the *Drexel Library Quarterly*, and Florida State's *Journal of Library History*. Lecture series may appear in print, e.g., Illinois' Windsor Lectures in Librarianship and Denver's Isabel Nichol Lectures. Institutes and conferences are frequently reported, as in Chicago's Annual Conference, begun some thirty-four years ago, and Illinois' annual Allerton Park Institutes, the first of which was published in 1954. Substantial book series, usually appearing irregularly, are represented by Columbia's *Studies in Library Service*. More ephemeral material may be found in such enterprises as

Illinois' *Occasional Papers*, founded in 1949, a processed pamphlet series on various professional subjects, appearing irregularly and reproducing manuscripts which are unsuited to printing in journals because of length, detail, or special nature.

For a successful publication program, a library school needs to make certain that it is properly nurtured and cared for. Manuscripts meriting publication may have to be sought to keep the program alive, unless it has a natural source of supply, such as an institute or lecture series. Even these ought to be planned in the beginning with eventual publication in mind. Editorial staff and space will be essential for any program of considerable scope.

Research studies on the nature and quality of library school publications, the need for publications in areas not now adequately covered, and problems of overlapping, would be of value. These studies would require access to a comprehensive collection of such publications, on the basis of which comparative analyses could be made as to the validity of the research involved, depth of treatment, style of writing, possible appeal for audience to whom material is directed, omissions, and attractiveness of format.

Finances

Due to the impact of various federal programs, the income and expenditures of library schools have increased substantially during the past few years. Grants have been generous for fellowships and scholarships, for special educational training programs, for conferences and institutes, for research projects, and for the purchase of materials.

The most recent figures reported found that in the fall of 1967 the incomes of the accredited library schools of the United States and Canada ranged from a high of $870,000 to a low of $112,000, with a mean of $358,299. Frank L. Schick (1969, p. 166) concludes:

> An examination of individual budgets indicates the basic problem of library education in the U.S.—there are too many schools insufficiently funded to offer meaningful programs. Estimates have been made that graduate programs require annual budgets of about $200,000.

> Research in problems of library school financing could profitably look into such matters as sources of funds for various types of activities, additional prospects for support, basic budgets, and student aid.

As a beginning, a useful research study could be based on data regularly collected from members of the ALA Library Education Division and the Association of American Library Schools, supplemented by U.S. Office of Education statistics.

Summary

Practically every aspect of library school administration has developed more or less pragmatically, unsupported by objective research. Unquestionably, current practices could be improved and library education strengthened by unbiased research studies to test the validity of many widely held concepts in such matters as administrative organization, physical facilities, faculty recruitment, student admissions and placement, curriculum, research programs, and financial support. On the administrative side, for example, is complete separation of library and library school administration, which has become the universal pattern, desirable in all instances? To what extent should the teaching faculty be expected to participate in a library school's administration?

References

Downs, Robert B. "Education for Librarianship in the United States and Canada: History and Present Status." In *Library Education, An International Survey,* edited by Larry E. Bone. International Conference on Librarianship, 1967. Urbana, Ill.: University of Illinois Graduate School of Library Science, 1968.

————. "Quarters and Facilities: An Administrator's Point of View." *Journal of Education for Librarianship* 7:84–89 (Fall 1966).

Journal of Education for Librarianship 5 (Summer 1964).

Land, Brian. "Library School Quarters and Space—the Ideal." *Journal of Education for Librarianship* 7:71–83 (Fall 1966).

Metcalf, Keyes D. *Planning Academic and Research Library Buildings.* New York: McGraw-Hill, 1965.

Rothstein, Samuel. "The Ideal Faculty Member—Qualifications and Experience." *Journal of Education for Librarianship* 7:65–70 (Fall 1966).

Schick, Frank L. "Education for Librarians and Library Manpower." *Bowker Annual of Library and Book Trade Information, 1969.* New York: Bowker, 1969.

Williamson, Charles C. *Training for Library Service.* New York: Carnegie Corporation of New York, 1923.

Lucille Whalen

Library School Faculty and Students

Definition of the problem

Of the many factors contributing to the total picture of library education, faculty and students are perhaps the most vital. Danton (1948, p. 291–96), in his comments on "The Library Educator" at the 1948 University of Chicago Library Conference, stated:

> The accomplishments of American libraries—their service to democracy, to education, to learning, to human progress, and hence the respect and prestige they are given in their communities—will be precisely as great as two things: the quality of students which American library schools educate and the quality of the faculties that teach those students.

To be effective, both groups must be of high quality. A top-notch faculty with a mediocre group of students is not only wasteful but also contributes adversely to the profession by sending mediocre graduates into it. Superior students, coping with a poor faculty, on the other hand, can only be frustrated, uninspired, and cynical. One rarely finds, however, that faculties or students are wholly poor or wholly superior; as with other groups, there are most often some of each kind.

Faculties and students, being components of the university complex, cannot be studied in a vacuum. Their effectiveness in their roles must be studied in relation to the overall academic policy of the institution, the needs of the library profession, the responsibility to the profession, and of the profession to society. The situation in both the university

100

and the profession today—as indeed in the world itself—is one of such rapid change that it is difficult to ascertain what roles faculty and students should play to effect needed improvement in library education.

One aspect of this change is an emphasis on the human person as a focus of primary concern. Librarianship, along with other professions, has felt the impact of this concern in educating its members. Henderson (1969, p. 506) points out:

> Engineers are becoming sensitive to the influence of technology in solving the problems of human beings. Architects have been shifting from concepts of city planning that are physical in nature to environmental design which takes account of the human problems. . . . Law schools, dissatisfied with graduating lawyers to serve affluent clients, are endeavoring to reorient their students toward the solution of human problems wherever they exist. Even the schools of business administration today use a "behavioral" approach to the study of administrative processes, a marked departure from their earlier emphasis on "scientific" management.

Library educators have perhaps to some extent been prodded to this reorientation by various student groups within the university. Recently, library school students themselves have formed groups demanding change. This type of group was brought before the profession quite dramatically during the 1969 ALA Conference when the Congress for Change presented its demands.

Probably for the first time, the student group will have some part in the shaping of library education for the future. It is not enough, however, that everyone in the academic community have a part in this; there must be a research base on which to draw for the decisions that must be made.

It is the purpose of this paper, therefore, to present the problems relating to students and faculties in library schools as shown in the literature, to offer some possible solutions and alternatives to these problems, and to make some specific recommendations for needed research.

Historical review

Although some of the studies relating to library school faculties have also treated the student problem, others concentrate on one or the other. For this reason, it might be well to trace studies relating to faculty first and then those relating to students.

Faculty

The earliest and probably most frequently cited study on librarianship is the Williamson Report of 1923. Interestingly enough, some of the criticisms regarding library school faculty by Williamson have been reiterated in almost every study since that time. Finding only 52 percent of the faculty members with college degrees, few full-time faculty, many with inadequate experience, and extremely low salaries, Williamson (1923, p. 138) recommended that every effort be made "to raise the quality of instruction in the schools by increasing salaries and making teaching positions more attractive in various ways to trained and experienced librarians of the highest quality."

Wheeler (1946) found the faculty situation greatly improved, due largely to increased salaries and the number of M.A.'s and Ph.D.'s that had provided recruits to the teaching staffs of library schools.

Danton (1946), however, was not so optimistic. In his study of 148 full-time faculty members, 50 had no higher degree than the B.A. or B.S., almost twice as many as had the Ph.D. While Danton recognized that faculties had improved over those of the 1923 study, he pointed out that they were "still far from being as good as they should be. Relatively speaking, they have not kept pace with the higher standards of academic preparation which have come to be required generally for college and university faculties." He further noted that of the thirty-four who held the rank of full professor, only eleven were not also the dean or director of the school. Although the financial burden was somewhat relieved by this practice, Danton felt that the schools suffered because of this dual responsibility of their directors. He recommended that more professors and associate professors be appointed to make it possible for the schools to attract highly trained and experienced librarians into teaching. Another recommendation was that the ALA seek funds for the endowment of four or five chairs, or "superprofessorships," which would make it financially possible for that number of schools to secure almost any librarian in the country for their faculties, thus increasing prestige of library education, and, it is to be hoped, attracting other well-qualified librarians

One of the Public Library Inquiry volumes (Bryan 1952) included a fairly extensive investigation of library school faculties by Robert Leigh. In comparing his data, collected from the 1948–49 academic year, with that of Williamson in 1921 and Wilson in 1937, Leigh found that salary averages, academic training and status, working conditions, opportunities for travel and study, provisions for security, although still inadequate, showed steady improvement over the years. In comparing

library school faculties with faculties of other professional schools, however, the library schools fell below average on most factors.

In regard to academic background, Leigh (1952) noted the improvement over that of the Wilson study, but added that the Ph.D. could
not be *the* criterion for the well-qualified library educator as he felt
Wilson seemed to imply. A faculty of Ph.D.'s with no practical experience could be as disastrous for the training of future librarians as "the
early library school faculties of practitioners teaching the tricks of their
trade in their spare time."

What Leigh's study pointed out most emphatically was the great
disparity among the faculties of the library schools. This is understandable in view of the fact that accredited schools included three types—
from undergraduate programs in teachers' colleges to advanced programs in universities. He did not hesitate to condemn "inherent weakness resulting from smallness, a weakness which cannot be cured by
any amount of valiant professional effort." His recommendation that
faculties be large enough to represent the several academic disciplines
with reasonable specializations and expertness—five or more members
at least—was well taken. When the 1951 standards came out, most of
the Type III or smaller schools were dropped from the list of accredited
schools.

At a 1965 institute held in Washington for library school administrators, Morton (1965, p. 3–9) summarized the changing picture of
library school faculties since the publication of the 1951 *Standards for
Accreditation* in which the standards regarding faculties became less
quantitative and more qualitative. She pointed out that the problem of
the part-time faculty was even more acute than in 1951, partly due to
the increase in the number of part-time students in most library schools.
Adequacy in number of faculty members was still not reached by the
majority of schools, although the educational level of the faculties was
considerably strengthened. The problem of professional growth of
faculty members was touched upon also. The acute shortages of well-
qualified personnel for library school teaching, however, seem to out-
weigh the formal study made possible through sabbaticals and faculty
leaves.

In a critique of the Morton paper, Dearing (1965, p. 10–12), president of the State University of New York, Binghamton, also pleaded
for full-time faculty adequate in number. He cited "the necessity of interaction and stimulation which is prerequisite to research productivity
and the vitality and excitement and validity in teaching which is thought
to be inextricably related." Although he used twelve as a minimum
number in an example, he hastened to add that it was not a magic

number. One might question, however, whether this kind of interaction is possible in faculties of four, five, or six members.

While the discussion of faculty adequacy in education and experience, research, and professional activities continues, the emphasis in the literature in the recent past seems to be more on the faculty member as a person and as a teacher, admittedly more difficult in assessment. Rothstein (1966), in describing the ideal faculty member, in fact, places teaching ability at the head of the list—at least from the point of view of a library school director.

In Bone's survey of library education, both Coughlin and Dunkin in their chapters raise the question of what makes a faculty member a good teacher. Dunkin (1968, p. 273–88), in suggesting his "Gadfly Method," describes the teacher as a person who " . . . can confront his student with questions which demand skeptical imagination," whose questions challenge the status quo, who constantly questions himself and what he really believes. For Dunkin, the teacher must have style, i.e., he must use the English language with skill—even slang, if it helps; and he must be a zealot, i.e., he "must show that he is himself caught up in the question he asks." The doctorate and experience are also important but even more is his "in-service training," meaning "creative and probing research."

Coughlin (1968, p. 289–316) emphasized the need for some training in teaching. She asked, "Why should librarians labor and experiment with large classes and a variety of teaching methods on a hit-or-miss basis only to discover what a professional teacher has known for years?" She discusses programs to improve college teaching in the U.S. in the past several years that have some relevance for library education programs.

Carnovsky (1968, p. 131–52), in the same volume and also in an earlier article (1967), relates faculty qualifications to accreditation standards. He points out that the Ph.D., faculty research, publication record, and professional activities do not necessarily reflect good teaching. He suggests that "background and the ability to communicate and stimulate may be far more important in library schools and perhaps should be the criteria for appointment and promotion." Accrediting teams, he adds, will probably find these qualities very difficult to measure, and there will always be an element of subjective judgment in this area of the evaluation.

More recently, the students and alumni have studied the library school faculty with a critical eye. Typical of such studies are the ones by Donaldson and Harvey (1966), who reviewed evaluations of faculty from Drexel students over a five-year period, and Randall (1968), who surveyed the students at the University of California, Los Angeles, during the spring quarter of 1968. In general, both groups rated such factors as "knowledge of the subject" and "spirit of helpfulness" high, but "stimulation of thought" and "encouragement of independent thinking" low. It seems likely that students in the future will not only have a part in faculty evaluation but may take part in the selection process also. The fact that the student group is represented at faculty meetings in many library schools today seems to point in that direction.

Students

If library school faculties have come under scrutiny, so, too, have the students. Many of the studies referred to above include sections on library school students or graduates. The early studies sponsored by the Carnegie Corporation—those of Williamson (1923), Munn (1936), and Wheeler (1946)—touched on the student problem, but only incidentally. Their comments centered mainly on recruitment, entrance tests, and field work. But no attempt was made to study specific groups of students.

One of the earliest research studies of students was Wilson's (1937), in which 808 students who completed work in 1926–27 and 1935–36 at the University of Illinois were studied. Findings indicated that students with library experience tended to achieve slightly higher degrees of success than those without experience. Other factors, however, such as undergraduate grades, amount of preparation in languages, type of college attended, and undergraduate major, had little effect on library school achievement.

A second was Howe's study (1940, p. 532) of the University of Denver's graduates from 1932–38. The composite picture of the library school student, drawn from these two studies is described by Howe as:

> . . . an unmarried women of 27 years of age, white, of American parentage. She is a graduate of an endowed college or university, where she made a "B" scholastic record, majored in English, and studied French and Latin, and probably German. She has had four years of library experience since college graduation. . . .

The description is probably typical of the average library school student of the 1930s.

A similar study was carried on by Danton and Merritt (1951) describing the University of California graduates from its first class in 1920 through the class of 1948. The study included data on age, sex, education, job satisfaction, professional activity, and other pertinent variables. They found that older students did slightly better than younger colleagues scholastically; that "while the correlation between entering grade point average and school grade point average is positive, it is

not sufficiently high to make too strong a point of requiring excep-
tionally good scholarship among applicants" and that " . . . there is
no appreciable correlation between high scholarship and success in the
profession as measured in terms of salary. . . ."

Douglass (1957), taking students of about the same period, 1947–
48, studied the extent to which the library profession selects members
exhibiting characteristics generally ascribed to librarians: extreme def-
erence, submissiveness, and respect for authority. One of his conclusions
was that the profession does tend to be selective in that direction. Words
used to characterize the students in the seventeen library schools included in the study were: conscientious, orderly, responsive, conservative, undominating, interested in people but not merely gregarious, and
"not neurotically anxious."

Leigh (1952) also examined the student population, but limited his
sample to the academic year of 1948–49, covering enrollment figures
in various types of programs, geographical distribution and costs, library experience, and admission requirements. Trends at this time indicated that certain competencies formerly required for library school
were now made prerequisites; the college degree, "formerly the sure
ticket of admission to the library school," was now being challenged as
a wholly adequate basis for admission; what had previously been only a
classroom in the academic library where classes were taught by the
library staff was in many places turning into a professional school of
graduate caliber with full-time staff. Leigh did not gather data on personal qualifications, intellectual capabilities, or work experience of individual groups of students; his data were gathered from catalogs, announcements, and other types of records.

Some studies attempted to discover factors that influence the choice
of librarianship as a career. Reagan (1957), who did the most comprehensive study of this type, limited it to factors in institutions of higher
education, the relative importance of these factors, and the way in
which they operated to influence college students to become librarians.
She found five major factors responsible for influencing students: individuals, publicity, use of libraries, work experience in libraries, and
library education—in that order.

McCreedy (1963) investigated factors influencing persons to select
school librarianship as a career. The most influential factors indicated
by the 2,154 librarians and library school students in her sample were
"enjoyment of books," "liking for people," and "desire for intellectually
stimulating work." Not surprisingly, the majority of the respondents
had been exposed to good school libraries in their own education.

Another type of study attempted to relate types of positions or library
work to professional preparation. In 1960, Rockwood studied "The

Relationship between the Professional Preparation and Subsequent Types of Library Positions Held by a Selected Group of Library School Graduates." Data were obtained from records at Florida State University Library School and questionnnaires sent to graduates. Responses from 251 graduates showed some relationship between elective courses in library school and present position, but not between undergraduate majors and positions. The author maintained that the findings justified the specialized rather than general approach to library education at Florida State University.

Bailie (1961) studied job success as it related to certain admission variables, such as grade point average, Graduate Record Examination scores, and the California Psychological Inventory scores for ninety-four graduates of the University of Denver. Results indicated that undergraduate grade point average and Graduate Record Examination scores correlated highly with success in library school; the correlation between success in library school and job success, however, was not so high.

Goldstein (1967, p. 121) edited a volume of papers presented at the University of Illinois Library Conference devoted entirely to evaluation of students. Such areas as essay and objective tests, course evaluation, grading principles, and other methods for evaluation were covered. The two most valuable sections of the book for the purposes of this paper are Simpson's "Developing Student Self-evaluation" (1967, p. 31–49), in which the author points out the advantages of student self-evaluation over the usual teacher monopoly of evaluation; e.g., the work is likely to become more purposeful to the student, and there are more opportunities for developing individual initiative and responsibility; and Boaz's "Library School Practices in Student Evaluation" (1967, p. 69–100), which, in addition to describing present practices, gives examples of innovative practices in student evaluation.

Another specialized study was that of Harmon (1967), who analyzed research problem sensitivity among library school students at the University of Denver. Students were asked to assess research problem statements on a specially constructed scale. Findings indicated that problem-sensitive students were on the average older, had attended more prominent undergraduate institutions, and had majored in problem-oriented disciplines.

Clayton (1968, p. 135) studies personality characteristics of a group of library school students who planned to be academic librarians. Students in this group were found to have lower mean scores than a composite of fourteen other occupations on all but the femininity scale. Also, 26 percent had profiles that were indicative of personality difficulties.

The most recent overall picture of the library school student was given by Shores in 1967. It is characterized by an older student—mentally, chronologically, and experientially; a higher percentage of men than ever before; a marked difference in students from metropolitan areas and from campus communities; an increase in foreign and minority group students; and a greater number of part-time students and those in trainee programs. Most library school faculty would agree with Shores' comment: "Whatever the library school student has been in the past, there are unmistakable signs in the present that his profile will be quite different in the future."

Summary and evaluation of the historical record

The literature on both faculty and students is replete with articles of the opinion type. Everyone, it seems, has an opinion on how to cope with faculty and student problems in the library schools. Most of the opinions, understandably, are not based on research, since, in fact, there have been relatively few real research studies in either of these areas. From those available, however, and the many opinion articles, certain problems and trends emerge.

Regarding faculty, most of the studies from Williamson to the present have been descriptive, i.e., those delineating characteristics of library school faculties, particularly academic background, previous library and teaching experience, publication record, and professional activities. This is understandable in the light of accreditation standards which placed high priority on these factors. Quality of teaching, a factor which has long been discussed, has not been studied to any great extent because of the inherent difficulty in ascertaining what effective teaching is and how it can be measured. In more recent literature, however, greater emphasis has been placed on this factor, and there is a shift from the merely descriptive and/or quantitative enumeration to the study of causal relationships.

One problem that has been recurrent in the literature from the beginning is the role of the part-time faculty. Has the pressure for more and more qualified faculty forced administrators to employ part-time instructors as a stopgap measure, or is there a significant role for them in library education?

Much has been written on the difficulty of obtaining good faculty, but little on the recruitment of faculty. Recent literature on the fellowship programs has touched on this, since one of the primary purposes of the funding was to recruit candidates for teaching, but research has yet to investigate the effectiveness of such programs.

Another topic recurring frequently in the literature is that of faculty benefits and what would be termed today "faculty rights." In many studies, faculties were compared to other faculties within the university with regard to status and privileges. In earlier studies, as with other emerging professions, library educators did not always fare so well. Today, however, library educators take their place with other members of the academic community and share in their benefits. There does not seem to be a problem except perhaps with respect to the question of how some of the privileges, such as sabbaticals, benefit the library school or the profession.

Finally, there is the problem of leadership in the profession. One might reasonably expect this to come from the faculties of the library schools, but generally this has not been true. Long (1965), in summarizing the need for this leadership, pleaded for philosophical ideas that would generate research and initiate action based on the findings of the research. She maintained that through ". . . this very proper emphasis on educators . . . will be bred the leaders who will solve the problems of education for librarianship and inspire their students to solve the problems of the rest of the library world."

The literature on students in many ways parallels that on faculty. Earlier studies concentrated heavily on describing characteristics of those in the library schools, i.e., number; educational background, with special emphasis on undergraduate major and test scores; and graduate school performance. Studies in the 1950s and 1960s began to relate these to such factors as job success, ability to do research, special abilities on the job, and personality questions.

Recruitment of students has been a long-standing problem, but, with the exception of the Reagan and McCreedy studies, little has been done at the research level in this important area. The evaluation of program and faculty has emerged in the most recent literature. Another problem, the role of the part-time student, although frequently mentioned in the literature, is no more defined than the role of the part-time faculty member; nor is the related problem of library experience as an indicator of success in either library school or the profession.

In addition to the literature about the student, there is more recently a fair amount of writing by students. More and more, as in other fields, the student is becoming vocal concerning his role in determining the kind of program he is pursuing in library school and the vital issues in the profession. The library school student, to an even greater extent than the faculty member, finds himself in the midst of protest and dissent. His concern is not only for his own professional life but with the larger concerns of the world in which most students today are caught up.

One other area that needs to be gleaned from the literature is that of the recruitment, selection, and retention of minority-group students and faculty. Much appears concerning library service to minority groups and the training necessary to work effectively with these groups, but little has been written on the problem of bringing minority-group members into the profession. Librarianship seems to lag behind other professions in this area, but it must begin to take steps toward its part in the solution of this national problem.

In summary, the literature regarding students and faculty most frequently revolves around the question of which factors are most important in determining effective recruitment, selection, performance, and evaluation of high-quality faculty and students. To answer this question, however, the profession has to know what kind of person it wants in the field today and what different kinds of jobs might this person have from librarians in the past.

Tentative solution

What are the tentative solutions to the problems posed: recruitment, the selection process, a better knowledge of attitudes and goals, the relationship between academic performance and job success, and evaluation methods?

Students

The recruiting problem can be attacked in various ways: reliance on career days; recruitment programs of national, state, or local library associations; publicity; and other such means. What has been less often attempted is the seeking out of applicants with particular competencies. This is closely tied to the selection process. A school can apply any of the time-honored methods of entrance requirements, e.g., the grade point average, Graduate Record Examination, or other general test scores, interviews, recommendations, any combination of these, or perhaps a special test suitable for library school applicants such as the Medical College Admissions Test given to pre-medical students.

Underlying the general problems of recruitment and selection is the specialized area applicable to minority groups. Library schools are faced with maintaining admissions standards and perhaps thereby excluding these students, or lowering standards, as has been done in some fields, and risking further failure. Another alternative might be setting up some specially designed program for pre-library school preparation. Essentially, the definition of quality must be derived from an analysis of those characteristics which are associated with dynamic, successful performance on the job.

In regard to job success, library schools must make objective decisions, based on the needs of the profession, on how best to educate their students for positions in the professional world. Studies sometimes offer conflicting solutions as to what are the best indicators of job success. And the question of what constitutes job success needs to be reconsidered also. What might have been considered a "successful" job by library school graduates five or ten years ago might be spurned by them today.

For evaluation methods, library schools have several alternatives—course exams, comprehensive exams, grades, or any of the other methods geared to traditional methods of teaching. Innovative teaching, which is under way in at least some library schools today, would seem to call for other evaluative methods. Some alternatives that might be employed are self-evaluation, group evaluation, or a nongraded system.

Faculty

To solve the faculty recruitment problem, which is certainly one of the most acute in the library profession, administrators and committees have recruited from other institutions; from among promising doctoral candidates, especially those in their own institutions if there is a doctoral program; from the field, especially administrators and specialists; and from among outstanding retired librarians.

The selection of faculty is usually based on those factors related to accreditation—doctoral degree, library experience, publication record, and good teaching record. In the absence of one or the other of these, administrators must often accept the choice between an applicant with a doctoral degree but little or no library experience, or a good teaching and library experience record with only the master's degree.

Faculty evaluation, closely related to the same factors, generally follows university policy for purposes of advancement—in rank, tenure, sabbatical leaves, and so forth. Although good teaching is included in this overall evaluation, it is difficult to assess in most cases. A recent trend is student evaluation of faculty; it could hardly be considered an alternative to the traditional methods, but it undoubtedly must be considered.

A number of peripheral problems cut across these major ones, e.g., the part-time faculty member and student, the foreign student, the doctoral student, the handicapped student. Library schools, in the absence of research data, have the alternatives of accepting some of these applicants with certain risks involved, of accepting them only under certain specified conditions, or of not accepting them at all.

The impact most of these solutions would have on existing programs would probably be very small. The solutions offered in most cases are those which administrators have been using for some time. Since most studies of faculty and student have generally been for one geographical area or even one school, or one facet of a larger problem, they did not always provide the research needed to select from alternatives.

Research needs

The two areas covered in this paper are very much in need of research on a national level somewhat similar to that of the Public Library Inquiry. The greatest need in library education today is for well-qualified faculty. In order to make progress toward fulfilling this need, a complete and thorough study of faculty in all its aspects is necessary. Or perhaps several studies, are needed, each taking some aspect of faculty background. From these data, it is hoped, new solutions can be found to old problems. Such a study would include data on recruitment and selection of faculty, the relative importance of research and publication, the role of the specialist and/or part-time faculty member, and perhaps most important, what factors contribute most to excellence in teaching.

A similar type of study is necessary for data needed on students. Included would be such factors as how and from where students are recruited; what their educational backgrounds are; what kinds of work experience they have had, library or otherwise; what their goals are; and what attitudes they brought with them to library school and whether these were changed or redirected during the time they spent in graduate education. In addition to these two major descriptive studies, some correlative and/or experimental studies would be needed to answer more causally related questions, as to, for example, which methods or techniques are most supportive in guiding new faculty members or doctoral candidates who are teaching assistants; which personality traits in library school students are most indicative of creativity and leadership; or which factors are most important in recruiting minority-group students.

Specific research proposals

The following are proposals for research projects relating to library science faculties and students:

1. A survey of library school faculty
2. A study of characteristics of library school students

3. An analysis of factors influencing the recruitment, selection, and retention of minority-group students
4. An analysis of factors influencing choice of librarianship as a career
5. A study of the relationship between admission standards for library school and academic success
6. An investigation of the relationship between faculty backgrounds and successful teaching
7. A survey of student attitudes and goals
8. A study of preprofessional library experience and its relationship to academic success and job success
9. An investigation of student involvement in policy-making decisions in library school
10. A study of the use of attitude and personality tests to predict academic success and job success.

The major studies (Nos. 1 and 2) would require research staffs of from five to ten persons—perhaps one group could do both studies—with a project director of the doctoral or postdoctoral level. Completing the studies would probably take approximately two years. (The Council on Social Work Education conducted a similar study of the faculties of seventy-two schools of social work, and it was completed in this length of time.) The cost of these studies would be extremely difficult to estimate, as it would depend on what group was conducting the research. It would appear to be less costly if these studies were conducted by the research institutes of one of the library schools.

The other studies could probably be done by doctoral students under competent direction. Projects 7 and 10, however, would have to be carried out by someone with a good background in psychology and probably under the direction of a psychologist. Costs would vary, but most projects could probably be completed for amounts ranging from $10,000 to $20,000.

It is possible that much of the work on the faculty study will be completed in two studies currently in process: one, on the occupation of the teacher of librarianship by Vincent Aceto of State University of New York, Albany; and the other, a study for the Manpower Project at the University of Maryland, by Rodney White.

References

Bailie, Gordon S. "An Investigation of Objective Admission Variables As They Relate to Academic and Job Success in One Graduate Library Program." Master's thesis, Washington University, 1961.

Boaz, Martha. "Library School Practices in Student Evaluation." In *Library School Teaching Methods: Evaluation of Students,* edited by Harold Goldstein. Urbana, Ill.: University of Illinois Graduate School of Library Science, 1967.

Bryan, Alice. *The Public Librarian.* New York: Columbia University Press, 1952.

Carnovsky, Leon. "Evaluation and Accreditation of Library Schools." In *Library Education: An International Survey,* edited by Larry E. Bone. Urbana, Ill.: University of Illinois Graduate School of Library Science, 1968.

————. "Faculty." *Drexel Library Quarterly* 3:115–19 (Jan. 1967).

Clayton, Howard. *An Investigation of Personality Characteristics among Library Students at One Midwestern University.* Brockport, N.Y.: State University of New York, 1968.

Coughlin, V. L. "Improving Library School Teaching." In *Library Education: An International Survey,* edited by Larry E. Bone. Urbana, Ill.: University of Illinois Graduate School of Library Science, 1968.

Danton, J. Periam. *Education for Librarianship: Criticism, Dilemmas, and Proposals.* New York: Columbia University School of Library Service, 1946.

————. "The Library Educator." In *Education for Librarianship,* edited by Bernard Berelson. Chicago: American Library Association, 1948.

————, and Merritt, LeRoy. "Characteristics of the Graduates of the University of California School of Librarianship." University of Illinois Library School Occasional Paper no. 22. Urbana, Ill.: University of Illinois Library School, 1951.

Dearing, G. Bruce. "Critique." In *Institute on Problems of Library School Administration,* edited by Sarah R. Reed. Washington, D.C.: U.S. Office of Education, 1965.

Donaldson, Mary Jane, and Harvey, John F. "Library School Instructor Evaluation." *College and Research Libraries* 27:470–77 (Nov. 1966).

Douglass, Robert R. "The Personality of the Librarian." Ph.D. dissertation, University of Chicago Graduate Library School, 1957.

Dunkin, Paul. "Good Teaching Methods in Library School Instruction." In *Library Education: An International Survey,* edited by Larry E. Bone. International Conference on Librarianship. Urbana, Ill.: University of Illinois Graduate School of Library Science, 1968.

Goldstein, Harold, ed. *Library School Teaching Methods: Evaluation of Students.* Urbana, Ill.: University of Illinois Graduate School of Library Science, 1967.

Harmon, Glynn. "Research Problem Sensitivity: A Professional Recruitment Criterion." *College and Research Libraries* 28:375–81 (Nov. 1967).

Henderson, Algo. "Innovations in Medical Education." *Journal of Higher Education* 40:505–19 (Oct. 1969).

Howe, Harriet E. "A Study of the University of Denver School of Librarianship Graduates, 1932–38." *The Library Quarterly* 10:532–44 (Oct. 1940).

Kauffman, Joseph F. "The Student Climate Today." *Illinois Libraries* 49:341–49 (May 1967).

Leigh, Robert. "The Education of Librarians." In *The Public Librarian,* edited by Alice Bryan. New York: Columbia University Press, 1952.

Library Education: An International Survey, edited by Larry E. Bone. Urbana, Ill.: University of Illinois Graduate School of Library Science, 1968.

Long, Marie. "Emphasis on Educators." *Journal of Education for Librarianship* 5:215–26 (Spring 1965).

McCreedy, Sr. Lucille. "The Selection of School Librarianship as a Career." D.L.S. thesis, Columbia University, 1963.

McCrossan, John A. "Library Science Education and Its Relationship to Competence in Adult Book Selection in Public Libraries." Ph.D. dissertation, University of Illinois, 1966.

Morton, Florrinell F. "Faculty Adequacy." In *Institute on Problems of Library School Administration,* edited by Sarah R. Reed. Washington, D.C.: U.S. Office of Education, 1965.

Munn, Ralph. *Conditions and Trends in Education for Librarianship.* New York: Carnegie Corporation of New York, 1936.

Parr, Mary Y. "Whatever Happened to the Class of 1962?" *College and Research Libraries* 28:208–16 (May 1967).

———, and Filderman, Marilyn. "Some Characteristics of Successful Alumni." *College and Research Libraries* 27:225–26, 238–39 (May 1966).

Randall, Michael H. "The Student Grades the Teacher." *Journal of Education for Librarianship* 9:89–94 (Fall 1968).

Reagan, Agnes. "Study of the Factors Influencing College Students to Become Librarians." Ph.D. dissertation, University of Illinois, 1957.

Rockwood, Ruth. "The Relationship Between the Professional Preparation and Subsequent Types of Library Positions Held by a Selected Group of Library School Graduates." Ed.D. thesis, Indiana University, 1960.

Rothstein, Samuel. "The Ideal Faculty Member—Qualifications and Experience." *Journal of Education for Librarianship* 7:65–70 (Fall 1966).

Shores, Louis. "Students." *Drexel Library Quarterly* 3:59–64 (Jan. 1967).

Simpson, Ray H. "Developing Student Self-evaluation." In *Library School Teaching Methods: Evaluation of Students,* edited by Harold Goldstein. Urbana, Ill.: University of Illinois Graduate School of Library Science, 1967.

Soffen, Joseph. *Faculty Development in Professional Education.* New York: Council on Social Work Education, 1967.

Wheeler, Joseph L. *Progress and Problems in Education for Librarianship.* New York: Carnegie Corporation of New York, 1946.

Williamson, Charles C. *Training for Library Service.* New York: Carnegie Corporation of New York, 1923.

Wilson, Eugene H. "Pre-professional Backgrounds of Students in a Library School." Ph.D. dissertation, University of Illinois, 1937.

Agnes L. Reagan

The Relationships of Professional Associations to Library Schools and Libraries

Definition of the problem

In this paper on research needs in areas involving the relationships of professional library organizations to library schools and libraries, three general limitations should be made clear. In the first place, the paper deals only with research needs in areas where the professional association is very much involved; it is not concerned with research into relationships that are for the most part between the schools and the libraries and where an association's involvement, if any at all, is likely to be minor. A second limitation holds the paper to a consideration of needed research in areas that relate directly to library education. For this reason, no attempt is made to delineate research problems growing out of an association's broader programs which, although they may include the concerns of library education, are not primarily focused upon these concerns. Finally, the paper, written in 1969, reviews the literature up to that date and is concerned with identification of research needs at that time.

Given these general limitations, several broad areas that involve the relationships of professional associations to library schools and libraries were identified. Identification was aided by two recent surveys of associational activities and concerns in the field of library education (Reed 1967; Lancour 1968, p. 373–84) and by a review of some of the major critiques and proposals dealing with library education, from the Williamson report in 1923 through the Asheim "Position Paper" in 1968. In addition to the broad area covering general relationships (not only of the associations to the library schools and libraries, but of the associations to each other), three other areas in which professional organizations have been thought to have a particular responsibility were selected: recruitment, standards and accreditation, and certification. To pinpoint current questions and problems in the selected areas and to obtain a sampling of current opinion and suggestions, selected references from the literature of the 1960s were also reviewed. While the four areas by no means exhaust the possibilities, they appear not only to have been, but also to be, of central concern to the profession and to contain a number of problems on which research at this time would be useful.

Historical review

Major critiques and proposals, 1923–68

Williamson (1923) had less to say about the responsibility of professional associations for recruitment than for accreditation and certification. He did emphasize, however, that recruiting is a responsibility of the total profession and that the library schools had theretofore been doing more than their share of it. On matters of accreditation and certification, he was much more explicit. Once Williamson had distinguished between professional and clerical work and the type of training required for each, he went on to stress the necessity for standards for professional education and means for their enforcement and to urge both accreditation of library schools and certification of librarians. To implement his recommendations, he proposed a national certification board, then under consideration by the American Library Association (ALA), which would inaugurate a voluntary system of national certification and, at the same time, formulate standards for library schools. Although Williamson noted that the ALA was not, in the strict sense of the word, a professional association, there was no question as to his preference for the ALA over the Association of American Library Schools (AALS) as the accrediting body for library schools. According to Williamson's assessment of the AALS at that time, "motives of self-interest and personal relationships" would hinder enforcement of standards by that body (Williamson 1923, p. 121).

By the time of Munn's report for the Carnegie Corporation in 1936, the ALA Board of Education for Librarianship (BEL) had been in operation for more than ten years; a program for the accreditation of library schools had been initiated; the 1933 standards, which were largely qualitative, had replaced the earlier quantitative standards developed by the board; and there was an oversupply of librarians. The report included a list of studies and projects which the BEL felt were desirable. Among them was an "organized effort to secure the adoption of certification for librarians" (Munn 1936, p. 29).

Ten years later, when Wheeler and Danton published their critiques of education for librarianship, the situation had changed considerably. There was a severe shortage of librarians, the 1933 standards were no longer considered adequate, and library education was being subjected to critical and careful examination. Wheeler (1946), reporting to the Carnegie Corporation, was frank in stating criticisms of the BEL—it had accredited weak schools and, in recent years, in part because of wartime restrictions, had not exerted the needed leadership. Although Wheeler felt that the functions of the AALS and its relationship to the BEL needed to be clarified, he also felt that the association had a definite role to play and that its activities need not duplicate those of the board. Wheeler saw the ALA Professional Training Round Table, a third group concerned with library education and the forerunner of the present Library Education Division (LED), as essentially a layman's organization which should function as "suggester, critic, forum, and balance wheel" (Wheeler 1946, p. 93). In short, he saw a need for each of the three groups but felt they should work together more closely.

In discussing recruitment, Wheeler emphasized that libraries, not library schools, should be the primary recruiting agencies, and he charged both the AALS and the BEL with certain responsibilities in this area. As for certification, Wheeler evidenced some concern as to whether a proper distinction would be made in employment of four-year and five-year graduates and noted that state certification plans would have to be worked out to provide for both groups.

In proposing three levels of library service and the education required for each, Danton (1946) called on the BEL and the AALS to work together for the implementation of the proposal. He felt that accreditation must be much stricter and that the BEL "must carry a big stick and be prepared to use it" (Danton 1946, p. 28). He also suggested that it should be possible to state minimums for such items as budget, number of faculty, and teaching load, below which a school would not be acceptable for accreditation. For accreditation to be really effective, he was convinced that there must also be national certification and, like Williamson, urged the establishment of a national certification board.

In 1948, the Council of National Library Associations (CNLA) sponsored a conference in Princeton to discuss issues in library education (Lancour 1949). In attendance were librarians and library educators, many of whom were active members of the various organizations interested in education for librarianship, including such specialized associations as the Special Libraries Association (SLA) and the Medical Library Association (MLA). Among the issues occupying a prominent place on the agenda were those that are the concern of the present paper: professional organizations and library education, accreditation, recruitment, and certification. The group concluded that there was a great deal of duplicated effort and activity in the several organizational units concerned with library education. They decided against the formation of another organization to represent the interests of all national library associations and recommended instead an informal joint committee within the framework of an existing organization for exchange of information between the library schools and the several associations. Special encouragement was given to the CNLA to establish such a committee.

The conference recognized recruitment as a responsibility of the profession at large and went on record in support of the work of the Joint Committee on Library Work as a Career, recently established by the ALA and made up of representatives of the several associations. In its discussion of certification, the group was mainly concerned with how persons completing only an undergraduate core curriculum in librarianship would fit into existing certification plans.

When it came to accreditation, conference participants agreed that it was necessary, that it should be done by a single agency, and that the BEL was the logical body to carry on the profession's accreditation program. Delegates active in the specialized associations disclaimed any wish on the part of their organizations to act as an accrediting agency. The group unanimously adopted a recommendation "that the Board of Education for Librarianship serve as the official accrediting body for library educational institutions of all types and at all levels, and that it take into consideration the interests of specialized library groups by adding suitable consultants to its membership" (Lancour 1949, p. 35).

In 1952, the personnel volume of the Public Library Inquiry (Bryan 1952) spoke directly to the relationship between accreditation on the one hand and certification and classification on the other: "Accreditation of professional library school programs is of no value in setting a minimum standard of education for the profession unless it is tied to a system of compulsory certification and scientific classification of professional positions" (Bryan 1952, p. 447). Accreditation of five-year programs was seen as the responsibility of the ALA, compulsory certification of professionals as state-administered.

Two years later, when Leigh (1954) suggested solutions to major problems in the education of librarians, he concluded that the BEL was the appropriate agency for the accreditation of graduate programs, while the American Association of Colleges for Teacher Education should be responsible for applying the undergraduate standards through accreditation. The importance of certification in any overall program of library education was emphasized, but its administration was believed to rest at the state rather than at the national level.

By 1962, when Western Reserve University and the U.S. Office of Education sponsored an Institute on the Future of Library Education (Schick and Warncke 1962), the 1951 Standards for Accreditation had been in effect for some ten years, the ALA Committee on Accreditation (COA) had replaced the BEL with many of the latter's responsibilities taken over by other units of the association, and library education was re-examining itself in light of the needs of libraries of the future. The group, which met by invitation at Western Reserve, was made up of both library educators and practicing librarians from the several types of libraries. Of the more than fifty suggestions and proposals that came from the institute, a number are pertinent to this paper, including the need for research related to accreditation standards at all levels and consideration of "a system of nationwide standards for the certification of librarians" (Schick and Warncke 1962, p. 59). A major recommendation approved by the total group pressed the ALA to "recognize more fully its responsibility to library education by increasing its administrative support of the Library Education Division and the Committee on Accreditation" and to seek whatever funds might be necessary for the development of a national plan for library education (Schick and Warncke 1962, p. 59). A final recommendation suggested that the AALS be actively involved in the study and implementation of the institute's recommendations.

In line with the recommendations of the institute, the ALA established later in that same year the Commission on a National Plan for Library Education. Composed of some sixty-five members representative of the various national library associations, library schools, fields of librarianship, and other fields concerned with information services, the commission in its 1964 report ("Report" 1967) identified what were seen as the critical problems in education for librarianship and related fields and those to which the profession should address itself. To carry out the work, the commission recommended that the ALA seek funds to establish "an office or center for research and experimentation in library education and personnel administration" ("Report" 1967, p. 420). The report also urged that the SLA, the American Documentation Institute—now the American Society for Information Science (ASIS)—the AALS, and the Joint Committee on Library Education of the CNLA be represented on an advisory board or involved in some other way in the center's development.

By 1968, when the Asheim "Position Paper" (*ALA Bulletin* 1968) was published, the recommendations from the Western Reserve Institute and from the commission's report had been partially implemented. Funds had been made available for an enlarged ALA program in library education and related fields, and the ALA Office for Library Education (OLE) had been established. Asheim suggested that the proposals contained in the "Position Paper" might have implications for accreditation which in the future might require a separate agency and increased financial support. The proposition that the standards for accreditation should be qualitative was reaffirmed; the necessity for involvement of the profession as a whole in their review and evaluation was emphasized.

Selected references from the recent literature

The recent literature has produced a fair number of articles and papers relating to professional associations and library education as well as to associational responsibility for recruitment, accreditation, and certification. From the articles available, several of the most pertinent have been selected for brief review.

In an appraisal of the two membership organizations which are devoted to library education—the AALS and the LED—Hintz (1967) concluded that, although both had done some useful things, neither had been able to exert any very strong leadership. He suggested that a merger of the two groups within the framework of the ALA might result in a more effective unit.* Such a merger does not appear likely, at least in the immediate future, since a recent survey (Rothstein 1969) of AALS membership opinion found that a great majority wanted an expansion of the association's activities and a broadening of its membership base.

In two articles published in 1967, Hunt discussed the obligation of associations for recruitment and spoke of the difficulties of evaluating the results of a specific recruiting program. Two years later, the Congress for Change (1969), in presenting demands to the ALA, urged an increase in the number of recruits from minority groups. The congress stated that librarianship is not a "relevant profession" to young people and directed the association to review and revise its recruiting policies (Congress 1969, p. 936).

Articles by Carnovsky (1965; 1967), Stallman (1967), and Asheim (*The Library Quarterly* 1968), all of whom had served as members of

---

*Although there has been no merger of the two groups, the AALS in 1968 changed its affiliation from the ALA to the LED in order to strengthen relationships.

the COA, described the ALA's accreditation policies and practices. They noted some of the problems involved in the evaluation procedure and suggested a number of questions related to standards and review procedures on which research would be useful. Galvin (1969) raised questions about the need for accreditation, the suitability of the ALA to conduct it, the use of library educators as evaluators, and the appropriateness of a single group exercising both regulatory and advisory functions. In the same year, Bundy (1969) proposed formation of a Council of Library and Information Work Education, composed of educators in librarianship and information science, whose accreditation committee would include representatives of the several professional groups, such as the ALA, ASIS, and SLA. A suggested alternative to the council was the AALS, provided its membership could be made sufficiently inclusive. Charging that accreditation procedures and standards are not relevant to present-day needs, the Congress for Change (1969) asked that the ALA relinquish accreditation to the AALS, which "would in turn invite students and new professionals to take part in the writing of new standards and participate fully on all future accreditation teams" (Congress 1969, p. 933).

Three articles dealing with certification complete this review of the literature. Two of these (Libbey 1967, Proctor 1967) discuss the experience of one library association—the MLA—with a program of certification. The third (Wight 1961) is a proposal for certification of library school graduates by the ALA or the AALS after a period of experience in an approved library. Wight suggests that specialist certificates be based upon examination by a panel of experts in the particular specialization.

Summary and evaluation of the historical record

The purpose of the preceding section was not to describe, or even to identify, activities and programs that individual associations are carrying on in the field of library education. Its purpose was simply to take a few of the problems that involve the relationships of professional associations to library schools and libraries and to see how these problems have been looked at over a period of time by different individuals and groups.

From the part of the review that touches on the general responsibilities, programs, and relationships of the associations, two general observations can be made. First of all, the number of associations with interests in library education and with units devoted to it has been increasing as specializations have developed and as new groups have been formed. In 1923, Williamson was concerned only with the ALA and the AALS; twenty-five years later at the Princeton Conference, eight groups operating at the national level were listed as having an involvement in library education. More recently, as librarianship has broadened its base, associations in such cognate fields as information science and audiovisual instruction have related interests. To the national associations can be added the state and regional organizations, as well as certain international groups, a number of which have library education committees. As the number increases, the relationships of the various units, both to each other and to the library schools and libraries, are bound to be more complex.

Secondly, although attempts have been made at closer communication and some coordination of effort, these do not seem to have been as successful as their initiators had hoped. It is probably safe to say that the following statement from the report of the 1948 Princeton Conference is still a fairly accurate assessment of the situation: ". . . There is a discernible overlapping of interests, a failure to achieve purposes and to fufill needs, duplication of activity, and to a not-inconsiderable extent a confusion as to which agency is charged with what responsibilities" (Lancour 1949, p. 8).

The second area of concern, recruitment, which was first viewed as primarily the responsibility of the schools, has come to be considered a responsibility of the profession at large. The profession's organized efforts at recruitment are carried out through the several associations which provide literature, scholarships, and overall coordination and direction of activities. From the reaction of the ALA membership at the Kansas City Conference to a proposed cut in the budget for ALA's Office for Recruitment, it appears that, for one association at least, recruitment will continue to be a major responsibility.

There is an indication in the record that the recruiting literature and techniques used by the associations may need to be examined with a critical eye. As the statement from the Congress for Change suggests, the appeals that have been thought effective in the past may be less so today for some of the groups the profession is attempting to reach. Also, if there are to be several career ladders in libraries, as the Asheim paper (*ALA Bulletin* 1968) proposes, persons with different kinds of qualifications will have to be sought for each of the ladders and the career expectations for those on each ladder made clear.

Over the years, the profession's accrediting agency has received its share of criticism. Sometimes it has been thought to be too strict and at other times not strict enough. On the one hand, it has been criticized for exercising too much authority, and, on the other, for failing to exert strong leadership. Questions have been raised at one time or another about the standards, the accreditation procedures, and the organizational structure of accrediting.

Criticism of accreditation, as well as interest in it, has been stronger during certain periods than others. When libraries and library service—and, consequently, education for librarianship—are undergoing substantial change, standards and procedures for accreditation are likely to be questioned for their adequacy. The year 1969 seems to be one of these times, and several alternatives to accreditation by the ALA have been proposed. Up to now, whenever the question has arisen, the decision has been to leave accreditation in the hands of the ALA and to strengthen the unit responsible for accreditation. This does not seem to have been done in opposition to the wishes of either the library schools or the other professional associations. How the present situation will be resolved remains to be seen.

The historical review makes clear the close relationship between accreditation and certification. The effectiveness of either can depend to a large extent upon the other. Although the proponents of certification would agree on the desirability of a fairly uniform system throughout the country, they have not always agreed on how it should be administered. Some have urged a national system of certification administered by the profession itself through its national organization; others have felt that the responsibility belongs to the states, with some standardization of requirements.

Whenever more than one level of personnel is discussed, certification is usually mentioned. If the proposal by Asheim (*ALA Bulletin* 1968) for recognizing several levels of work in libraries is accepted by the profession, it seems reasonable to assume that the question of certification will receive even more attention in the next few years.

Tentative solutions and their effects on library education

If the record can be trusted, the relationships of library organizations to each other and to the library schools, in the area of education, could be more productive and useful than they presently are. An evaluation of the programs and activities of the various associations should provide a basis for judgment as to how each can contribute most effectively to the improvement of library education. If, after such an evaluation, changes were to be indicated, they might include dissolution or combination of certain units, redefinition of responsibilities, coordination of activities by an existing agency, or formation of a new coordinating body. It is to be hoped that whatever changes are suggested would result in meeting needs not presently being met, in reduced duplication of effort, in more effective utilization of staff and membership talent, and in improved relations between library schools and libraries.

As was pointed out above, the effectiveness of the recruiting programs of library associations has been questioned. To improve these programs, much more must be learned about what kind of appeals would most likely be effective with particular groups of people. Also, any critical assessment of associational recruitment literature and techniques would be aided by more precise information on what the personnel needs of libraries are than is presently available. Not nearly enough is known about the profession's personnel requirements—in terms of numbers of people needed at the professional and supportive levels for different kinds of positions in metropolitan and more sparsely populated areas of the country. If this type of information were available, recruiting appeals could be based on something a little more solid than the need for a specified, but often unqualified, number of "librarians." The data might show, for example, that the need is not uniform and general—that in some geographic areas, the supply of librarians has caught up with the demand; that the need is much greater for recruits with certain characteristics, backgrounds, and specializations than for persons with different sets of qualifications; or that the real personnel needs are in the supportive rather than the professional ranks.

Not only would data such as these provide for a much sounder recruitment program for the profession, but they would give the recruit a much better picture of what he can expect in the way of opportunities. They would also be helpful to library schools in admissions, counseling, and placement, and might even serve as a brake or an encouragement —depending upon the particular situation—to the establishment of a new school.

What are the alternatives for the organizational structure of accreditation? The several professional fields offer a number of possible patterns. Responsibility may be lodged in the general professional association, as it now is in librarianship; in an association of professional schools or educators, such as the AALS; in a joint committee established by two associations; or in a council arrangement under which the various organizations in the field have official representation. In librarianship, the nearest equivalent to the last-named at the present time is the CNLA. Other possibilities include the separate agency with its own staff, which was mentioned by Asheim (*ALA Bulletin* 1968). The question as to which of these structures might be most appropriate for librarianship is still to be explored, as is the most feasible method of financing accrediting, a matter that is closely related to structure.

A question frequently asked about accreditation standards concerns the extent to which they should be either qualitative or quantitative. The 1951 Standards for Accreditation, under which graduate library school programs are presently accredited, are qualitative; yet the suggestion has been made that it should be possible to establish definite minimums for certain items, below which a school would not be accredited. If this were done and the figures were applied, the results might be both good and bad. With something very definite to work toward, schools below standards might work all the harder to raise themselves, but, having reached the minimum, might be tempted to relax their efforts.

If nationwide certification of library personnel at the various levels is determined desirable, some decision will have to be reached as to how best to achieve it. Some of the possibilities were suggested in the literature review—certification in the hands of the states; a system administered by a national association; licensing of library specialists, such as medical and law librarians, by a board or by the several special library associations. Additional alternatives may very well be found in other professional fields.

If a suitable model for certification could be found for the library field, its implementation could very well put more "teeth" into accreditation and thereby raise the standards of library education. If certification were to be withheld from graduates of unaccredited programs, then, as Danton (1946) suggested, the schools offering these programs would have little choice but to improve themselves or to go out of business.

Research needs and proposals

In this section, the research needs and proposals which have been hinted at in the foregoing sections (and in some cases actually stated) are delineated in somewhat more detail. While some of the proposed studies appear to be comparatively simple to carry out, others will probably require fairly sophisticated research techniques. The suggestions are not all of equal importance, but each appears capable of contributing useful information that, in the long run, will contribute to the betterment of library education. Given adequate staff and clerical assistance, it would seem that most of the projects are subjects for individual rather than team research.

In the area of associational relationships and programs, a study is needed to determine the degree of duplication and coordination in the programs and activities of the professional associations or units concerned with education for librarianship and related fields. The proposed study might cover the period 1960–69 and include national associations in the library, information science, and audiovisual fields, as well as any international, regional, and state associations with programs directly related to library education. The basic data should be available in the publications or archives of these associations. The study appears to be one that might appropriately be carried out under the general direction of the CNLA or the AALS.

In the area of recruitment, it would be helpful if someone would devote himself to the construction of an adequate sample of libraries and a valid survey instrument to be used to determine personnel needs in libraries. To furnish the kind of data needed, the sample and instrument should be so constructed as to provide information on both actual and anticipated needs in different geographic areas (with distinctions made between urban and rural), at various levels of work, in special fields, and by size and type of library. Once the sample and instrument are devised, they could be used periodically by the ALA Office for Recruitment, or some other appropriate agency, to verify personnel needs and to make these needs known to the schools and the field.

Other research needs in this same area are a critical evaluation of the literature and techniques of recruitment used by the various library associations in relation to a realistic assessment of library manpower requirements, and a study of the effectiveness of various kinds of recruiting appeals for different types of potential recruits. Both studies should take into account the several levels of work in libraries and the several groups to be reached.

Since there is more than one possible organizational structure for accreditation, it would be helpful to have a study to determine the differences, if any, in the effects on professional education of different organizational structures for accreditation. The study, which would draw its data from a number of different professional fields, might be made by a nonlibrarian who is knowledgeable about higher education and the field of accreditation in general.

The scope and organizational structure of an accrediting program generally indicate the sources to which the accrediting agency must look for support. But, whatever the scope and structure are, more exact information on the actual costs of accreditation would be useful. Many of the costs are hidden. It is not known, for example, how much it costs to accredit a library school program or, for that matter, not to accredit a program—from the first letter of inquiry through final notification of the institution. The basic data could be supplied through a cost study of accreditation.

A third need in the area of accreditation, one which relates to the standards and their application, is a study to determine the extent to which quantitative data are an index to the quality of a library school. The kinds of data available and some of their limitations are pointed out by Carnovsky (1967) and Asheim (*The Library Quarterly* 1968). Investigations that provide further information on this subject would be welcome.

Since there are a number of other professions which have had experience in certification, it would be instructive to have a study of the applicability of certification practices of other professions to the library field. Such a study should not only be concerned with the practices of the other professions but should also take into account the experiences of such associations as the Medical Library Association and the American Association of Law Libraries. The consequences of various certification practices, if adopted by the library field, should be a part of the study. Sources of data would include publications and archival materials, as well as correspondence and interviews with individuals knowledgeable in the subject. The study is one that might suitably be conducted under the direction of the ALA Library Administration Division, in whose field of interest it seems to fall.

References

Asheim, Lester E. "Education and Manpower for Librarianship: First Steps toward a Statement of Policy." *ALA Bulletin* 62:1096–1106 (Oct. 1968).
———. "The State of the Accredited Library Schools, 1966–67." *The Library Quarterly* 38:323–37 (Oct. 1968).
Bryan, Alice I. *The Public Librarian.* A Report of the Public Library Inquiry. New York: Columbia University Press, 1952.
Bundy, Mary Lee. "An Accreditation Proposal," May 1969. A Challenge Paper presented for the Congress for Change, June 20–22, 1969.
Carnovsky, Leon. "Accreditation: Panel Member No. 2." In *Problems of Library School Administration.* Report of an Institute, Apr. 14–15, 1965. Washington, D.C.: U.S. Office of Education, 1965.
———. "The Evaluation and Accreditation of Library Schools." *The Library Quarterly* 37:333–47 (Oct. 1967).
Congress for Change. Statements read at membership meeting, American Library Association, June 25, 1969, Atlantic City, N.J. *ALA Bulletin* 63:932–36 (July-Aug. 1969).
Danton, J. Periam. *Education for Librarianship: Criticisms, Dilemmas, and Proposals.* New York: Columbia University School of Library Service, 1946.

Galvin, Thomas J. "The Accreditation Controversy: An Essay in Issues and Origins." *Journal of Education for Librarianship* 10:11–27 (Summer 1969).

Hintz, Carl. "LED and AALS." *Drexel Library Quarterly* 3:196–201 (Apr. 1967).

Hunt, Donald H. "Associations and Recruitment." *Drexel Library Quarterly* 3:371–74 (Oct. 1967).

———. "Recruiting." *Drexel Library Quarterly* 3:46–51 (Jan. 1967).

Lancour, Harold, ed. *Issues in Library Education:* A Report of the Conference on Library Education, Princeton University, December 11th and 12th, 1948. Council of National Library Associations, 1949.

———. "Library Associations and Library Education." In *Library Education: An International Survey,* edited by Larry Earl Bone. Urbana, Ill.: University of Illinois Graduate School of Library Science, 1968.

Leigh, Robert D., ed. *Major Problems in the Education of Librarians.* New York: Columbia University Press, 1954.

Libbey, Miriam Hawkins. "MLA Certification: The Certification Program and Education for Medical Librarianship." *Bulletin of the Medical Library Association* 55:5–8 (Jan. 1967).

Munn, Ralph. *Conditions and Trends in Education for Librarianship.* New York: Carnegie Corporation of New York, 1936.

Proctor, Vilma. "MLA Certification: Its Present Problems and Future Development." *Bulletin of the Medical Library Association* 55:9–12 (Jan. 1967).

Reed, Sarah R. "Education Activities of Library Associations." *Drexel Library Quarterly* 3:375–90 (Oct. 1967).

"A Report from the Commission on a National Plan for Library Education." *ALA Bulletin* 61:419–22 (Apr. 1967).

Rothstein, Samuel. "The Future of AALS." *Journal of Education for Librarianship* 9:301–307 (Spring 1969).

Schick, Frank L., and Warncke, Ruth, ed. "The Future of Library Education: Proceedings of an Institute . . . Cleveland, Ohio, April 25–28, 1962." *Journal of Education for Librarianship* 3:1–80 (Summer 1962).

Stallman, Esther. "Accreditation." *Drexel Library Quarterly* 3:185–95 (Apr. 1967).

Wheeler, Joseph L. *Progress & Problems in Education for Librarianship.* New York: Carnegie Corporation of New York, 1946.

Wight, Edward A. "Standards and Stature in Librarianship." *Journal of Education for Librarianship* 2:59–67 (Fall 1961).

Williamson, Charles C. *Training for Library Service.* New York: Carnegie Corporation of New York, 1923.

Page Ackerman

The Library School and Requirements for Staffing Libraries

Definition of the problems

Problem I

We are perplexed by a situation in which there is confusion and ambiguity about the roles, the tasks, and consequently the educational preparation appropriate for librarians as compared to that appropriate for other staff categories, especially as between beginning librarians and experienced subprofessional staff members.

Problem II

Rapid increases in the size and complexity of libraries and library systems, in the application of automated technology to library procedures and in the size and scope of the bibliographical universe, have placed demands on experienced working librarians for new skills (including but not confined to planning, cost and production control, personnel, systems analysis, and academic subject specialization in many disciplines). These skills are not usually taught in the graduate library curricula, and, unless they are gained in some other way, there is a troubling incongruity between preparation and responsibility.

Problem III

New applications in technology, larger libraries and library systems, and the development of new forms of library cooperation and inter-dependence (e.g., the centralization of processing activities) are also

130

creating changing tasks and roles for subprofessional employees, whose rate of turnover is likely to be high and whose background and training are both varied and limited. The more effective use of librarians depends heavily on the ability of subprofessionals to support them at higher levels of responsibility and competence. Therefore, the development of skill in training and training methods is of immediate concern to librarians.

Not only are these problems not new, they are so basic that they have been argued about in library literature for at least fifty years. The following survey makes no pretense of being exhaustive, intensive, or evaluative. Literature outside the field of librarianship is not covered. The review does attempt to focus attention on relevant recent research and, where appropriate, to provide a historical frame of reference.

Literature survey—library manpower

Supply and demand

Manpower needs. Although, in attempting to forecast 1970 professional library vacancies, Drennan and Reed (1967) labored under the usual handicap of fragmentary and noncomparable information, they produced a useful synthesis of available statistical information. By relating vacancy projections to information on staff composition by age, to the ALA Standards for School Library Programs, and to the output of both accredited and unaccredited library schools, they identified both school and public libraries as possible crisis areas in the 1970s. Drennan and Reed depended heavily upon the basic Drennan and Darling study of school and public library manpower, conducted as part of the Post-censal Study of professional and technical manpower, and published in 1966.

Characteristics of the work force. From the manpower utilization point of view, Drennan and Darling's median age data (which indicate that by 1975 roughly half of the public and school librarians in 1960 will have to be replaced), in conjunction with the information about the tasks done by librarians, are noteworthy. Among public librarians, 78.4 percent indicated supervision as the most frequently conducted activity, while 41 percent listed it as the most time-consuming. Among school librarians, 59.2 percent listed supervision as an activity, while 21.2 percent listed it as most time-consuming. In both settings, supervision seems to be a statistically significant aspect of the librarian's role. Are replacements being appropriately prepared for that aspect?

On the other hand, record-keeping (which should be suspect as a professional activity) is reported as a most frequently conducted activity by 71.2 percent of the public and 77.7 percent of the school librarians, and as most time-consuming by 14.3 percent of public and 17.9 percent of school librarians. Are professional replacements now being recruited for semi- or subprofessional jobs, thus perpetuating a costly misuse of personnel?

Schiller's findings (1968) on librarian roles and responsibilities in college and university libraries reinforce Drennan's data on the importance of supervision among the librarian's tasks. Of Schiller's respondents, 50 percent supervise from one to five employees, and 25 percent supervise more than five. One of every seven academic librarians is a head librarian, and 25 percent of these work in very small libraries with a maximum of two subordinate staff members. The tremendous spread in size of institution is reflected in the fact that 35 percent of all academic librarians work in fifty institutions.

A relevant characteristic of academic librarians, documented by Schiller and not covered by Drennan's data, is what she refers to as the "enormous variety" of job activities carried on. Fifty-three percent of her respondents cited nonlibrary specializations as their primary activity (including subject fields, geographical areas, specialized materials, foreign languages, and "other"—budget control systems, analysis, personnel work, etc.).

Schiller also tried to gauge the degree of satisfaction with librarianship as a career, finding 11 percent actively dissatisfied primarily because of the lack of stimulating "professional?" work and a desire for more decision-making responsibility. Since this question was asked in terms of expectations, it is possible that low levels of expectation kept the dissatisfaction ratio from being higher.

Salaries

Frarey's annual 1968–69 *Library Journal* placement and salary survey of ALA accredited library schools presents an approximation of what new graduates of accredited library schools were offered in base salaries for the working conditions they elected to accept. He emphasized the consistency of the situation over time: a continuing shortage of graduates as compared to reported openings and a gradual 4 percent increase in salary level, but no change in librarians' salaries as compared with other professionals. Frarey's figures indicate a gradual and perhaps important change in the choice pattern. School and special library categories, although fluctuating over the years, have remained relatively stable, while there has been a steady gradual trade-off between public and academic choices. By 1968, 51 percent of the current graduates were entering college and university or special libraries as compared with 44 percent in 1951–55. A continuation of this trend could have significant implications for professional library education.

The implications of current library manpower studies have been spelled out by Ginsburg (1967). He cited as major problems the lack of a systematic relationship between education received and work assignment, a dependence upon local manpower, a high proportion of women, the relatively advanced age of incumbents, low salaries, the need for specialization, the suborganizational nature of libraries, and variations in size and mission. Ginsburg attempted to place these major problems in the larger context of the labor market, i.e., heavy competition for persons and dollars, increased demand for service related to population increase, higher incomes, and new federal programs. Within this context, he suggests that actual shortages are no worse for librarianship than for other professions. He points out, however, that because high turnover is characteristic of fields with a majority of women workers, it will be essential to develop much stronger in-service training programs, no matter how much progress is made in strengthening formal library education programs.

Education and training—functions and tasks

Education and training

Looking backward. Since the early days, library educators have been deeply concerned about what Ginsburg described as the loose linkages between educational preparation, work assignments, and required competence. Williamson (1923) insisted on the necessity for differentiating between clerical and professional work as a basis for efficient library operation and for planning professional education. He insisted on the bachelor's degree—symbol of a liberal education—as a prerequisite for professional education, recognized the need for specialization beyond the first graduate year, and paid particular attention to the proper and systematic training of clerical workers.

Twenty years later, Danton (1946) still saw lack of such differentiation as a major obstacle to the development of a professional curriculum and added to it the increasing difficulty of training for school, college, public, and special librarianship in one year. He identified three levels of library work and training: (a) subprofessional (last year of junior college), (b) a middle service for beginning librarians (four-year bachelor's degree), and (c) upper service for the administrative or subject specialist (one semester of fundamental techniques plus one year of specialization by type of library and type of work).

Reece (1949) gathered information from all types of libraries to guide library schools in determining the future curriculum, focusing attention not on what libraries do, but upon "offices that fall properly within their purview but have not been assumed sufficiently or at all." He identified these roughly as: a more significant and aggressive role in systematic education, in the support of scholarship and research, and in the provision of informal education and recreation. Among the skills needed, but identified as lacking among librarians, were: expertness in analysis, capacity for research, and the ability to see the library enterprise in its broadest context. Knowledge so identified included administrative science, theories and nature of research, and sociology and psychology. Reece's respondents showed strong interest in establishing the traditional library school program in an undergraduate year or years, thus reinforcing Danton's proposals. Moreover, Reece himself emphasized the necessity for administrative tools, such as personnel policies and classification plans, which would differentiate between levels of preparation needed before a multi-level educational system could be successful.

Looking ahead. Asheim's position paper (1968) on *Education and Manpower for Librarianship* represents the profession's latest attempt to synthesize and integrate library education and training for all levels of library work. It makes explicit two important assumptions: that the library occupation is broader than the library profession; and that the library profession is responsible for the establishment and maintenance of educational norms for library work at all levels. It proposes five occupational levels corresponding to five educational levels: (1) clerical—high school, business school, or commercial course; (2) technical assistance—junior college degree or the equivalent; (3) preprofessional-library assistance—four-year B.A. or equivalent; (4) librarian—M.A. in librarianship; and (5) professional specialization—education beyond the M.A. Here for the first time, the librarian's preparation is seen, not as a one-year graduate program added to whatever undergraduate preparation he brings with him, but as a program of general and special education covering five or more years.

In the official Criteria for Programs to Prepare Library Technical Assistants (1969), the ALA Library Education Division took a first step in recognizing overall responsibility for the library occupation. The criteria made a distinction between library technical assistants and other supporting staff categories—defining their work, describing the abilities required, and listing the duties and responsibilities to be assigned to this classification. Although, as the criteria state, identification of tasks assigned to library technical assistants has been helped by modern management practices and mechanization of library operations, the key definitions of such work are still couched in negative terms. (Library assistants do *not* do "tasks which require a full *professional* knowledge of librarianship. . . .") There still is a great variety of opinion as to what library positions actually require such knowledge. There still is suspicion, borne out by some of the evidence in studies already cited, that librarians are, on the one hand, doing the work of technical assistants, for which they are overprepared, or, on the other, that of professional specialists, for which they are underprepared.

Functions and tasks: the library occupation

General

Now in progress under the directorship of Robert Case (1971), the School Library Manpower Project is an ambitious attempt by the American Association of School Librarians (AASL) to plan a training and education program on the basis of specific and detailed information about the tasks, roles, and functions performed by school library personnel at all levels. Recommendations for the content of future training programs were based on in-depth analyses of tasks done in a broad sample of the most outstanding school library programs across the country. The analysis led to development of new occupational definitions for school library media personnel and to the identification of the competencies needed to carry out the functions formulated in this work. There are now six experimental higher-education programs which are based upon the seven major areas of competency identified by the project. The methods as well as the results of this study should be studied closely for their usefulness in other library settings.

The librarian

In another ambitious and comprehensive study, the University of Maryland School of Librarianship and Information Science research team is identifying manpower requirements and exploring the educational preparation and utilization of manpower in the library and information professions. Frankly focused on the future, the Maryland project considers change a positive value and increased professionalization a major instrument in producing it. Studies are designed to: (1) contrast and compare traditional and innovative libraries and information organizations, (2) understand the change administrator as distinguished from the nonchange administrator, (3) identify personality characteristics associated with the choice of a career in innovating organizations in the field, and (4) study professional education in terms of its contribution to the shifting requirements of practice.

Hall (1968) investigated the relationship between the critical knowledge, skills, and abilities needed in public service activities in large public libraries in relation to the preparation given in ALA-accredited library schools. Her respondents, like Reece's, placed a high priority on complex intellectual skills and abilities—comprehension, application, analysis, synthesis—and on knowledge in psychology, human relations, sociology, education, and management. Her study indicated that, while most factual knowledge related to librarianship was thought to be adequately taught in library schools, the development of the higher intellectual skills was neglected as were principles and theories of related subject areas. Presumably Hall's respondents felt underprepared for their responsibilities.

Librarian or technician: the twilight zone

In a recent study of matched pairs of reference librarians in seven medium-sized middlewestern public libraries, Bunge (1967) tried to provide objective data on the relationship between library education and effectiveness in answering reference questions. He hypothesized that professionally trained librarians would be able to answer more questions correctly within a given time than untrained staff members, and that the difference would be related to the librarian's use of a more systematic reference technique. He found that: (1) although professionally educated librarians as a group produced accurate answers more quickly, their superiority did not seem to be related to use of a more systematic reference technique; (2) nonprofessionals can answer a broad range of factual-type reference questions successfully; (3) their ability to do so was improved by in-service training; and (4) the use of nonprofessionals in answering reference questions was widespread and favored by administrators.

McCrossan (1967) undertook a similar investigation of the relationship between library science education and competence in adult book selection in small public libraries. Like Bunge, he found a significant but not large difference in favor of the library school graduate. He suggests that it would be particularly important to try to discover under what circumstances "blurring between library school graduates and experience and in-service or other training leads to insignificant differences."

A survey by Rosenthal (1969) of the specific tasks assigned to nonprofessionals in five university libraries throughout the country indicates that increasing use is being made of them in simple original cataloging (a blurred area) and that administrators look forward to an extension of such assignments. He points out that all of the institutions studied have relatively sophisticated personnel programs and classification systems and a relatively high degree of work specialization, and that they share higher turnover rates. He emphasizes the crucial importance of training (whether in-service or academic) to the successful transference of marginal work.

Training methods

The management literature on training and staff development in public service and industry is voluminous, and the *Training and Development Handbook* (1967) summarizes advanced theory and method in the field. Although library literature has its share of how-to-do-it articles and pleas for more and better in-service training programs, systematic studies designed to evaluate the methods or measure the results of such efforts are rare. Among recent articles, two are of unusual interest because they examine the effectiveness of self-administered instructional units.

At System Development Corporation, Wallace (1968) created and tested self-administered modules of instruction in system analysis, Russian-to-English transliteration, and reference tools for use in on-the-job training of professional and nonprofessional personnel in scientific and technical libraries. Testing the participants immediately after the course was taken established the fact that learning had taken place in all areas, although the subjective opinions of the participants in one area—the system analysis tests—were preponderantly critical and negative. A significant problem encounted in field-testing was the difficulty encountered by most of the libraries in providing the time required to take the instruction and do the testing.

Another experiment with programmed learning, this time with library school students, was conducted by Walker (1968), who used control and experimental groups in the first segment of a cataloging and classification course. The control group was taught in the traditional lecture-laboratory format, while the independent group used a programmed text, an index, and other materials developed especially for this purpose. He concluded (1) that learning achievement was sufficiently high to justify use of such materials, (2) that student reaction was favorable, and (3) that the retention of subject matter was not significantly lower than that of the control group.

Both Wallace and Walker concluded that self-administered instructional units can be effectively used in both academic and on-the-job situations.

Summary and evaluation of the historical record

As this small sample indicates, the literature on the use of manpower in libraries is not systematic and cumulative, but fragmentary and suggestive. For that reason, I have decided to summarize common themes and indicate interrelationships in connection with specific research problems rather than present them in a summary section.

I have tried to describe projects which would in some way relate to and build upon work that has already been done. At the same time, I have consciously stayed away from topics on which work appears to be in progress (specifically, the role and function of the administrator and the specialist now being explored in the Maryland studies). Although it was tempting to recommend comprehensive, systematic explorations of library tasks and functions (the method used in the School Library Manpower Project 1969) in all library settings as the essential knowledge base from which to start in any direction, I concluded that smaller, less time-consuming, more sharply focused inquiries would be useful. My suggestions reflect my own conviction that the appropriate training and placement of beginning librarians is of major importance for effective manpower use, as is exploration of the extent to which librarians must be educated, not only as librarians, but as supervisors, managers, and trainers.

Research needs and proposals

Investigation of the role of the library school in providing basic training in the use of supervisory and management tools.

Problem statement:

Supervision and management are statistically significant aspects of professional work in all types and sizes of libraries (Drennan 1966, Schiller 1698). Proposals for the increasing use of library technicians place heavy emphasis on the role of librarians in supervision and direction (Asheim 1968). The rapid growth of the "system concept," particularly in the public library fields, is increasing the size of library units and consequently emphasizing the need for the management skills of planning, coordination, and control. There is a large and somewhat controversial body of literature on principles, tools, and methods of supervision and management. Many librarians believe that their training in the field has been inadequate. For these reasons, the provision of better basic education still is an urgent problem of librarianship.

Alternative approaches to provision of
supervisory and management training:

1. On-the-job training
2. Graduate courses in library schools
3. Graduate courses outside of library schools (business, administration, public administration, etc.)
4. Undergraduate preparation
5. Self-study, experience, or a combination of the two.

Information needed:

1. Nature of typical supervisory and management tasks assigned
   (first five years)
2. Effect of library size, type, and function on the nature of typical
   tasks assigned
3. Specific management and supervisory principles, tools, and skills
   appropriate for these tasks
4. Extent to which respondents have received training in these principles, tasks, and skills:
   a. From on-the-job training
   b. From graduate courses in library school
   c. From graduate courses in other disciplines
   d. From undergraduate study
   e. From self-study (including professional workshops, reading, ex-
      perience).

Answers to these questions would enable the profession to identify
the management and supervisory principles, tools, and skills most useful to the working librarian; to compare the effectiveness of present
formal and informal sources of such training; and to develop library
school course content more closely related to reality. Further, they
would provide library administrators with a basis for justifying, developing, or improving on-the-job and staff-development training programs. They would provide the profession with a sounder basis for con-
centrating institutes and workshops in these areas. Finally, they might
well enable schools, the profession, and library or municipal administrators to work together in given localities to integrate and improve
available training opportunities.

Method and sponsorship:

The study should be directed by a qualified researcher with appropriate background in management and librarianship. The method used

could combine questionnaires covering a wide population base with intensive interviewing of sample populations to check responses against reality. Graduate students might be used in interviewing. Sponsorship should be broad, including library administrators, educators, and representatives of all types of libraries.

Use should be made of studies already completed or under way. In this case, determination of the population base for the questionnaires and of the interviewing samples might be tied in with the Schiller study, the Maryland studies, and the Case School Library Manpower Project.

Exploration of the extent to which job responsibilities and education are matched at the beginning professional level.

Problem statement:

Throughout the literature on librarianship, there has been continuing concern about the placement of library school graduates in basically subprofessional positions where there is little opportunity to make use of professional preparation. Graduate library schools have recognized a growing need for more sophisticated, theoretical, and specialized educational programs, but have been frustrated in meeting that need by the library administrator's demands for vocational competence (Williamson 1923, Danton 1946, Harlow 1966). If responsibility for vocational competence could be responsibly shifted downward, the graduate curriculum might include areas now felt to be neglected (Reece 1949, Hall 1968).

Asheim's position paper (1968) on *Education and Manpower for Librarianship* and the recent *Guidelines for the Education of Library Technicians* (American Library Association May 1968) have theoretically defined the duties and responsibilities of borderline positions which could be filled by candidates with less than graduate library education. Junior college programs for the training of library technicians are developing rapidly (Boelke 1968). The next several years will see a large number of incumbents of retirement age replaced (Drennan 1966). Under these circumstances, it seems important to test theory against reality—to determine whether fifth-year graduates are, in fact, taking beginning positions whose duties could be performed by library technicians. If that is the case, it is equally important to explore the reasons for such placements and to develop alternative ways to remedy the situation.

Information needed:

Before alternatives could be developed, the facts would have to be established over a three- or four-year period. Needed would be:

1. Standardized information about the level of duties and responsibilities and the salary range for beginning openings for librarians
2. The name, location, size, and type of recruiting institution
3. The number and location of positions whose responsibilities and duties appear to fall substantially within the library assistant or library technician specifications.

If the number of such openings were significant, step four (below) could be omitted. We would have at that point, however, much better information than we now do on beginning professional openings by location, size, and type of library. If the number of borderline positions were significant, the data would produce important information about the market for library technicians; moreover it would:

1. Identify areas where training programs should be encouraged
2. Provide a factual basis for their justification
3. Identify locations in which, although training facilities exist, administrators are not using them
4. Encourage administrators to reassess the allocation of duties and responsibilities between librarians and support staff.

Method and sponsorship:

Such a project would seem to fall within the scope of both the Library Education Division and the Library Administration Division of ALA and could be a logical follow-up to the work of the Interdivisional Ad Hoc Committee on the subprofessional or technician class of library employees. It would also supplement the annual *Library Journal* study of beginning placements. Data-gathering problems would include:

1. Identification of recruiting institutions. This could be approached in a variety of ways—through sampling of libraries by type, size, and location, or through lists of recruiting institutions obtained from accredited library schools
2. Development of a standard position reporting form designed to produce information which could be related to the library technician specifications. This might well be done under the supervision of the Office for Library Education, possibly by members of the former Interdivisional Ad Hoc Committee
3. The obtaining of a high enough ratio of position descriptions to produce a valid sample. Since such reporting would require some effort on the part of library administrators, cooperation would need to be actively solicited. This writer believes that many administrators would recognize the value of either negative or positive results as a way of testing their own practice

4. If results were positive, the information about reasons for recruiting at the professional level would require a follow-up either in the form of questionnaires or interviews, which could be developed and conducted by advanced students interested in administration.

Exploration of the role of the graduate library school in the development of tools and the education of librarians for in-service training responsibilities.

I have tried for some time, and failed, to define a research project in this area. Nevertheless, I am impelled to add here a plea for special attention to the state of the art of in-service training in libraries and to ways in which it could be improved.

Every study cited in this paper on the ability of subprofessionals to perform marginal tasks in "blurred areas," whether in public service, technical processes, or acquisitions, stresses the determining influence of the quality of in-service training available. Moreover, libraries now, like other institutions, have a growing responsibility for recruiting, placing and training job applicants from educationally disadvantaged groups.

In business, industry, and education, staff development and training techniques and tools—including new methods for self-instruction—are becoming more sophisticated and more effective, but, so far as I know, the mounting need for training in libraries is not generally being matched by a comparable increase in the expertise needed to plan and implement successful programs. Neither individual libraries nor library systems seem equipped to cope individually with a problem that is, essentially, an educational responsibility.

References

American Library Association. Interdivisional Ad Hoc Committee of the Library Education Division and the Library Administration Division "The Subprofessional or Technical Assistant." *ALA Bulletin* 62:387–97 (Apr. 1968).

———, Library Education Division. *Criteria for Programs to Prepare Library Technical Assistants.* Chicago: The Association, Jan. 1969.

———, Library Education Division Interdivisional Committee on Training Programs for Supportive Library Staff. "Guidelines for the Education of Library Technicians." ALA Library Education Division *Newsletter* (May 1968).

Asheim, Lester. "Education and Manpower for Librarianship." *ALA Bulletin* 62:1096–1106 (Oct. 1968).

Boelke, Joanne. *Library Technicians, a Survey of Current Developments.* Minneapolis, Minn.: ERIC Clearinghouse for Library and Information Science. Review Series No. 1. Sept. 1968. ERIC microfiche ED 019 530.

Bunge, Charles A. *Professional Education and Reference Efficiency.* Urbana, Ill.: University of Illinois Library Research Center, Sept. 1967. ERIC microfiche ED 019 097.

Case, Robert N., and Lowrey, Anna Mary. *School Library Manpower Project: A Report on Phase I.* Chicago: American Library Association, 1971.

Craig, Robert L., and Bittel, L. R., eds. *Training and Development Handbook.* New York: McGraw-Hill, 1967.

Danton, J. Periam. *Education for Librarianship: Criticisms, Dilemmas, and Proposals.* New York: Columbia University School of Library Service, 1946.

Drennan, Henry T., and Darling, Richard L. *Library Manpower; Occupational Characteristics of Public and School Librarians.* Washington, D.C.: U.S. Office of Education, 1966.

Drennan, Henry T., and Reed, Sarah. "Library Manpower." *ALA Bulletin* 67:958–60 (Sept. 1967).

Frarey, Carlyle J., and Rosenstein, Richard S. "The Placement and Salary Picture in 1968." *Library Journal* 94:2425–29 (15 June 1968).

Ginsburg, Eli, and Brown, Carol A. *Manpower for Library Service.* Conservation of Human Resources Project. New York: Columbia University, Sept. 1967. ERIC microfiche ED 023 408.

Hall, Anna C. *An Analysis of Certain Professional Library Occupations in Relation to Formal Educational Objectives.* Pittsburgh: Carnegie Library, 1968. ERIC microfiche ED 021 606.

Harlow, Neal. "Who's Afraid of Melvil Dewey?" *PNLA Quarterly* 31:10–17 (Oct. 1966).

McCrossan, John A. *Library Science Education and Its Relationship to Competence in Adult Book Selection in Public Libraries.* Urbana, Ill.: University of Illinois Library Research Center, 1967. ERIC microfiche ED 019 096.

Reece, Ernest J. *The Task and Training of Librarians.* New York: King's Crown Press, 1949.

Rosenthal, Joseph A. "Non-professionals and Cataloging: A Survey of Five Libraries." *Library Resources and Technical Services* 13:321–31 (Summer 1969).

Schiller, Anita R. *Characteristics of Professional Personnel in College and University Libraries.* Urbana, Ill.: University of Illinois Library Research Center, 1968. ERIC microfiche ED 020 766.

Walker, Richard D. *Independent Learning Materials in Library Science Instruction.* Madison, Wis.: University of Wisconsin Library School, 1968. ERIC microfiche ED 025 296.

Wallace, Everett M., et al. *On-the-Job Training of Library Personnel (Interim Report)*. Santa Monica, Calif.: System Development Corporation, May 1968. ERIC microfiche AD 680 788; ED 027 933.

Wasserman, Paul, and Bundy, Mary Lee. *A Program of Research into the Identification of Manpower Requirements, the Educational Preparation and the Utilization of Manpower in the Library and Information Professions*. College Park, Md.: University of Maryland School of Library and Information Services, 1969. ERIC microfiche ED 023 938.

Williamson, Charles C. *Training for Library Service*. New York: Carnegie Corporation of New York, 1923.

James J. Kortendick, S.S.

Continuing Education for Librarians

Definition of the problem

Potential recruits to a career in librarianship are advised that, among other advantages, because of the materials they handle and the people they serve, they will be continually stimulated to growth in knowledge and understanding. The new graduate is told: "Now you begin to really learn what you have been studying." Education has as its main objective, asserts John Gardner, the shifting to the individual of the burden of pursuing his own education.

Although the ultimate responsibility for continuing education rests with the individual, the library profession has a corporate responsibility to society to provide opportunities easily available to all librarians who are motivated to a lifetime of learning. As knowledge in every discipline advances, the public has a right to expect librarians to advance with it and to supply the maximum information service in the most efficient manner possible. The rapidity and technical complexity of new knowledge and technical advances soon overwhelm a librarian who does not develop a continuing system of study. As it is, improvement in academic qualifications at the graduate level is often and soon negated by the actions of supervisory personnel who may have received no increments of training since graduation.

As has often been suggested, if librarians do not supply the services desired by society, society will inevitably turn to other members of society for such services. There are many evidences that librarians have failed to satisfy the newly emerging user demands for information.

145

Klempner (1968) asserts that the lack of continuing education for librarians is a major factor in contributing to this inability to meet newly emerging user demands.

Whatever the habits of lifelong learning practiced by the individual librarian, it appears that they are not adequate to this day of rapid societal and technological change. Although there have been some excellent continuing education and training programs and workshops sponsored by library schools, professional associations, and individual library systems, they have been accessible and convenient for too few and have not provided sufficiently for continuity in any given topic. Lorenz (1964) states "The effort toward systematic development of the library personnel at all levels and in all types of libraries has been insufficient, indeed." The trouble with continuing professional education, writes Rothstein (1965), is that it is a "peripheral activity within librarianship. As professional people, as librarians, especially, we owe it to ourselves and to our clientele to go on learning in a more purposeful, planned, and effective way than we now are doing. If we really set store by our continuing education, let's do it properly."

Other professions have identified continuing education of their practitioners as their greatest concern. The research literature in medicine, law, education, pharmacy, engineering, business and industry, and public administration have demonstrated the need, and further research and development activities are directed toward cooperative and coordinated planning and implementing programs on national, regional, and local levels.

Much has been said and implied in the library literature on the need for varying kinds of formal and informal continuing education, but there is a dearth of research-based and evaluation information available. Advanced degree programs on the post-master's and doctoral levels are within the reach of a tiny percentage of the profession. Our primary concern in this paper is for the bulk of the practitioners and their professional growth and the delegation of responsibility among the various segments of the library profession to provide for this growth. Monroe (1967) has written helpfully on the responsibility of the graduate library school, the library association, and state agencies for cooperatively developing state-wide plans which will focus on four chief aspects of continuing education: foundation learning, remedial learning, emergency education, and, finally, specialization for the experienced librarian.

If our profession is to meet its responsibilities to its members, answers must be developed to such basic questions as:

1. What *are* the continuing education needs of professional librarians?

2. How can these needs be analyzed, interpreted, and translated into meaningful recommendations for action?
3. How and by whom will objectives be defined and priorities of effort and support be established?
4. How best can we capitalize on the good programs that have been offered by library schools, associations, and library systems to re-activate, improve, and extend their effectiveness through repetition and communication exchange?
5. What factors motivate individuals to continue their professional learning? What administrative strategies can be implemented to achieve wider participation?
6. What instructional methods and techniques at this level are most effective in achieving objectives?
7. What standards and criteria for evaluating and measuring out-comes of programs are needed? How and by whom are they to be developed?
8. How can the library profession select from, interpret, and dis-seminate concepts and research findings from other disciplines that are relevant to the professional growth of librarians?

Historical review

A search of the literature reveals many references to the exponential growth of knowledge and the obsolescence of librarians. Although re-ports appear frequently on individual meetings and conferences, work-shops and institutes, seminars, and short courses, proceedings and eval-uations are seldom available. All have in varying degrees and ways stimulated and supported continuing education, but the general effect has been sporadic, haphazard, and splintered. Rarely, if ever, does li-brarianship appear in comparative studies of the professions and their continuing education programs. Material that does discuss the factors associated with professional growth generally has not been based on research inquiries, surveys, and experimentation. Typically, it has been based on individual opinion and observation.

There has, however, been some research that has implications for continuing library education. In the area of background characteristics of various types of librarians, studies have been done by Alvarez (1939), Harvey (1957), Morrison (1969), Douglas (1957), Drennan and Darling (1966), and Schiller (1968).

In the past few years, several aspects of continuing education have been the subject of special attention, and these provide an approach to an overview of the field. One recent effort showing an increasing interest in continuing education has been the annual publication, "Continuing Education for Librarians—Conferences, Workshops, Short Courses" (Reed 1964, 1966; ALA 1967, 1968, 1969).

Symposia on continuing education appearing in library journals include the following: One, planned by Foster Mohrhardt for the ALA Midwinter Meeting in 1967, features papers presented by Houle, Kortendick, McJenkin, Monroe, and Stevenson (*ALA Bulletin* Mar. 1967). Taken as a whole, these provide a survey of various aspects of the subject and stress the importance of continuing education to the profession, identifying various types of programs, and indicating areas of need for further programs and study. Another, appearing in the January 1967 issue of *Special Libraries,* includes articles by Sloane, Davis, and Shank. A third covers four phases of continuing education as presented by Alvarez, Boaz, Duncan, and Kennedy in the July 1969 issue of the *California Librarian.*

Unresolved problems as well as research needs in the area of continuing education were briefly outlined in an article by Boaz in 1967. That year also brought emphasis on the manpower problems of the profession, many of which have direct implications for continuing education: (1) initiation of the Library Manpower Study at the University of Maryland School of Library and Information Services by Wasserman and Bundy; (2) ALA President Gaver's program at the ALA Conference in San Francisco; and (3) the Ginsburg and Brown Report from the Conservation of Human Resources Project of Columbia University, which gives an in-depth analysis of the educational-occupational linkages within the profession.

Asheim's widely circulated position paper (1968) emphasized the importance of continual learning for all library manpower, but especially for the "professional specialist."

The library schools' formal post-MLS programs for continuing education as they existed in eleven accredited library schools were surveyed by Fryden (1968). On the basis of his research, he raised some pertinent and troubling questions and concluded with the practical suggestion that other occupational groups be examined to see what they did to promote continuing education beyond the first professional degree. Under the auspices of the ALA, Danton (1970) of the University of California has further analyzed sixth-year programs.

Jesse and Mitchell (1968) examined the extent of staff development opportunities available to academic librarians as revealed by questions answered by fifty-two research librarians. The research by Stone (1969) dealt entirely with the continuing education of librarians and specifically sought an answer to the question, "What motivates and deters librarians in their participation in professional development activities?" It also identifies the activities that the librarians themselves consider the most important for their professional growth and presents a profile showing what librarians are actually doing now in this area. The population on which the research was based was drawn from a representative sample of academic, public, school, and special librarians. Recommendations were in three main areas: to the individual librarian, to the library administrator, and to the profession at large.

Another study (Kortendick and Elizabeth W. Stone 1971) which deals exclusively with the area of continuing education is that on the continuing education needs at the post-MLS level of middle and upper-level personnel in the federal libraries. This study is based on actual on-the-job needs and on the demands of this group for both formal courses and for short-term institutes and workshops. Findings are translated into recommendations for action in the area of continuing education, and a data bank is presented which has potential value for the graduate library school planning post-MLS courses or workshops. It is found through comparison with the findings of the other studies mentioned above that the profile of federal librarians is comparable to that of other segments of the profession in age, length of service, educational background, and job activities. Other segments of the profession, however, should be surveyed in a somewhat similar fashion to develop a wider base of information related to needs for continuing education.

Under a grant from the Knapp Foundation, the School Library Manpower Project (Case and Lowrey 1971) is being conducted by the American Association of School Librarians on educational needs of school media center personnel, which is in some ways parallel to the study on federal librarians. An earlier study by Woodworth (1967) examined and identified the areas needing research in school librarianship and found that 26.4 percent of the people in the study thought continuing education was an "absolutely essential" area for research and that 50.89 percent thought it was "very important."

"Recommendations for Training Media Service Personnel for Schools and Colleges" (C. W. Stone 1964) is an excellent example of thoughtful planning of professional career paths, in the area of formal continuing education, by a library school. Learning-program designs include identification of information to be acquired, as well as needed application, production, and research skills at the entrance level for four types of media specialists, and for fifth-, sixth-, and seventh-year programs.

The final recommendation of the Ginsburg and Brown Report (1967), which is especially pertinent to any development in the area of continuing education, is "that the field of librarianship broaden and deepen its knowledge about itself. There are too few facts, and the facts available are frequently of such questionable quality that a responsible leadership cannot formulate action programs and press for solutions. If the leaders are to lead and not be pushed by events, they must devote more time and energy to encouraging systematic research into their profession. Only with sound knowledge of the past and the present, will it be possible to formulate plans for the future.

Tentative solutions

Because the problems of continuing education are nationwide, and because continuing education is one of the most important problems facing librarianship today, and because the gap between new knowledge and concepts and actual application in terms of service grows greater every year, practical methods will have to be found to meet the actual needs of individual librarians at a national level through the participation of those concerned.

The basis of criticism of the present state of continuing education of librarians is seen to be the lack of long-range cooperative planning based on research of actual needs and optimal ways of meeting these needs.

A blueprint is suggested to meet this lack, which will provide for equal, coordinated educational opportunities with the ultimate goal the establishment of a national center for continuing library education.

The plan should incorporate such concepts as a research data bank, the use of systems design, the behavioral approach to learning, systematic evaluation, the use of media, and the organized distribution and dissemination of program elements.

Further, it is believed that to promise any measure of success, certain criteria and standards in the development of programs will be necessary: excellence in content; opportunities for a wider choice of programs; continuity of opportunity; and accessibility and convenience of opportunities.

With this in mind, the research proposals suggested here in regard to continuing education are all oriented toward action. All embrace in some phase a part that can be planned by the library schools.

In several of the proposed target areas, major elements are suggested which should be carried on simultaneously. Then the findings and recommendations of each substudy suggested or added should be synthesized in a report which should be published and widely circulated among the educators and the profession at large. A variety of research methods is suggested or implied. Although all studies should proceed from an awareness of the past, the present and the trends and prospects for the future should occupy the major amount of time, effort, and cost of each project.

Specific research proposals

A feasibility study of a national program of continuing education for librarians.

Objectives:

Such a study would lead to a conceptual and practical blueprint for the provision of equal, coordinated, educational opportunities throughout the country for those who need, want, and will continue lifetime postgraduate learning. Possible items to include in this study would be:

1. Analysis of national continuing education programs being developed in other professions, profiting from their experience
2. A study of alternative structures and operational guidelines for a national committee representing the various interests and segments of the profession
3. An outline of the elements that contribute to a national policy, such as objectives, scope, roles of various agencies, and ways and means of equalizing opportunity, etc.
4. A description of the necessary mechanics for an information clearinghouse function in the plan
5. A description of a systems design capable of achieving the coordination of activities and program.

Manpower needs:

This study is conceived as a team project, with the team consisting of a director, a research staff, and a group of selected consultants representative of the interests and activities of the total profession, and consultants from other fields who have had experience in developing national or regional continuing education programs.

Related studies:

Dryer (1962) for medicine, Hewitt (1965) for pharmacy, Taylor (1967) for law, the National Education Association (1964) for education, McMahon (1968) for adult education, and Dubin (1968) for engineering.

A national survey of continuing education needs of librarians: A study of educational needs, job dimensions, and professional and personal characteristics.

The feeling is widespread that there is need for improving our manpower programs as they relate to continuing education, but that general feeling does not produce a detailed understanding of the particular needs as the librarians and their supervisors see them. Some studies have been done, but with limited population groups. Now, it would seem important, before any nationwide program is embarked on, to bring continuing education within easy access of every librarian, that time and resources be taken into account to discover what the chief needs are on a national basis.

Objectives of the National Survey:

1. To determine the self-perceived educational needs for professional librarians
2. To determine the job dimensions—what the librarians actually do in their jobs. As Corson (1966) pointed out, only on the basis of a clear understanding of what professionals do in a given profession, what activities consume their time, what responsibilities they bear, and hence what talents are required, can sound decisions be made as to kinds of programs to develop.
3. To collect data on the personal characteristics such as age, sex, marital status, geographical location, level of supervisory responsibility, years in the profession, etc. It is imperative in educational planning from a systems point of view to know the background of the students and what they bring into the course.
4. To determine attitudes of librarians toward continuing education needs as related to their job, supervisory functions, and library
5. To recommend methods for providing continuing education programs to keep librarians up-to-date
6. To provide the organization of these data so that profiles of a group of librarians in terms of a number of variables may be supplied on demand
7. To provide a means for continual updating of these data.

Manpower needs:

The research could be broken down into smaller segments to be carried out by Ph.D. candidates or library school professors under the coordination of a project director to ensure that uniform information is obtained. This is essential if a national data bank is to be built up which will meet the needs. A programmer, statistician, and consultants from each type of library service would be necessary.

Related studies:

Corson (1966), Dubin (1968), Dryer (1962), Ginsburg (1967), the Graduate School of the Department of Agriculture Handbook (1967), Kortendick and Stone (1971), McKeachie (1965), Morrison (1969), Schiller (1968), Stone (1969), and Taylor (1967).

Motivational factors related to participation in continuing education activities.

This study would seek to establish the importance of the individual librarian's motivation toward continuing education and also the importance of top management, showing every participant why he should undergo training and how the course content meets his training needs. Without this influence from top management, Likert (1967) points out that training may not have value, and, as a matter of fact, may do more harm than good.

Objectives:

1. To find out what motivates librarians to engage in continuing education
2. To find out what deters librarians from pursuing continuing education
3. To establish the criteria necessary in planning for continuing education if there is to be wide participation by the librarians
4. To discover the most effective strategies that administrators may use in motivating the individual librarian to engage in continuing education
5. To determine how actively and with what results the library school instills in the student the need for a lifelong program of continuing education
6. To determine the types of continuing education activities librarians consider most important for their professional growth
7. To determine the degree and kind of support administrators give to their employees regarding participating in continuing education activities.

Manpower needs:

A director with some background in social psychology and administration, with a modest supportive staff, several consultants who have done research in motivation, a statistician part-time, and a part-time programmer.

Related studies:

Anderson (1961), Clegg (1963), Dubin (1969), Jerkedal (1967), Herzberg (1959, 1968), Stone (1969), Swanson (1965), and Taylor (1967).

Development of a model for continuing education and staff development in libraries.

A continuing education and staff development program set up to accomplish a number of specific objectives is composed of many elements. For such a development program to be maximally effective, all these elements must be integrated into a system, designed to accomplish the objectives at a minimum cost. Various principles and techniques of learning must be applied in the development of the system.

Objectives:

1. To develop a model which could be used by any practicing librarian responsible for continuing education or staff development for any population size or typical library and which should provide decision-making criteria
2. To provide for the combination of the elements in a rational way to make up a complete system which would not only be responsive to internal factors but to elements outside the specific program developed, such as the attitude and motivation of those participating in the programs, the climate of the library or library system in which the program takes place, and the attitude of the administration of the given system toward continuing education and staff development.

Manpower needs:

A professor in a library school who would direct a series of doctoral studies related to the study and be responsible for coordinating the whole.

Related studies:

Garrison (1967), Smith (1966), Odiorne (1965), and Likert (1967).

Development of a comprehensive model for managing and evaluating short-term institutes and workshops for the continuing education of librarians.

The need for a more comprehensive approach to educational planning for short-term institutes and workshops has been emphasized as projects (a) become longer and more complex, (b) call for greater allocations of money and personnel, and (c) cover a wider range of subject areas. Although short-term institutes and workshops provide one of the major avenues of continuing education available to librarians today, there are at present no models in library science that apply to every important phase of a project from its inception to its termination. Topics to be covered would be identification of sponsoring body, its qualifications for this project, stated purposes, development, learning applications, validation of effects, training methods, and the techniques and use of multi-media facilities.

Objectives:

1. To analyze and evaluate library institutes and workshops to provide background material for a data base. The study would include workshops funded by federal legislation and those which had been locally sponsored
2. To develop a model which could be used by (a) those who write proposals, (b) those who operate projects, and (c) those who evaluate the programs. The use of such a model should result in improvement of programs by providing specific criteria from the conception to the culmination of a project and by providing feedback data throughout
3. To include in the model the following elements: statement of criteria for proposal development, assessment of needs, objectives relevant to needs, priority considerations, staff and management, program activities and curriculum, facilities, evaluation, assurances, and appraisals.

Manpower needs:

The model would be developed by a director with consultants and supportive staff. The director or an assistant might work with the U.S. Office of Education staff and thus have access to relevant records in that office. The surveys of individual short-term courses could be done by one or more Ph.D. candidates.

Related studies:

Richard Miller (1968), Garrison (1967), Merrell (1965), and Andrews (1957, 1961).

Communication and research information exchange in library science.

The American Psychological Association, under a grant from the National Science Foundation (1963) made a two-year study on scientific information exchange in psychology and found that there were four processes that could be identified in any successful system of scientific exchange of information: the origin of information, its transmission, its user, and information conveyance devices that have both transmission and storage functions.

Objectives:

1. To identify the institutions associated with the source, the user, and the information conveyance devices that have transmission and storage functions in library science and to identify the scope of each agency in fulfilling these roles
2. To analyze the types and categories of information exchange activities
3. To study the persons now initiating, guiding, or actively engaged in scientific research and the modes of communication they chiefly use; to determine roles of formal and informal communication; to derive information (from questionnaires and interviews) on the individual's research and the information exchange related to his research
4. To discover the information exchange between foreign and American librarians and information scientists
5. To determine the membership patterns in library and information science organizations and the information exchange among their members
6. To investigate the production, distribution, and use of technical reports, and the use made by librarians of such reports
7. To ascertain the nature of the scientific products of library associations, especially the research content of convention programs
8. To use the convention as a source of scientific and professional information; to report the dissemination of information at library and information science conventions and meetings
9. To study the information exchange activities at regional, state, and local library and information science meetings
10. To analyze the journal publication dates of papers presented at library and information science meetings

11. To study the collection, preparation, and use of scientific and professional information disseminated at a large library meeting or convention
12. To make a study of library and information journal authors, users, and reviewers, including the evaluation of journals and journal images
13. To determine the role of the invisible college in librarianship.

Manpower needs:

An association executive director familiar with the interdisciplinary exchange of information and also the framework and patterns of library associations and publications. The major elements of the study could be carried on simultaneously. The findings and recommendations of each sub-study should then be synthesized in a report which would be reviewed by the total staff and by a group of specialists (consultants) before publication. This complex project, it is estimated, would require at least two years and entail a large staff of research associates and assistants assigned to segments of the overall study. Computer facilities would be necessary for parts of the project. Major funding would be required and could be sought from a number of funding agencies.

Related study:

Reports of the American Psychological Association's research on scientific and information exchange (1963).

The development of model packaged programs of study in selected, defined areas pertinent to the needs of in-service librarians for updating and expanding their knowledge of advances in the field.

Objectives:

1. To identify the topics for which need and interest have been demonstrated, e.g., concepts and use of program budgeting in libraries, data for planning and decision-making on such topics as automation of library processes, on library insurance programs, Marc II tapes, etc.
2. To delineate the objectives of the unit
3. To develop the materials and techniques of presentation best calculated to achieve the objectives
4. To package a syllabus with a selected annotated bibliography illustrative charts, diagrams, photographs, and, depending on the topic, perhaps film strips, tapes, slides, programmed text or teaching machine program

5. To include some form of self-evaluation in the development of the package program
6. To develop methods of effective distribution of the package program.

Manpower needs:

An appropriate faculty member of a library school working with graduate students, an educational technologist, and an educator would constitute a minimum staff.

Related studies:

Dryer (1962), Wallace (1968), and Walker (1968).

Evaluation of the potential capabilities of various media for use in the continuing education of librarians: A feasibility study.

Objectives:

1. To experiment with the matching of media to educational objectives to obtain optimal results
2. To research and develop new methods and materials for continuing education of librarians
3. To study and evaluate the capabilities of EVR (Electronic Video Recording System) for the presentation of continuing education instruction
4. To study and to evaluate the capabilities of talk-back TV
5. To study and evaluate the use of a telephone dial-access tape recording system
6. To study and evaluate the use of video-tape
7. To study and evaluate instruction using TV fixed service
8. To study and evaluate the use of programmed instruction, which would include programmed texts, teaching machines, and computer-assisted programmed learning
9. To study and evaluate the possible use of correspondence courses
10. To study and evaluate the use of films and slides for use in the continuing education of librarians
11. To analyze and synthesize the end results, which would indicate in what kinds of situations and for what kinds of learning each of these major media might be most effectively used.

Manpower needs:

A team of researchers consisting of a technology specialist, a learning specialist, a subject specialist, and consultants would analyze and synthesize the results from the individual parallel studies.

Related studies:

Faegre (1968), Hamreus (1967), Briggs (1967), Gagne (1965), and Ofiesh (1969).

Toward closer reciprocal relationships between library science professors and practicing library administrators: An exploratory study.

Mosher (1968) emphasizes the serious threat inherent in the fact that there is an ever-widening gap in higher education between the professors and the administrators who make the decisions in society. He presents the hypothesis that, as scholars proceed more deeply into their subject matter, the problem of converting their findings and their wisdom into social policy becomes even greater and more important. In librarianship there would be many gains if professors in the graduate schools were to have closer working relationships with the practicing administrators of libraries.

Objectives:

1. To determine how university resources might be developed for helping library administrators improve their effectiveness
2. To determine the order of preference among the suggested ways in which professors of library science might best serve practicing library administrators, as viewed by the administrators and as viewed by the practicing professors in library schools
3. To determine whether the professors and the practicing administrators agree concerning the value-ranking of the ways in which professors of library science may best serve practicing administrators
4. To determine which of the suggested ways for professors of administration to best serve practicing administrators are viewed as most helpful by the total group of professors and practicing library administrators
5. To determine which of those ways are viewed as *least* helpful by the total group
6. To determine what understanding, knowledge, and skills should be emphasized in the program of leadership development for practicing library administrators
7. To ascertain which methods the administrators would prefer and which alternatives they would suggest to returning to the library school for continuing education.

Manpower needs:

The director should be a professor of library administration with supportive staff and selected library administrators as consultants.

Related study:

Mosher (1968).

Postgraduate internships and trainee programs in librarianship: An evaluation of existing programs and a proposal for development of the internship concept in continuing education for librarians.

Few library schools, libraries, and library systems have developed such programs. The internship concept has long been accepted in other professions as an integral part of professional training. It has not been regarded as such in librarianship. Yet, it would seem to be a very significant approach to continuing education for librarians. The internship approach might also be useful at various levels, say, immediately following the master's degree, or at mid-career for those showing special potential for top-level administration, or as part of the doctoral program (before, during, or after).

Objectives:

1. To evaluate existing intern programs in librarianship
2. To present the case for and against internship
3. To construct alternate internship plans
4. To make recommendations to the profession.

Methodology:

1. Content analysis of the literature on the concept of internship
2. Survey of existing programs, history, objectives, and elements of each program
3. Development of criteria for evaluating the programs
4. Evaluation:
   a. Questionnaires directed to those who completed the program and those currently involved in it
   b. Interviews with directors of programs
   c. Interviews with employers
5. Summarization of results and the reaching of conclusions
6. Development of alternate plans based on findings.

Manpower needs:

Director should probably be a faculty member who has taught and done some research in library administration. A programmer and statistician would probably be required for computer analysis of questionnaire and interview data. Consultants would be selected library administrators and others with experience in planning internships and training programs.

Related studies:

See related studies in librarianship, such as Stallman (1963), Wilson (1963), Kenney (1969), Brodman (1960), and Postell (1960) and internship reported on as master's theses at the University of Texas, for example: Ayres (1961), Bentley (1961), and M. H. Stone (1958).

A study of attitudes and responses to participation of mid-career librarians in community affairs as stimulators and effectors in continuing professional growth.

Library schools and the library literature stress the importance of the librarian's involvement in the interests and activities of the community he serves. The hypothesis is that such involvement can lead to a deeper sense of social responsibility, a mark of the professional whose growth should be personal as well as professional. Absorption in internal organization concerns can restrain serious thought in a groove and ultimately lead to superficiality. Social responsibility broadens a person's view of the total social system within which and for which the library makes its unique contribution.

Methodology:

The research would test the hypothesis through a series of interviews with a structured sample of mid-career librarians to determine their attitudes on social responsibility and to measure in some way its relative effect on their professional growth. Since related studies in other professions have revealed that an important factor in the amount of interest and activity given to community affairs is the example and encouragement of chief administrative offices, there is indicated a follow-up sampling of the attitudes of the bosses and their expectation and encouragement of staff to community involvement as a means of staff development toward a more enlightened and more sharply focused service.

Findings, if they follow the pattern of the other studies, may be somewhat negative, perhaps revealing conviction with little application. But, at the same time, the findings will identify gaps in training to which library education programs should address themselves today.

Manpower needs:

This project was conceived as one for an individual, preferably a library educator with special interests, experience, and training in sociology and social philosophy.

Related studies:

Several studies in related disciplines include: Mee (1968), Dillman (1961, 1962), Lazarus (1968), and Blizzard (1956).

References

Adelson, Marvin. "The System Approach—A Perspective." *SDC Magazine* 9:1–3 (Oct. 1966).

Allen, Lawrence A. *An Evaluation of the Community Librarians' Training Courses with Special Emphasis on the Entire Training Function in the Library Extension Division of the New York State Library.* Albany: New York State Library Extension Division, Jan. 1966. ERIC microfiche ED 024 406.

Alvarez, Robert Smith. "Continuing Education for the Public Librarian." *California Librarian* 30:177–86 (July 1969).

———. "Qualifications of Heads of Libraries in Cities of over 10,000 Population in the Seven North-Central States." Ph.D. dissertation, University of Chicago, 1939.

American Library Association, Office for Library Education. *Continuing Education for Librarians—Conferences, Workshops, and Short Courses 1967–1968, 1968–1969, 1969–1970.* Mimeographed. Chicago: American Library Association, 1967, 1968, 1969.

American Psychological Association. *Reports of the American Psychological Association's Project on Scientific Information Exchange in Psychology.* vols. I and II. Washington, D.C.: American Psychological Association, 1963.

Anderson, Frederic. *Factors in Motivation to Work Across Three Occupational Levels.* Ph.D. dissertation, University of Utah, 1961.

Andrews, Kenneth R. "Is Management Training Effective? I. Evaluation by Managers and Instructors." *Harvard Business Review* 35:85–94 (Jan.–Feb. 1957).

———. "Is Management Training Effective? II. Measurement, Objectives, and Policy." *Harvard Business Review* 35:63–72 (Mar.–Apr. 1957).

———. "Reaction to University Development Programs: As Reported by More than 6,000 Executives Who Went Back to School." *Harvard Business Review* 39:116–34 (May–June 1961).

Asheim, Lester E. "Education and Manpower for Librarianship: First Steps Toward a Statement of Policy." *ALA Bulletin* 62:1096–1106 (Oct. 1958).

Ayres, S. F. "Report of an Eleven-Month Internship in the Library of Yale University, July 1959 to June 1960." Master's thesis, University of Texas, 1961.

Bentley, B. "Report of an Internship Served in the Abilene (Texas) Public Library February 1 to August 1, 1960." Master's thesis, University of Texas, 1961.

Blizzard, Samuel W. "The Minister's Dilemma." *The Christian Century* 73: 509–10 (25 Apr. 1956).

Boag, Walter R. *The Minicourse Rationale and Uses in the Inservice Education of Teachers.* Berkley, Calif.: Far West Laboratory for Educational Research and Development, 1968. ERIC microfiche ED 024 647.

Boaz, Martha. "Continuing Education." *Drexel Library Quarterly* 3:151–57 (Apr. 1967).

———. "Education A-Go-Go Continuing . . ." *California Librarian* 30: 187–90 (July 1969).

———. "More than Deliberate Speed." *ALA Bulletin* 60:286–88 (Mar. 1966).

Briggs, Leslie J., et al. *Instructional Media: A Procedure for the Design of Multi-Media Instruction, A Critical Review of Research and Suggestions for Future Research.* Pittsburgh: American Institutes for Research, 1967.

Brodman, Estelle. "Internships as Continuing Education." *Medical Library Association Bulletin* 48:412 (Oct. 1960).

———, et al. "Continuing Education of Medical Librarians." *Medical Library Association Bulletin* 51:354–83 (July 1963).

Brunner, Edmund De S., et al. *An Overview of Adult Education Research.* Washington, D.C.: Adult Education Association of the U.S.A., 1959.

Bundy, Mary Lee. "Public Library Administrators View Their Professional Periodicals." *Illinois Libraries* 43:397–420 (June 1961).

———, and Wasserman, Paul. "Professionalism Reconsidered." *College and Research Libraries* 29:5–26 (Jan. 1968).

Case, Robert N., and Lowrey, Anna Mary. *School Library Manpower Project: A Report on Phase I.* Chicago: American Library Association, 1971.

Center for Documentation and Communication Research. *Education for Hospital Library Personnel: Feasibility Study for Continuing Education of Medical Librarians.* Interim Report no. 2 and Interim Report no. 3. Cleveland: Case Western Reserve University, 1968.

Clegg, Denzil. "The Motivation of County Administrators in the Cooperative Extension Service." Ph.D. dissertation, University of Wisconsin, 1963.

Cohen, David, and Dubin, Samuel S. "A Systems Approach to Updating Professional Personnel." In *National Seminar on Adult Education Research.* Toronto, 9–11 Feb. 1969. State College, Pa.: The Pennsylvania State University, Feb. 1969. ERIC microfiche ED 024 718.

Commission on Engineering Education. *Computer Sciences in Electrical Engineering, An Interim Report on the COSINE Committee.* Washington, D.C.: Commission on Engineering Education, Sept. 1967. ERIC microfiche ED 020 128.

Cook, Desmond L. *The Impact of Systems Analysis on Education.* Columbus, Ohio: Ohio State University Educational Research Center, 1968. ERIC microfiche ED 024 145.

———. "An Overview of Management Science in Educational Research." In *Symposium on Management Science in Educational Research,* 15th

International Meeting of the Institute of Management Science at Cleveland, Ohio, 11–13 Sept. 1968. Columbus: The Ohio State University College of Education, 1968. ERIC microfiche ED 024 002.

Corson, John J. "Equipping Men for Career Growth in the Public Service." *Public Administration Review* 23:1–9 (May 1963).

———, and Paul, R. Shale. *Men Near the Top: Filling Key Posts in the Federal Service*. Baltimore: John Hopkins Press, 1966.

Cross, K. Patricia. "When Will Research Improve Education?" *The Research Reporter* 2:1–4 (1967). Berkeley, Calif.: University of California Center for Research and Development in Higher Education, 1967. ERIC microfiche ED 025 206.

Cuadra, Carlos et al. *Technology and Libraries*. Santa Monica, Cal.: Systems Development Corporation, Research and Technology Division Technical Memorandum TM–3732, 1967. ERIC microfiche ED 022 481.

Culbertson, Jack. "Differentiated Training for Professors and Educational Administrators." In *Annual Meeting of the American Educational Research Association*. Chicago, 8–10 Feb. 1968. ERIC microfiche ED 021 039.

Cummings, Roy J. "Removing Intuition from Course Development: Methods at FAA to Prevent Overtraining and Undertraining." *Training and Development Journal* 22:18–27 (Jan. 1968).

Danton, J. Periam. *Between MLS and Ph.D*. Chicago: American Library Association, 1970.

Davies, Don. "Professional Standards in Teaching: Moving From Ideas to Action." *Journal of Teacher Education* 13:191 (June 1962).

Davis, Richard A. "Continuing Education: Formal and Informal." *Special Libraries* 58:27–30 (Jan. 1967).

Dill, William R. et al. "Strategies for Self-Education." *Harvard Business Review* 43:119–30 (Nov.–Dec. 1965).

Dillman, Beryl R. "The Professional Growth of Teachers as Perceived by Members of Other Professions—Physicians, Lawyers, Clergymen." Mimeographed. Research paper presented at the American Educational Research Association National Annual Convention. Pick-Congress Hotel, Chicago, 25 Feb. 1961.

Douglass, Robert R. "The Personality of the Librarian." Ph.D. dissertation, University of Chicago Graduate Library School, 1957.

Drennan, Henry T., and Darling, Richard L. *Library Manpower: Occupational Characteristics of Public and School Librarians*. U.S. Office of Education Publication OE–15061. Washington, D.C.: Government Printing Office, 1966.

Dryer, Bernard V., ed. "Lifetime Learning for Physicians: Principles, Practices, Proposals." *Journal of Medical Education* 37:1–134 (June 1962).

Dubin, Samuel S. "Keeping Managers and Supervisors in Local Government Up-To-Date." *Public Administration Review* 29:294–98 (May–June 1969).

————, and Marlow, H. LeRoy. *Highlights—A Survey of Continuing Professional Education for Engineers in Pennsylvania.* University Park, Pa.: Pennsylvania State University, 1968.

————; Alderman, Everett; and Marlow, H. LeRoy. *Educational Needs of Managers and Supervisors in Cities, Boroughs and Townships in Pennsylvania.* University Park, Pa.: Pennsylvania State University, 1968.

————; Alderman, Everett; and Marlow, H. LeRoy. *Highlights of a Study on Managerial and Supervisory Educational Needs of Business and Industry in Pennsylvania.* University Park, Pa.: Pennsylvania State University, 1968.

Duncan, Margaret. "Making the Special Librarian Special: The Case for Continuing Education." *California Librarian* 30:191–98 (July 1969).

Evans, Richard K., and Leppman, K. *Resistance to Innovation in Higher Education.* San Francisco: Jossey-Bass, 1967.

Faegre, Christopher L. et al. *Analysis and Evaluation of Present and Future Multi-Media Needs in Higher Education.* Communication Research Program, American Institutes for Research, 1968. ERIC microfiche ED 024 351.

Fitch, Vera E. "In-Service Training in Public Libraries." Research report. Los Angeles: University of Southern California School of Library Science, 1957.

Frenckner, T. Paulsson. "Development of Operational Management Methods: What does it Mean for the Education of Managers?" *International Social Science Journal* 20:29–34 (1968).

Fryden, Floyd N. "Post-Master's Degree Programs in Some American Library Schools." Mimeographed. Research paper. Chicago: University of Chicago Graduate Library School, 1968.

Gagne, Robert M. "Learning Decisions in Education." In *The Conditions of Learning.* New York: Holt, Rinehart and Winston, 1965.

————, and Bolles, R. C. "A Review of Factors in Learning Efficiency." In *Automated Teaching,* edited by E. Galanter. New York: Wiley, 1959.

Gardner, John W. *Self-Renewal: The Individual and the Innovative Society.* New York: Harper and Row, 1964.

Garrison, Lloyd N. et al. "Developing a Model for In-Service Education." In *Operation PEP, Symposium on the Applications of System Analysis and Management Techniques to Educational Planning in California.* Chapman College, Orange, Calif., 12–13 June 1967. Burlingame, Calif., June 1967. ERIC microfiche ED 023 181.

Gaver, Mary. "Is Anyone Listening? Significant Research Studies for Practicing Librarians." *Wilson Library Bulletin* 43:764–72 (Apr. 1969).

Ginsburg, Eli, and Brown, Carol A. *Manpower for Library Service.* New York: Columbia University, Conservation of Human Resources Project, Sept. 1967. ERIC microfiche ED 023 408.

Goheen, Robert F. "The Teacher in the University." *American Scientist* 54:221–25 (June 1966).

Goldstein, Harold, ed. *Proceedings*. Monograph Series no. 1. National Conference on the Implications of the New Media for the Teaching of Library Science, Chicago, 1963. Urbana, Ill.: University of Illinois Graduate School of Library Science, 1963.

Gomersall, Earl R., and Myer, R. Scott. "Breakthrough in On-The-Job Training." *Harvard Business Review* 44:62–72 (July–Aug. 1966).

Hamreus, Dale G. *Self Instructional Materials for Research Training: Supporting Documents to a Final Report*. Monmouth, Oreg.: Oregon State System of Higher Education Teacher Research Division, 1967. ERIC microfiche ED 021 778.

Hanzas, Barbara. "On-The-Job Training Procedures for Library Assistants." Master's thesis, Western Reserve University, 1953.

Harvey, John Frederic. *The Librarian's Career: A Study of Mobility*. ACRL Microcard Series No. 85. Rochester, N.Y.: University of Rochester Press, 1957.

Herzberg, Frederick. "Job Enrichment Pays Off." *Harvard Business Review* 47:61–78 (Mar.–Apr. 1969).

———; Mausner, Bernard; and Snyderman, Barbara. *The Motivation to Work*. 2d ed. New York: Wiley, 1959.

———. "One More Time: How Do You Motivate Employees?" *Harvard Business Review* 46:53–61 (Jan.–Feb. 1968).

Hewitt, Gordon B. *Continuing Education in Pharmacy: A Report*. British Columbia. Pharmaceutical Association, Province of British Columbia. Mar. 1965. ERIC microfiche ED 019 545.

Holton, Gerald; Watson, Fletcher G.; and Rutherford, F. James. *Harvard Project Physics Progress Report*. Three speeches delivered to the American Association of Physics Teachers (AAPT) Meeting, Feb. 1967. Washington, D.C.: American Association of Physics Teachers. ERIC microfiche ED 020 117.

Holzbauer, Herbert. "Inhouse ADP Training." *Special Libraries* 58:427–28 (July–Aug. 1967).

Honey, John C. "A Report: Higher Education for Public Service." *Public Administration Review* 27:294–321 (Nov. 1967).

Horn, Francis. *Tomorrow's Targets for University Adult Education*. 10th Annual Seminar on Leadership in University Adult Education. Lansing: Michigan State University Continuing Education Services, 1967. ERIC microfiche ED 019 536.

Houle, Cyril O. "The Role of Continuing Education in Current Professional Development." *ALA Bulletin* 61:259–67 (Mar. 1967).

Jerkedal, Ake. *Top Management Education: An Evaluation Study*. Stockholm, Sweden: Svenska Tryckeri Bolagen, 1967.

Jesse, William H., and Mitchell, Ann E. "Professional Staff Opportunities for Study and Research." *College and Research Libraries* 29:87–100 (Mar. 1968).

Katz, Saul M. *Education for Developmental Administrators: Character, Form, Content and Curriculum*. Paper presented at the Conference on Research and Teaching of Public Administration in Latin America, Rio de Janeiro, Brazil, Nov. 1967. Pittsburgh: University of Pittsburgh Graduate School of Public and International Affairs, 1967.

Kennedy, Maxine. "An Internship." *Medical Library Association Bulletin* 49:425 (July 1961).

Kenney, Louis A. "Continuing Education for Academic Librarians." *California Librarian* 30:199–202 (July 1969).

Klassen, Robert. "Institutes for Training in Librarianship: Summer 1969 and Academic Year 1969/1970." *Special Libraries* 60:185–89 (Mar. 1969).

Klempner, Irving M. "Information Centers and Continuing Education for Librarianship." *Special Libraries* 69:729–32 (Nov. 1968).

Knezevich, S. J. *The Systems Approach to School Administration: Some Perceptions on the State of the Art in 1967.* Paper presented at the U.S. Office of Education Symposium on Operations Analysis of Education, Washington, D.C., 19–22 Nov. 1967. ERIC microfiche ED 025 853.

Knox, Alan B. "Continuing Legal Education of Nebraska Lawyers." Nondegree study report. Lincoln, Nebr.: Nebraska State Bar Association, 1964.

———, and Booth, Alan. "Decisions by Scientists and Engineers to Participate in Educational Programs Designed to Increase Scientific Competence." Nondegree study report. Washington, D.C.: National Science Foundation, 1966.

Knox, Margaret Enid. "Professional Development of Reference Librarians in a University Library: A Case Study." Ph.D. dissertation, University of Illinois, 1957.

Kortendick, James J. "Continuing Education and Library Administration." *ALA Bulletin* 61:268–72 (Mar. 1967).

———. "Trends in Professional Education: Curriculum-Administration." *Drexel Library Quarterly* 3:92–103 (Jan. 1967).

———, and Stone, Elizabeth W. "Highlights of a Study on Federal Librarians and Post-MLS Education: A Preliminary Report." *DC Libraries* 41:71–76 (Fall 1969).

———, and Stone, Elizabeth W. *Job Dimensions and Educational Needs in Librarianship.* Chicago: American Library Association, 1971.

Kreitlow, Burton W. *Educating the Adult Educator, Part 1. Concepts for the Curriculum.* Bulletin 573. Mar. 1965. Madison: University of Wisconsin College of Agriculture Experimental Station, Mar. 1965. ERIC microfiche ED 023 969.

———. *Educating the Adult Educator, Part 2. Taxonomy of Needed Research Report.* Madison: University of Wisconsin Development Center for Cognitive Learning Adult Re-Education Project, May 1968. ERIC microfiche ED 023 031.

Lazarus, Charles Y. "Quest for Excellence—A Businessman's Responsibility." *Bulletin of Business Research* 43:1–5 (May 1968).

Likert, Rensis. *The Human Organization: Its Management and Value.* New York: McGraw-Hill, 1967.

Lorenz, John G. "The Challenge of Change." *PNLA Quarterly* 29:7–15 (Oct. 1964).

McConnell, T. R. *Research or Development, A Reconciliation.* Bloomington, Ind.: Phi Delta Kappa International, 1967.

McJenkin, Virginia. "Continuing Education for School Librarians." *ALA Bulletin* 61:272–75 (Mar. 1967).

McKeachie, Wilbert J. "Research in Teaching: The Gap Between Theory and Practice." In *Improving College Teaching,* edited by Calvin B. T. Lee. Washington, D.C.: American Council on Education, 1967.

———. *The Learning Process As Applied to Short-Term Learning Situations.* Preconference Workshop, Conference Proceedings. West Lafayette, Ind.: Purdue University National University Extension Association Conference and Institute Divison, Apr. 1965. ERIC microfiche ED 019 532.

McMahon, Ernest E.; Coates, Robert H.; and Knox, Alan B. "Common Concerns: The Position of the Adult Education Association of the U.S.A." *Adult Education Journal* 18:197–213 (Spring 1968).

Mager, Robert F. *Developing Attitude Toward Learning.* Palo Alto, Calif.: Fearon, 1968.

———. *Preparing Instructional Objectives.* Palo Alto, Calif.: Fearon, 1962.

Mee, John. "Participation in Community Affairs—The Role of Business and Business Schools." Research paper. Indiana University, 1968.

Merrell, V. Dallas. *An Analysis of University Sponsored Executive Development Programs.* Los Angeles: University of Southern California, 1965. ERIC microfiche ED 019 531.

Miller, Richard I. *A Comprehensive Model for Managing an ESEA Title III Project from Conception to Culmination.* Fairfax, Va.: Fairfax County Public Schools Center for Effecting Educational Change, 1968. ERIC microfiche ED 024 842.

Monroe, Margaret E. "AIM: An Independent Study Program in Library Science." *Journal of Education for Librarianship* 6:95–102 (Fall 1965).

———. "Variety in Continuing Education." *ALA Bulletin* 61:275–78 (Mar. 1967).

Moon, Eric. "The Library Press." *Library Journal* 94:4104–109 (Nov. 1969).

Morrison, Perry David. "Career of the Academic Librarian: A Study of the Social Origins, Educational Attainments, Vocational Experience, and Personality Characteristics of a Group of American Academic Librarians." Ph.D. dissertation, University of California, 1969.

———. *The Career of the Academic Librarian: A Study of the Social Origins, etc.* Chicago: American Library Association, 1969.

Mosher, Frederick. *Professional Education and the Public Service: An Exploratory Study. Final Report.* Berkeley, Calif.: University of California Center for Research and Development in Higher Education, 1968. ERIC microfiche ED 025 220.

Nakata, Yuri Ike. "An Analysis of Various Quantitative Differences Among Library Schools Based on Standards for Accreditation." Master's thesis, University of Chicago Graduate Library School, 1966.

National Education Associaton, National Commission on Teacher Education and Professional Standards. *The Development of the Career Teacher: Professional Responsibility for Continuing Education.* Washington, D.C.: National Education Association, 1964.

———. *What You Should Know About New Horizons.* A condensation of *New Horizons in Teacher Education and Professional Standards.* Washington, D.C.: National Education Association, 1962.

National Institute of Mental Health. *Training Methodology.* Public Health Service Publication 1862. Washington, D.C.: U.S. Government Printing Office, 1969.

Noonan, Fannie Sheppard. "In-Service Training in Catalog Departments of Public Libraries." Master's thesis, Columbia University, 1948.

Odiorne, George S. "A Systems Approach to Training." *Training Directors* 19:11–19. (Oct. 1965).

O'Donnell, Cyril J. "Managerial Training: A System Approach." *Training and Development Journal* 22:2–11 (Jan. 1968).

Ofiesh, Gabriel D. "The New Education and the Learning Industry." *Educational Leadership* 26:760–63 (May 1969).

O'Toole, John F., Jr. "Systems Analysis: A Rational Approach to Decision-Making in Education." *SDC Magazine* 8:1–6 (July 1965).

Pfeiffer, John. *New Look at Education: Systems Analysis in Our Schools and Colleges.* Poughkeepsie, N.Y.: Odyssey Press, 1968.

Poorman, Lawrence Eugene. *A Comparative Study of the Effectiveness of a Multi-Media Systems Approach to Harvard Project Physics with Traditional Approaches to Harvard Project Physics.* Ph.D. dissertation, Indiana University School of Education, 1967.

Porter, Elias H. *Manpower Development: A System Training Concept.* New York: Harper and Row, 1964.

Postell, William D. "Some Practical Thoughts on an Internship Program." *Medical Library Association Bulletin* 48:413 (Oct. 1960).

The Professional Education of Media Service Personnel: Recommendations for Training Media Service Personnel for Schools and Colleges. Preliminary edition. Pittsburgh: University of Pittsburgh Graduate Library School Center for Library Educational Media Studies, 1964.

Randall, Raymond L., and Simpson, Dick W. *Science Administration Education and Career Mobility.* Summary of Proceedings and Working Papers on the University Federal Agency Conference, 7–9 Nov. 1965. Bloomington, Ind.: Indiana University Institute of Public Administration, 1966. ERIC microfiche ED 019 563.

Ranta, Raymond R. "The Professional Status of the Michigan Cooperative Extension Service." Ph.D. dissertation, University of Wisconsin National Agricultural Extension Center for Advanced Study, 1960.

Reed, Sarah R., ed. *Continuing Education for Librarians—Conferences, Workshops, and Short Courses, 1964–1965.* Washington, D.C.: U.S. Department of Health, Education, and Welfare, Office of Education, 1964.

————, and Toye, Willie P., eds. *Continuing Education for Librarians—Conferences, Workshops, and Short Courses, 1966–1967.* Washington, D.C.: U.S. Department of Health, Education, and Welfare, Office of Education, 1965.

————. *Continuing Education for Librarians—Conferences, Workshops, and Short Courses, 1966–1967.* Washington, D.C.: U.S. Department of Health, Education, and Welfare, Office of Education, 1966.

————. "Education Activities of Library of Library Associations." Paper read at the Drexel Institute of Technology Library Association Administration Workshop, 10 Nov. 1966, Philadelphia. Mimeographed.

————, ed. *Problems of Library School Administration.* In Report of Institute, April 14–15, 1965. Washington D.C.: U.S. Department of Health, Education, and Welfare, Office of Education, 1965.

Rees, Alan M. et al. *Feasibility Study for Continuing Education of Medical Librarians. Interim Report.* Cleveland: Case Western Reserve University Center for Documentation and Communication Research, 1968.

Reisman, Arnold, ed. *Engineering: A Look Inward and a Reach Outward.* Proceedings of the Symposium. Milwaukee: University of Wisconsin College of Applied Science and Engineering, 1967.

Ripley, Kathryn Jane. "PERT As a Management Tool for Educators." Paper presented at the Management Training Program for Educational Research Leaders. Ohio State University, 24 Apr. 1968. Columbus: Ohio State University Educational Research Management Center, 1968. ERIC microfiche ED 023 368.

Roberts, T. J. *Developing Effective Managers.* London: Institute of Personnel Management, 1967.

Rothstein, Samuel. "Nobody's Baby: A Brief Sermon on Continuing Professional Education." *Library Journal* 90:2226–27 (15 May 1965).

Ryans, David G. "A Model of Instruction Based on Information System Concepts." In *Theories of Instruction,* edited by James B. Macdonald and Robert R. Leeper. Washington, D.C.: Association for Supervision and Curriculum Development, 1965.

Schiller, Anita R. *Characteristics of Professional Personnel in College and University Libraries.* Urbana, Ill.: University of Illinois Library Research Center, May 1968. ERIC microfiche ED 020 766.

Schramm, Wilbur. *The Research on Programmed Instruction: An Annotated Bibliography.* U.S. Department of Health, Education, and Welfare Bulletin, 1964, no. 35. Washington, D.C.: U.S. Government Printing Office, 1964.

Shank, Russell. "Administration Training in Graduate Library Schools." *Special Libraries* 58:30–32 (Jan. 1967).

Sloane, Margaret N. "SLA Chapters and Continuing Education." *Special Libraries* 58:24–26 (Jan. 1967).

Smith, Robert G., Jr. *The Design of Instructional Systems.* Technical Report 66–18. Alexandria, Va.: The George Washington University Human Resources Research Office, 1966.

Special Libraries Association. "Continuing Education for Special Librarianship . . . Where Do We Go from Here?" Proceedings of a planning session sponsored by the Education Committee, 2 June 1968, in conjunction with the Special Libraries Association annual conference in Los Angeles. Mimeographed.

Stallman, Esther L. *Library Internship: History, Purposes and a Proposal.* Library School Occasional Paper no. 37. Urbana, Ill.: University of Illinois Library School, Jan. 1954.

———. *The Library Internship Program Maintained for Students in the University of Texas Graduate School of Library Science.* Austin, Tex.: University of Texas Graduate School of Library Science, June 1963.

Stevenson, Grace T. "Training for Growth—The Future for Librarians." *ALA Bulletin* 61:278–86 (Mar. 1967).

Stolurow, Lawrence M. *Some Educational Problems and Prospects of a Systems Approach to Instruction.* Technical Report no. 2. Urbana, Ill.: University of Illinois Training Research Laboratory, Mar. 1964.

Stone, C. Walter, ed. *The Professional Education of Media Service Personnel: Recommendations for Training Media Service Personnel for Schools and Colleges.* Pittsburgh: University of Pittsburgh Graduate Library School Center for Media Studies, 1964.

Stone, Elizabeth W. "Administrators Fiddle While Employees Burn . . . or Flee." *ALA Bulletin* 63:181–87 (Feb. 1969).

———. "Continuing Education: Avenue to Adventure." *School Libraries* 18:37–46 (Summer 1969).

———. *Factors Related to the Professional Development of Librarians.* Metuchen, N.Y.: Scarecrow Press, 1969.

———. *Training for the Improvement of Library Administration.* Urbana, Ill.: University of Illinois Graduate School of Library Science, 1967.

Stone, M. H. "Report on an Internship Served at the Enoch Pratt Free Library, Baltimore, September 16, 1957–July 1, 1958." Master's thesis, University of Texas, 1958.

Suppes, Patrick. "On Using Computers to Individualize Instruction." In *The Computer in American Education,* edited by Don D. Busnell and Dwight W. Allen. New York: Wiley, 1967.

Swank, Raynard C. "Sixth-year Curricula and the Education of Library School Faculties." *Journal of Education for Librarianship* 8:14–19 (Summer 1967).

Swanson, Harold B. "Factors Associated with Motivation Toward Professional Development of County Agricultural Extension Agents in Minnesota." Ph.D. dissertation, University of Wisconsin, 1965.

Taylor, Edward Bunker. "Relationship between the Career Changes of Lawyers and their Participation in Continuing Legal Education." Ph.D. dissertation, University of Nebraska, 1967.

Thornton, James W., and Brown James W., eds. *New Media and College Teaching.* Washington, D.C.: National Education Association the Department of Audio-visual Instruction in collaboration with the American Association for Higher Education, 1968.

Tough, Allen M. "The Teaching Tasks Performed by Adult Self-Teachers." Ph.D. dissertation, University of Chicago, 1965.

Trow, William Clark. *Teacher and Technology: New Designs for Learning.* New York: Appleton-Century Crofts, 1963.

U.S. Department of Agriculture, Graduate School. *Faculty Handbook, Part II: Improving Teaching.* Washington, D.C.: Department of Agriculture Graduate Schools, 1967.

Walker, Richard D. *Independent Learning Materials in Library Science Instruction.* A report of a series of experiments on the efficiency of a programmed text developed in the articulated media program at the Library School of the University of Wisconsin, 1968. ERIC microfiche ED 025 296.

Wallace, Everett M. et al. *Planning for On-The-Job Training of Library Personnel.* Santa Monica, Calif.: System Development Corporation, Mar. 1968. ERIC microfiche ED 027 932.

————. *On-The-Job Training of Library Personnel (Interim Report).* Santa Monica, Calif.: System Development Corporation, May 1968. ERIC microfiche ED 027 933.

Walrath, Donald C. "A Systems Approach to the Training Program." *Training in Business and Industry* 2:22–24 (Jan. 1965).

Wasserman, Paul, and Bundy, Mary Lee. "Manpower for the Library and Information Professions in the 1970's: An Inquiry into Fundamental Problems." College Park, Md.: University of Maryland School of Library and Information Services, 1966.

Welch, Wayne W. *Harvard Project Physics Research and Evaluation Bibliography.* Cambridge, Mass.: Harvard University, Harvard Project Physics, Nov. 1968. ERIC microfiche ED 025 424.

Wilson, Celiana I. "Professional Internship: A Program and a Proposal." *Library Journal* 88:2201–205 (1 June 1963).

Woodworth, Mary L. *The Identification and Examination of Areas of Needed Research in School Librarianship.* Madison: University of Wisconsin, 1967. ERIC microfiche ED 018 243.

Leon Carnovsky

Research Needs Relating to the Role of the Library in the Community

Introduction

Since the program of any library school is conditioned by the society it exists to serve, it is essential that the school be aware of the character of the community to be served and of the changes occurring within that community. Otherwise, the school is in danger of continuing a program which may be only partially relevant, or may even be obsolete. However important its concerns with internal matters—such as student selection, faculty recruitment and assignments, placement procedures, and the like—it cannot lose touch with the society outside and still retain a viable program.

Whether all library schools can maintain a comprehensive research program is problematical. Many, perhaps most, are patently service institutions, established and operated to provide practitioners for traditionally functioning libraries. But even schools without a research orientation cannot remain immune to social changes, especially changes which have affected the libraries themselves. Indeed, the criticism recently voiced about the irrelevance of library education—whether justified or not—stems from the accusation that schools have not sufficiently, if at all, recognized the changes in society. Therefore, the critics continue, library instruction is geared to earlier times when social demands were different, when libraries functioned in ways appropriate to the nineteenth century. They feel libraries are not ready to meet current demands because library schools have not prepared their students for these responsibilities.

For present purposes, it is unnecessary to respond to these accusations. Whether they are correct and to what extent they are applicable to all schools, the implication is clear: The library school program must be relevant to the needs of its constituency. This statement has been invoked most forcefully with respect to the public library, but it is no less applicable to school, academic, and special libraries.

The problem as stated is really twofold: philosophical and operational, or ends and means. Is it the proper role of the public library, for example, to accept responsibility for serving the needs of all citizens regardless of their literacy, their interest in reading or in ideas in whatever form, and their capacity for comprehension? To put it in the broadest terms, we know that virtually every library is used (however "use" is defined) by a minority of the community, and by a very small minority of the adults in the community. Does the library have an obligation to the majority who never come near it?

Suppose the answer is "yes"; what then? *Can* it do anything that would effectively attract the non-user, and even more important, can it do anything that would make a significant difference in the patron's life or in the community's welfare? These questions are difficult to answer, and it may be doubted if investigations thus far of the effects of reading have done more than scratch the surface. (See, for example, Waples, Berelson, and Bradshaw 1940.) However, librarians, like others, have a strong faith that reading does make a difference, even if the difference cannot be scientifically demonstrated. But, given such faith, the question still remains as to whether persons for whom reading is a chore, or virtually impossible, can be induced to use the library at all.

These questions may be pleasantly speculative to the philosopher; they are realistic to the librarian who sometimes is expected to do something about them. He must inevitably consider how best to allocate the funds he' has—to determine whether he can afford to engage in experimental programs at the expense of conventional services, whether personnel are available for such programs, and ultimately, whether the society, or community, that supports his library expects him to reach beyond those activities to which it has become accustomed.

Each library must face these questions in terms of its philosophy, its community, and its financial, bibliographic, and personnel resources. At this point, we can do no more than suggest some of the research possibilities that in the long run may help to reach the answers. At the same time, these investigations may benefit the library school in two ways: (1) If the investigations are conducted in the schools, students are provided an invaluable opportunity for research experience; (2) if the studies lead to conclusions that might affect the direction of library development, the schools have an opportunity to revise their curricula and to prepare their students for services not currently offered. In this sense, at least, the schools might exert a profound influence on the direction to be taken by the library of the future.

The library and its community

There have been numerous studies concerning the question, Who uses the library? This is a question that can never be given a final answer. This is because communities differ so markedly from one to another that the pattern revealed in one may be quite different from that in another. Moreover, even in a single community, the character of the population may change significantly from one time to another. This in itself is sufficient to justify renewed attention to the use of the library and failure to use it.

Studies of library use have been reported in a number of publications. They have been summarized (as of 1949) in Berelson's *The Library's Public* and subsequently considered by Ennis and Fryden (1960, p. 253–65). Ennis (1965) probes further into the question of library use and concludes with suggestions for appropriate library programs in the light of each "community's needs and power structure." Library priorities, he says, cannot be the same in all cities, because the cities themselves are not alike. In one city, service to the business community may be stressed, especially if no "special" libraries exist to serve it; in another, the library might become "the educational and cultural auxiliary to whatever agencies are working to improve the opportunities for the deprived groups." Whatever the presumed implications for the library, there can be no doubt that community analysis should constitute an important element in library investigation.

The emphasis in community analysis has recently been placed on the so-called underprivileged—the economically insecure and the educationally deprived segments of an urban population—for whom the conventional library with books of some sophistication is largely, even completely, irrelevant. Yet on the assumption that the library has a responsibility to engage interest and patronage of those groups, questions may be raised about their numbers and geographical distribution, levels of literacy, language ability, interest in taking advantage of library programs, and the kinds of programs that would attract them. Such information may lead to administrative decisions of far-reaching significance and stimulate the provision of services far beyond those once envisaged as the limits of library responsibility. The High John project of the University of Maryland (Moon 1968) is illustrative of the type of program that might be undertaken, once we know where to place it and the most useful form it might take.

Yet this is only the beginning of research in this area. What happens, for example, when a special program is set up; specifically, what happens to the users of High John (and of similar programs undertaken in many large communities)? What proportion of the patrons are new, and how large a proportion of the underprivileged residents do they represent? What are their satisfactions and frustrations? Can anything more, or different, be done for the underprivileged who still do not come? For those who do, what is the nature of their involvement with the library—attending lectures or movies, borrowing books (and of what kind), using the facility as an escape from a depressing home environment, or whatever? These are only a few of the questions that a library might ask. The answers to many of them might well be that the *community*, rather than the library, has the responsibility for coping with the problems of the underprivileged through institutions other than the library, and that the library lacks the means to deal effectively with such problems.

There are other matters worth exploring, not only with respect to the underprivileged, but also relating to library use in general. For example, how good is the bookmobile, as a substitute for a fixed, or permanent, branch of a library, or as a means of introducing library service into areas where it was formerly not available? The word "good" immediately requires definition: good in terms of what? If *something* in place of *nothing* is accepted as "good," then no further study is necessary. But one may ask, how effective is the bookmobile in reaching adults? Is the bookmobile essentially a service to children, and does it actually repel rather than attract adults? (See Carnovsky Nov. 1967, p. 13–16.) (Even the implied generalization needs qualification; reaction in one community may not be at all representative of reaction in another, dominated by a different type of resident.) Questions of this kind may be raised for all types of extension outlets: how they are used, by how many, with what frequency, etc., and the answers may throw light on a realistic policy of branch establishment. If library school students were to undertake such studies, they would benefit greatly, not only through experience in objective measurement and in defining concepts in quantitative terms, but also from the opportunity to learn through observation, and possibly through participation, how people react to library facilities conventionally provided and assumed to be altogether satisfactory. Beyond this, there might be intensive cost studies of branches and other extension outlets, not for the purpose of determining whether a given service is *worth* what it costs, but for providing a realistic basis for assessing costs, which would contribute to the budgeting process.

The study of library use by adults should be supplemented by studies of student use. The recent Baltimore studies (Martin 1963) revealed clearly the impact on the public library made by the increase in school enrollments. How successful the library generally has been in accommodating the flood of students—how its experience may be related to its size, the character of the community, the quality of school libraries —are all considerations that might indicate a different role for the library, or different methods for performing its role.

Another matter that has rarely been studied is the effect of crowds of students in libraries upon adult attitudes toward the library and how this affects their patronage. Do students demand so much attention that other patrons are neglected? Do they pre-empt all the seats and many of the books that adults want? Since libraries and communities differ so widely from one another, the findings in one city may not apply to others. Studies of communities that differ significantly should therefore be welcome, and library schools can perform a real service to the profession by sponsoring them. At the same time, their own teaching and course content might be affected by the results. Can service to students be given more efficiently through better-equipped school libraries, accessible even when the school itself is not open? But before acting on the assumption that the answer lies in better school libraries, we would do well to determine how effectively the public library serves students and how student use of the library affects the rest of its clientele.

Although we have written of "students" and "adults" as though they were homogeneous groups, we know that this is so in only a limited sense, and their demands on the library are likely to vary as widely as does human curiosity. Nevertheless it is useful to differentiate among *types* of demand by identifiable groups, however defined. Consider, for example, the industrial community. What are its needs? How and to what extent can the public library satisfy them? These questions involve a host of other considerations, such as the definition of the industrial community, its size and character, the identification and classification of its needs that may be met through bibliographical resources, the possibility that other kinds of library or bibliographical centers may meet them, and the cost involved. As such information is made available, the library school itself—with specific population components in mind—may find it desirable to shape its curriculum, particularly in reference work and information retrieval, to give its students more realistic preparation.

The industrial community is only one of a virtually unlimited number of enterprises that make up the life of any large city. Newspapers, insurance firms, investment houses, for example (or individuals with similar concerns), are constantly in search of information, frequently of an esoteric kind, for which they depend on the public library. Or they would, if they felt the library was in a position to help them. It is, of course, true that many of them maintain their own "special" libraries, but they must often still look beyond their own resources for assistance. The possibility of interdependence should be studied, not only for its immediate value, but also for what it can contribute to the library school student in his own approach to the provision of needed information.

Although we have used the public library as our point of departure, this discussion inevitably leads to other kinds of libraries and to individuals with interests beyond "something to read." The focus is service to the community: How can it best be provided? With emphasis on the potential reader in need of information, the solution may be found, not in any existing library, but in the rapidly expanding field of investigation into methods of bringing to bear the needed information, wherever stored, on inquiries, however unusual or difficult.

From adults, we turn to children. Surely no area is more important than library service to children, and libraries have probably achieved their greatest success in attracting and introducing children to books. At the same time, the disciplines of psychology and education have developed a monumental literature on how children learn, their reading behavior, satisfactions, and frustrations. It is difficult to say to what extent such studies have affected the preparation of children's and school librarians; indeed, it may well be that most investigations are too far removed from library involvement to bear much relevance to library practice. However, in spite of work already done, the sociology of reading with particular reference to children seems a fruitful field. What is the relationship, for example, between the kinds of library books read and the child's background? How is library reading affected by other sources, such as friends' collections, bookstores, and the like? How is reading affected by television and other distractions, or does television stimulate rather than distract from reading? (See Himmelweit 1958.) No less important are studies of the effects of reading: What happens to a child's attitudes as a result of reading? To what extent, if at all, are a child's prejudices, likes, and animosities nourished by what he reads? Strictly speaking, this may not be a library problem; still, since the librarian inevitably plays a role in determining at least *some* of the reading of *some* children, the better equipped he is in knowledge of children *as well as* in knowledge of books, the more effective his contribution to the child and to society.

These are merely illustrations of possible investigations into children's relative motivation to read. Children as a group are no more homogeneous than adults. The more we know about influences on the reading patterns of children of different backgrounds and environments, the better we may be able to prepare the specialist in library work with children. Aside from this, we might speculate that such investigation would suggest striking changes in the curriculum in this area, adding strong components of child psychology and urban sociology to the conventional areas of children's literature, storytelling, and administrative problems.

The school library has received considerable attention, particularly in recent years, and a set of standards has been developed to serve both as guidelines and as evaluative instruments. Investigations have subsequently been made to determine the extent to which given libraries meet or exceed the standards. But, beyond such studies, one might look at school library *performance*, especially since the standards themselves say nothing about measurement of service. One might examine the relationship between size of collection and amount of student use per capita, or use by groups differentiated according to scholarship, major interests, family backgrounds, etc. Since library use is the *end* toward which the standards are implicitly directed, studies of use might lead to a reconsideration—perhaps an evaluation—of the standards and might suggest revision in some of the details. A standard might specify that seating in the library should be provided for X percent of the student body. On what is this figure based? If it can be shown to apply satisfactorily in a given school, can it be generalized to apply to *all* schools, or to schools where the curriculum or teaching method or student characteristics are different? No given standards or formulas should be blindly accepted without raising the question: How do we know? And are these prescriptions universally applicable?

Needless to say, such investigations should have an impact on library school instruction in the school library field. As in other segments of the curriculum, the library school should do more than inculcate an awareness of current practice and officially accepted standards. The school should continually encourage students to ask how we know that a given practice is best for a given situation, even though it conforms to present standards. These standards may be suspect because they are out-of-date or were originally adopted on the basis of necessarily limited evidence.

The current preoccupation with the library as a larger unit of service seems more closely related to government than to community problems. In fact, the two coalesce, for changes in structure derive solely from presumed community needs and expectations which cannot be fulfilled by the conventional structure. The larger unit makes sense in light of its ability to accomplish certain things that are difficult or impossible for the typical small library. Now the question arises, how has the nature of library service—what the library *does*, not what it is prepared to do—been affected by the transformation of the institution into system membership? Some results are readily identifiable: circulation to communities formerly deficient in availability of library service, perhaps a larger circulation, and possibly the expansion of the types of materials loaned. Others are worth examining: Since at least one outcome that was envisioned by the larger unit was the availability of a larger and more diversified collection than the independent library could possibly provide, how has the *character* of the library circulation and reference use been affected? This, of course, does not question the desirability of the larger unit, but only suggests that the results as revealed in community use be studied. The Nelson Associates study (1969, p. 246) observes: "Few libraries know whom they are serving, and almost none can assess accurately the costs of the various services they provide." This observation is elaborated in the following passage (p. 258):

> There are now no adequate measures for the values of many library services to the patron. The problem is not only to devise new measurements but also to translate the value into dollars. If this is to be done, much more needs to be discovered about the cost of services. There are no existing cost figures that can be used with any degree of assurance; figures are assembled in a variety of ways with varying care, and include different things.

Many additional questions for investigation are suggested (see especially p. 259–61), and library schools should bring their students' attention to them. It would be difficult to point to another area so fruitful in giving the schools the opportunity to lead, rather than merely reflect, the trend in library organization and service.

Closely related to the larger unit is the metropolitan area. As the central city library has expanded its holdings, as it has moved into the acquisition of books, periodicals, and documents in little demand but invaluable to the serious student, it has reinforced its position as a magnet, as the focus for attracting patrons wherever they live in the city and from surrounding communities as well. Highways and interurban transportation facilities have all but wiped out the distinction between city and suburb and the territory beyond; the service area of a large city library goes far beyond the area responsible for its support. This whole process of dependence on the central city is one that could be usefully studied: How great is the external impact in terms of circulation, reference use, demands on personnel, etc.? What are the implications for external financing—by county, state, or federal government? The more we know the answers to such questions, the better we can plan library expansion and financing—and the better we can prepare students for a useful role in such planning (Carnovsky Jan. 1967, p. 489).

Before leaving consideration of the public library's role in its community, we shall devote some attention to the question: Does the library have a special role in improving community race relations? What is this role and how can it be exercised? It is, of course, naive to assume that the library alone, or that reading in general, can significantly influence attitudes among racial or national or religious groups. Nevertheless, the social implications of race relations are so serious that, at the very least, the library should ask what it could do, if only to make a slight contribution.

The problem, though currently in the forefront of local and national concerns, is not new. An outbreak of racial violence in Detroit in 1943 led the Detroit Public Library to issue a pamphlet and reading list on race relations, and libraries have always been alert to the possibilities of contributing to the understanding and amelioration of social disturbances. The problem of racial animosities, particularly in large urban centers, has been aggravated by a number of factors which need no elaboration at this point. But the question remains: What, if anything, can the library do? Certain things seem obvious. It can try to attract the newly arrived resident to the library or to a branch; it can take the library (via deposits or bookmobile) to him; it can provide him reading matter he can grapple with; it can offer significant programs by film, lecture, or records. The library can also provide materials to prepare him for successful job performance.

All these activities and more may be identified through field studies, correspondence, or analysis of the professional literature, and the listing alone might well prove suggestive to librarians in general and to students looking forward to a library career. But there are other aspects which are clearly worth investigation. What has happened as a result of the programs? How many people have been affected, at least to the extent of attending special classes or lectures? Can any figures be given on cost? Can the special programs be operated by conventional library personnel, or are they more properly conducted by social workers, formal educators, or others? If so, are there implications here for a change in library school curricula to provide a different kind of training, either instead of that presently offered or in addition to it?

We may conclude this section by repeating one of the questions raised in this inquiry: How can the role of the library in the community, present and future, be determined and influenced? The question has already been raised as to whether the library has a responsibility for all citizens regardless of their literacy and the presence of other inhibiting factors. There is likely to be some difference of opinion on this point, ranging from an unequivocal "yes" to a much more qualified response. For example, Banfield has stated: "The proper business of the public library is with the *serious* reader and—assuming that the library cannot be an effective instrument for educating the lower class —with him alone" (Conant 1967, p. 109). And, in the same vein, Burchard comments: "I believe the library should do its special job for those who need and want it and that other institutions, such as better settlement houses or youth houses equipped with smaller libraries, should prepare some youngsters to need and want the larger service, just as the schools and the hearths may prepare others" (p. 194). These observations will strike a sympathetic chord with many; they will strike others as deliberately closing the door of opportunity to the disadvantaged. Whether the open door can actually lead to enrichment, to growth, or even to small satisfactions, is a question that might usefully occupy the attention of many of our library schools.

From the focus on persons indifferent to the library or incapable of using it, we turn now to the opposite extreme—those for whom excellent resources may still not be sufficient. These, too, make up part of the community. How can library schools prepare their students to cope with the needs of these persons? Or, to put the question in a somewhat different context, what part can libraries play in the development of our communications and information-exchange. networks? This is a major consideration of the National Advisory Commission on Libraries.

This area is currently receiving the serious attention of information scientists, whether or not under the aegis of library schools. Much more is involved than the designing of hardware to make communication of information more efficient. What is required is investigation into the actual needs of scholars and scientists and the difficulties and frustrations they experience in meeting them. One might visualize greater library expansion, specialization, and interdependence as the most efficient and least costly approach to a solution. Or one might ask if something still better is needed, which would bring into play the whole panoply of technological devices aimed at the speedy retrieval of information without regard to its physical format or place of storage. Basically, however, we need to know how the advanced student and research worker can be aided in their scholarly pursuits. To learn this, we must begin with *them*, not with the mechanisms.

Research methods

Thus far we have tried to pinpoint certain problem areas where research might contribute to possible solutions, as well as how it might affect the character of library education. A word now about methods for the collection and analysis of data. There is nothing particularly new in the methods necessary to pursue most of the studies, though this is not to deny the difficulties involved in many of them. Studies of reading and the distribution of reading matter have depended on the analysis of circulation statistics, questionnaire responses, observations, and, infrequently, diaries. (See Carnovsky 1957, Tauber and Stephens 1967.) Needless to say, caution must be exercised to ensure as much accuracy as possible, particularly in questionnaires and checklists. And since many studies will invariably rest on population sampling, some knowledge of statistical techniques is indispensable. Should training in research methods form part of the library school program? The same question might be raised about investigations centering on information storage and retrieval, where advanced mathematical and statistical competence is likely to be essential. That such training must be provided is beyond dispute, but that it should form part of the library school curriculum is doubtful. The important thing is that the potential investigator be equipped with the necessary tools, not that his preparation be limited to the library school. Particularly now, when all schools are part of colleges or universities which provide courses in mathematics, statistics, sampling methods, etc., it may be hoped that the student would be encouraged to take advantage of such courses where his own background may be limited.

The type of research suggested in this paper is not unique; it has long been conducted in the social sciences, and the literature of research methodology is plentiful. Perhaps only relatively few students will have an interest in investigation and the competence to pursue it, but the results should redound to the benefit of the library profession, and, in time, may be reflected in the library school curriculum and perhaps in the creation of a corps of individuals for whom the study of library problems will be a lifelong adventure.

Conclusion

The library's role in its community has served in this discussion as the point of departure for considering research needs. Hence, the emphasis has been placed on actual and potential library *users*, ranging from the most sophisticated to the least, at least so far as access to library materials and information generally is concerned. Library use certainly does not constitute all of librarianship, but without it the institution loses much of its reason for being. Implicit in this emphasis on the user is the vague concept of social value—benefits to society at large as well as to the individual. This point has been so well expressed by the National Advisory Commission on Libraries, that we may conclude by quoting one paragraph from its report:

> One theme emerges throughout all the activities of the National Advisory Commission on Libraries since its first meeting in November

1966. This is a strong social-benefit awareness, a service orientation that pervades every existing and conceivable library and information function. Perhaps it is not too soon to propose the criterion of social value as the most important in decision-making—whether for broad central planning, more specific planning, or immediate problem-solving. We should look at the value to our people and our culture that accrues from the activities of the user whose functions are to be enhanced by improved availability of library and information services. A library can be understood only as it enhances a socially valuable function, one of which—and one that all libraries can enhance—is the personal intellectual and ethical development of every individual in our society. The variety of the other socially valuable functions determines the need for variety in kinds of libraries.

References

Berelson, Bernard. *The Library's Public*. New York: Columbia University Press, 1949.

Carnovsky, Leon. "Changing Patterns in Librarianship: Implications for Library Education." *Wilson Library Bulletin* 41:484–91 (Jan. 1967).

———. "The Mansfield Public Library: Suggestions for a Future Program." Mimeographed. Mansfield, Ohio: Mansfield Public Library, Nov. 1967.

———. "Methodology in Research and Applications." *Library Trends* 6:234–46 (Oct. 1957).

———. "Survey of the Use of Library Resources and Facilities." In *Library Surveys,* edited by M. F. Tauber and I. R. Stephens. New York: Columbia University Press, 1967.

Conant, Ralph W., ed. *The Public Library and the City*. Cambridge, Mass.: M.I.T. Press, 1967.

Ennis, Philip. "The Library Consumer." In *The Public Library and the City,* edited by Ralph W. Conant. Cambridge, Mass.: M.I.T. Press, 1965.

———, and Fryden, F. "Use Studies Revisited." *The Library Quarterly* 30:253–65 (Oct. 1960).

Himmelweit, Hilde T. *Television and the Child: An Empirical Study of the Effect of TV on the Young*. London, New York: Oxford University Press, 1958.

"Library Services for the Nation's Needs: Report of the National Advisory Commission on Libraries." *ALA Bulletin* 63:67–94 (Jan. 1969).

Martin, Lowell A. *Students and the Pratt Library: Challenge and Opportunity*. Deiches Fund Studies of Library Services, No. 1. Baltimore: Enoch Pratt Free Library, 1963.

Moon, Eric E. "High John: Report on a Unique Experiment in Maryland Designed to Initiate Change in Public Library Service and Library Education." *Library Journal* 43:147–55 (15 Jan. 1968).

Nelson Associates. *Public Library Systems in the United States*. Chicago: American Library Association, 1969.

Waples, Douglas; Berelson, Bernard; and Bradshaw, Franklyn R. *What Reading Does to People*. Chicago: University of Chicago Press, 1940.

Part Two

Determining Research Priorities

Kevin D. Reilly

The Delphi Technique:
Fundamentals and Applications

Background on the Delphi Technique

Not all decisions men are called upon to make can be improved upon by study. The "bold man of action" has his place. However, a man disdainful of study, who repeatedly is called upon to make decisions, is likely to quickly erode his reputation for success and ultimately remove any claim to the right of further decision-making. But there is a Charybdis corresponding to the Scylla of decisions without information; it is information without decisions. A would-be decision-maker can become so enmeshed in detailed facts or in rhetoric that he becomes paralyzed to act. A compromise between these two extremes is surely desirable. It has been achieved, to some extent (in business circles principally), in the form of a "people-based" information retrieval system; that is, the decision-maker surrounds himself with a small group of advisors who gather information and "package" it appropriately for specific information needs (Wilson 1970). Seen in this context, the bold man of action, with his instantaneous decisions based on hunch or some sixth sense, begins to be perceived as an element from the realm of mythology.

The decision-maker who relies heavily on others must, however, guard himself against the fate depicted by the aphorism that a man is no better than his advisors. He may achieve some degree of protection by being an avid reader and an attentive listener, by being able to "read between the lines" of reports and absorb added and alternate meanings on the basis of advisors' facial expressions. Nevertheless, his personal fact data bank and psychological talents are likely to be found wanting more than just occasionally. Thus, any new technique which promises potentially rapid response with concise, directly relevant information is highly welcome. The Delphi Technique is such a method.

The name of the technique arouses at least a modicum of interest in all who come upon it for the first time. Immediately, the famous oracle comes to mind; the question arises: "What does a Delphi Technique have to do with the scientific method which this generation so highly reveres? Have we become so confused with the complexities of life that we have become disenchanted with the orderly scientific approach and have returned to listening to the ravings of a priestess who has thrown herself into a trance by drinking waters from hallowed springs, chewing consecrated bay leaves, shaking a laurel branch, and breathing vapors mystically rising from the earth?"

A more solid clue to the modern use of the term "Delphi" can be gained from a look at the early days of the oracle, when careful collection and shrewd use of information prevailed (Fine 1970). A number of devices were employed at Delphi to gather information, including a network of "spies," who mingled among the patrons of the oracle as they waited (sometimes for a very long period) to receive its blessings and extracted every morsel of available information from them. The oracle was then able to confirm courses of action that had already been decided upon and choose when to vary from its otherwise firmly established policies of vagueness and ambiguity in all foretellings, avoidance of decided positions on political matters, and maintenance of a conservative base on religious and philosophical issues.

The goals of the Delphi Technique are much the same as those of the oracle: to predict the future and to evaluate alternative courses of action, although not by deliberate use of vagueness and ambiguity! That is, a new methodology reigns: The "spies" have been replaced by researchers and the respondents are actually accomplices in the prediction enterprise. The details of this camaraderie will be laid bare as this chapter proceeds.

Conducting a typical Delphi study

A Delphi study involves at least two groups of individuals: the researchers who conduct the study and the respondents, generally a group of experts in the field under investigation, who answer the questions posed by the researchers. Although uniform to the extent of being in the same field, the respondents are normally chosen to represent the varying perspectives of managers, researchers, analysts, planners, educators, and any others for whom the questions have some special meaning. A study frequently begins with the researchers making an informal inquiry of the respondents as to what significant events are likely to occur in the field under investigation within a given period of time (usually a ten- to thirty-year segment of the immediate future). In some cases, only a portion of the respondents are involved in this initial phase of the effort. In an even smaller number of cases, the listing of events is supplied by individuals who are not otherwise involved in the study. The researchers generate a questionnaire whose questions or proposals are conducive to eliciting precise responses as to: (1) when, (2) with what probability, or (3) with what degree of benefit certain events or conditions will obtain. The questionnaire is then sent to the respondents by mail. (Speculations are that this might occur some day via a computer-based communications system not unlike that envisioned by EDUCOM [Brown 1967].)

The responses are developed in private—a fundamental element in the Delphi approach. This is done to avoid certain undesirable effects of face-to-face communication, such as specious persuasion, the unwillingness to abandon publicly expressed opinions, and the bandwagon effect of majority opinion (Helmer 1959). Additions to this list include the effect of the dominant individual—he who speaks loudest and longest wins the day!—and "semantic noise"—that portion of the conversation directed to matters other than the question at hand (e.g., to establish pecking order in the sponsoring professional organization's hierarchy).

When they are returned, the answered questionnaires are analyzed by the researchers. Some basic statistic, such as the median, is calculated, and it, along with the original questionnaire, is sent back to the respondents for a second "round." On occasion, some of the questions may be omitted, e.g., in the case of events which all respondents believe will never happen. Alternatively, modifications may be called for if certain flaws in the questions become apparent, e.g., if the comments of respondents indicate that an altered form of a particular question may be more appropriate. Additional information may be sent to the respondents, or an inquiry may be made as to why a question was answered in the manner it was, especially when the answer is unusual. The purpose of doing this is to make the individual more rigorously question his views and encourage him to express them; if his reasonings are sound, the whole group may gain insight on a subsequent round. The purpose of this feedback (or iteration) element in the Delphi Technique is to effect interaction or concert among the respondents, who otherwise would be operating in a totally independent manner. This element distinguishes the Delphi approach from conventional survey research. Viewing the method from this perspective reveals it to be a contribution to the survey research art.

Second and subsequent rounds in a Delphi study generally produce a degree of convergence of opinion. The basic tendency of humans to be not overly extreme probably lies at the heart of this. Convergence, however, may well be countermanded, at least to some extent, as a consequence of the very "expertness" of the experts, who, it might be surmised, feel little pressure to change a position, once taken, when confronted by the (differing) opinions of others.

Early Delphi studies

The Delphi Technique was first discussed in detail in a monograph by O. Helmer (1966). This, along with another pair of reports by Helmer (1957, 1967), reveals much of the philosophical underpinning of the methodology as well as portraying a number of the early applications. The Delphi Technique is described as a "new form of procedure within the scientific establishment." Helmer endeavors to categorize it in relation to a general scientific methodology, which is undergoing many changes, and, in particular, being extended in a variety of new directions under the impact of computers, more sophisticated statistical analysis, multidisciplinary team approaches, and increased role for conferences and other people-to-people forms of communication. The phrase coined to represent the newer methodologies (also the title of Helmer's monograph), "social technology," purports to contrast the almost operations research emphasis of these new approaches with the emphasis of the more conventional "social science" methodologies, which the new methods complement. This "technology" espouses the systems approach and exploits every possible benefit from mathematical modeling and simulation in the move toward greater precision. Helmer is quite the optimist about these developments and, in particular, about their potential application in helping to solve mankind's social, economic, and technological problems:

> The newly discernable willingness to examine the applicability and refine the use of such tools in the social-science area, together with the computer capabilities on the horizon, convince me that we are entering an era of potentially remarkable social progress.

Were his comments directed more precisely toward library science, they would be highly reminiscent of those of Pierce Butler (1933) who long ago pressed for the foundation of a "science" of librarianship as opposed to the almost entirely humanistic librarianship of the time. His plea for statistics and his appeal to the magic of numbers ("Theories of relationship derived from quantitative ratios usually involve the least danger of subjective misunderstanding") came at a time when statistics was dominated by methods more appropriate to the controlled experiment of the physical sciences. It would seem to follow that Butler's enthusiasm for "social technology" might even exceed that which he showed for "social science."

Time prediction studies

Beyond these more philosophical matters, the papers by Helmer contain the results of a wealth of individual Delphi studies illustrating the broad scope of the method. The appendixes of *Social Technology* present a series of studies involving, for the most part, prediction of the time when certain events or conditions will obtain. The very first study, for example, focuses on predicting the advent of certain technical and scientific developments having "general public interest," such as: synthesis of artificial life, production of artificial plastic and electronic organs, and control of gravity through means of gravitational field modification. The timing for the appearance of these developments was left open even to the extent of their never happening at all, a fate bestowed in large measure by the respondents on the use of telepathy and ESP in communications. The resulting predictions are presented as house-shaped pictographs (now almost a universal characteristic of Delphi project reports), which display the median response along with the inter-quartile range or other appropriate central and dispersion measures.

A number of other time prediction studies were performed and are reported in Helmer's appendixes: one on general automation (of labor, medical diagnosis, education, transportation, etc.); one on space progress (a Mars landing and return; a Pluto fly-by, etc.); and another on weapons systems (battlefield computers, robots, incapacitating biological agents, etc.).

By compiling results from several independent Delphi studies and taking the cross-sections for a given year, a composite picture of the likely state of development of technology, human resources, etc., at that time can be formed. Appendix I of Helmer's book presents such composites for the years 1984 and 2000. Results compiled in this manner constitute a form of packaged information useful as input ("feed-in") for further Delphi predictions. For example, predictions on educational needs in library and information science in the year 2000 would probably be more sound if predictions of technological developments, the general state of human knowledge, and perhaps other factors were made available to respondents.

Evaluation studies

As part of the study on automation, ten proposed measures for abating automation-produced unemployment were rated according to the three parameters of *effectiveness*, *desirability*, and *probability* of their being utilized. The evaluative scales covered negative, nil, neutral, minor, moderate, and high, while the probability scale spanned minor, moderate, and high. Most of the proposals were prosaic ones—e.g., creation of new (unspecified) types of work, retraining, government aid to depressed areas, legislation proscribing certain kinds of automation activities—and none of them emerged with a high rating across the board, the highest set of ratings being achieved for the creation of new types of employment: high on desirability, moderate to high on effectiveness, and moderate to high on potential.

Another evaluation study concerned foreign policy proposals, for which the same three criteria were employed. In this case, only a condensed scale was utilized involving high, medium, and low values. If substantial agreement was obtained for any of these scale values, it is underlined in the report; e.g., if one-third of the group assigned a high value, one-third a low value, etc., there is no underline. But if 60 percent assigned a low value and 20 percent a high value, etc., the "low" value appearing in the table of results is underlined. Underlining appears frequently in the table of results, indicating that substantial agreement was not a rare event. High scores across the board were given only to three proposals, all of which dealt (basically) with defensive military initiatives.

Experimental studies of the Delphi methodology

A new method such as the Delphi must undergo thorough examination if only to ascertain whether its early promise can be sustained. Experiments on the Delphi Technique have begun in earnest, and some results are already available concerning such matters as: What constancies exist from study to study? What form (if any) of interaction between the researchers and respondents is optimal; and the most basic question of all—how accurate can a method of this type be? It is convenient to separate the experiments into two classes: (1) those concerned with collecting, comparing, and cataloging the results of typical Delphi studies; and (2) those concerned fundamentally with accuracy of results. The former generally constitute a more straightforward form of examination in the sense that they can be performed on *any* Delphi study. Such examinations may nevertheless be quite detailed, requiring statistical knowledge ranging from the elementary to the most complex.

The latter type of examination is quite special and involves the concept of error. In order to measure error, a synthetic Delphi procedure must be developed, one in which the answers to the questions are known or can be estimated accurately. A series of studies by N. Dalkey and his co-workers (1969, 1970, 1970, and Brown et al. 1969), which constitute the basic corpus to date for assessment of Delphi methodology and which treat these matters, will now be reviewed.

Study of elementary characteristics

Among the data that can be readily collected in any Delphi study are those relating to (1) the issue of reliability, or more specifically, the effect of group size on reliability; (2) the likelihood and magnitude of respondents' opinion change on one round as a function of distance from the median on a previous round; (3) change of opinion as a function of sex; and (4) the form of the distribution of responses on the various rounds.

1. Reliability is important for any experimental procedure. For the Delphi Technique, reliability presupposes that different groups of equal expertise produce similar results. Reliability obviously depends on group size, the expectation being that, as group size increases, reliability increases. Experimental results indicate that reliability, measured by the correlation coefficient taken over a collection of questions for pairs of respondent groups of varying sizes, behaves in this expected fashion.
2. Questionnaire feedback is of such central importance in the Delphi approach that any experiment analyzing patterns of convergence is of great value. First of all, there exists an undeniable "pull of the median." That is, a respondent's answer on a second round is likely to move toward the group median. Within limits, this pull increases as a function of the distance of the respondent's answer from the median: The likelihood of change is effectively a linear function for smaller distances from the median, leveling off for larger changes, presenting an overall $\curlyvee$-shaped appearance when graphed. The magnitude of change demonstrates a similar tendency but not quite so clearly cut.
3. A complete study of male-female effects involves more than a simple comparison of opinion change from a first to a second round, but the basic result on this single issue is in accord with the layman's view: Women do live up to their image of changeability. Other aspects of this topic are discussed later.
4. The form of distribution of responses for first-round answers to questions requiring numerical estimates appears to be log-normal,

suggesting that respondents were directing their thoughts to orders of magnitude rather than to the precise numerical values of the answers. Second-round answers appear to deviate somewhat from this distribution and cannot be assigned a standard (i.e., "name") distributional form. If it could be shown that a certain distributional form tends to accompany more accurate answers, techniques might be employed even in single-round surveys to reduce it.

Study of errors

Error measurements suitable for the Delphi context can be formed in either of two ways: (1) the absolute difference between the group median and the correct answer; and (2) the stated difference divided by the correct answer, more appropriate when interest is directed to percentage of error. The concept of error is thus simple to form. However, real-life Delphi studies deal almost exclusively with questions for which answers are not known and cannot be discovered by any conventional means. Therefore, error cannot be measured in most studies. It is possible, however, to create a synthetic Delphi procedure using questions for which answers exist, but which are almost certainly not known to the respondents. Ideally, the questions will be of such a nature that the respondent's efforts in arriving at answers to some degree simulate the act of opinion formation, as opposed to factual responding (as would be the case with the "handbook" type of questions on, say, Avogadro's number with physical scientists). Perhaps the most suitable choice, that which Dalkey and co-workers picked, is to create questions from information in almanacs. Such questions are frequently quantitative and are of such a nature that the respondent can often calculate a "ballpark answer." A typical question might be: "What was the population of France in 1650?" or "When was gunpowder invented?"

Questions of the type just described can be used to perform experiments concerning fundamental assumptions of the Delphi method, such as demonstrating that error diminishes with increasing group size—a result comparable to that for reliability. Moreover, they have the added appeal that supplementary facts can be supplied along with the question; e.g., the population of England in 1650 might be provided in the attempt to elicit the population of France in the hypothetical question mentioned above. Such a variation on the basic method is but one of the many possible avenues for further experimentation with the technique in the hopes of improving accuracy, the most important purpose of the study of error. Other potentially productive error-reducing techniques center on the possible elimination of questions on subsequent rounds of the questionnaire feedback, other variations in the form of the feedback, and respondent self-ratings.

Elimination of questions on subsequent rounds of the feedback procedure rests on the basic fact that convergence does not always produce desirable effects. For example, when the initial median is different from the correct answer and the deviation is small, further convergence toward the median draws the almost correct answer away from the correct value. Although the answers displaced from the median on the side opposite the correct answers are drawn closer to the true value, over-all error may increase. The suggestion then arises that questions for which the (relative) deviation is small be eliminated from the questionnaire on subsequent rounds. Despite this logic, however, no very significant improvements in over-all error have been achieved through this means. The fact that questions for which the error standard deviation is small do not contribute a very large fraction of the over-all error perhaps plays a significant role here.

Hoped-for reductions in error which proved elusive in the simple approach just outlined have been sought through more complex forms of feedback. A spectrum of feedback levels has been used in the experimental framework: Respondents can be given (1) none; (2) medians; (3) medians and inter-quartile ranges; (4) simple percentile ratings (for each individual's response); (5) statistical feedback (usually medians) plus additional information in the form of "soft facts," i.e., facts of a more subjective quality, such as the reasons given by respondents whose answers were outside the quartiles; and (6) statistical feedback plus additional "hard facts," i.e., facts in the form of related or comparative values, upper or lower bounds, or even qualitative facts.

Utilization of no feedback provides the control level for the standard Delphi procedure: For, if feedback does not produce an improvement over iteration without feedback, the rationale of the Delphi Technique is destroyed. However, feedback does produce an improvement both in terms of the number of respondents whose answers improve as well as in over-all group error. A subtle point exists in connection with the latter measures: Improvement in them does not necessarily imply a better median result; i.e., the roof of the "house" may become steeper with the apex remaining in the same place, resulting in (perhaps) the same median and less over-all error.

The second, third, and fourth options above, dealing with the basic level of statistical feedback, prove not to be significantly different in their consequences, a result that is not intuitively obvious. Even less obvious is the fact that no improvement is achieved through supplying supplementary "soft facts" in the form of giving the reasons of those whose answers were farthest from the median; giving the reasons of those whose answers were closest to the median seems not to have been tried.

The finding with supplementary "hard facts" is that they do prove successful in lowering group error. Three different kinds of such facts have been used: comparative, qualitative, and upper- or lower-bound. Providing the population of England in 1650 in attempting to elicit the population of France in the same year is an example of a comparative fact. That the Chinese invented gunpowder is an example of a qualitative fact. An upper-bound fact is exhibited by providing the career home-run total of Babe Ruth in attempting to elicit the number of home runs he made in a given year.

Sex differences in Delphi response characteristics have practical consequences, since the proportions of sexes can affect the results. The significant factor is that women take greater advantage of "hard facts," resulting in greater improvement than that shown by men on subsequent rounds. Though women are less accurate on the initial round, their greater changeability tends to dispose of any difference on the final round.

Reduction of error via self-ratings has perhaps the longest tradition and the best prospect. Early examples of their use are included in Helmer's book and the doctoral dissertation by Campbell (1966). Two kinds of self-rating can be identified—competence and confidence. Although these terms may frequently be assigned simultaneously to one and the same respondent, they are not necessarily synonymous. A respondent can realize that a question is in his field of expertise and that it is not one for which he can supply a good answer. Conversely, one can be confident of knowing an answer to a question outside his immediate specialization. (Most studies have involved either one of these two, but Campbell [loc. cit.] used a combination of the two.) An important initial finding is that any individual who rates himself highly does not do better consistently than the group as a whole. The earlier statement to the effect that an individual is not as accurate as a group over a range of questions can be strengthened to read that no single expert, no matter how confident and/or competent, can be expected to be as accurate as the group. Though individually assigned high ratings cannot be exploited, group ones can. Those questions on which the group as a whole feels confident or competent are those for which group accuracy is highest. These results probably can be ascribed in large part to the mechanism responsible for decreased error with increased group size, a mechanism that operates for competent and/or confident respondents as well as for the "ordinary" individuals in the group.

An implication of these several findings has been verified by experiment: Accuracy can be improved by selecting a subgroup of sufficiently large size to overcome the small group effect and for which the average self-rating is significantly higher than that of the rest of the group.

These criteria are such that a subgroup cannot be devised for some questions. In a particular study, the high rating subgroup consisted (by choice) of at least seven members. The need to extract significantly higher average self-ratings led to the result that a subgroup could be devised for only 156 of 240 questions. The outcome, comparing the high-rating subgroup to the entire group, was that the high-rating subgroup was more accurate on 95 questions and less accurate on 52, the groups being the same on nine questions. These results, while making it clear that self-ratings are no panacea, clearly indicate that the use of self-ratings shows promise.

Library-information science related studies

The discussion above suggests that the Delphi Technique has reached a stage of sufficient maturity that it can profitably be applied to solving problems in many different areas. A critical area of application in library and information science is the identification of major research needs in education for the profession. Two other studies in closely related fields warrant attention: that of Helmer (1966) on general educational issues; and that of Bjerrum (1968) on forecasting technological developments in computers and their applications.

An education study

Helmer's report begins with background issues in planning for educational innovation. He outlines the potential scope of the Delphi Technique in this context, including applications at all levels of education from grade school to university. This sets the stage for a particular application in which the respondents were presented a large number of proposed educational innovations with instructions to distribute the monies of a hypothetical budget among the proposals. The proposals were classified into several groups under the following headings: increase in student participation, educational R&D, model facilities, administration of school systems, internal administration of schools, professional staff, costly new equipment, reorganization of instruction and program, adult retraining, education in the home, and education of the underprivileged. The results were published in terms of these categories. The individual proposals were also categorized, according to cost, in three categories. Different groups of respondents were then called upon to supply their evaluations in each of these categories. The technique used to produce the evaluations—i.e., distributing a fixed budget over many viable proposals—represents a particular kind of variation of the Delphi Technique that simulates the decision-making environment which frequently exists in political and other organizations. The situation in the study was somewhat ideal in that there was an enormous budget to allocate and there were no special-interest groups, no persuasive rhetorics, and no threat from the voter to remove or restrict freedom of action. Nevertheless, the technique seems to provide a means for avoiding what can easily happen when a group of respondents is asked to pick and choose among a set of good alternatives; Almost all of them are given a moderately good rating, thereby leading to no clear resolution as to which choices ought to be made.

Helmer stressed the need to keep technological change in mind in making long-term projections for education. However, doing so would seem to require a more complex kind of survey than was employed in his study—perhaps one in which technological developments are predicted in an initial survey and the results of this study are packaged and used as supplementary fact feed-in to the participants in a later (evaluative) study to assess the educational impact. That this more complex mode of inquiry was not utilized in this study may well be the cause of why the bulk of the monies for innovation were assigned to conventional rather than highly innovative technology-based proposals. This is not meant to deny the existence of. needs in the areas chosen (e.g., teachers' salaries and scholarships). However, the spectre of the old Delphi arises: "maintenance of a conservative base" and confirmation of "courses of action that had already been decided upon."

A computer development and application study

Because much of the background of the inventors and popularizers of the Delphi Technique has been technological and/or technologically related, there have been a number of Delphi studies with a technological slant. Many of these are, of course, of great interest to information scientists. Some of the automation results reported in the appendix to Helmer (1966) fall into this class. A study of this type—developments in computers and their applications potential—is that of Bjerrum (1968, and Reilly 1969). Computer development questions in this study dealt with memory systems, input/output devices, software emulating hardware, computer sizes, prospects for computers that "learn," and prices of typical hardware. Applications covered the areas of industry, taxation, transportation, medicine, education, libraries, and the home.

The logical dependency of the computer-applications predictions upon the computer-developments predictions suggests that the predictions on the developments should be made known to the respondents before eliciting their predictions on applications. Although this was not done in Bjerrum's study, the study itself provides discussion of a number of significant issues of direct concern to the future of library and information sciences. The very general applications scope, which includes libraries, leaves room for more specific studies in each of the areas it impinges upon, as well as for tightening up the methodology.

References

Bjerrum, Chresten A. *Forecast 1968–2000 of Computer Developments and Applications.* Copenhagen, Denmark: Parsons and Williams, Inc., 1968.

Brown, Bernice B.; Cochran, Samuel; and Dalkey, Norman C. *The Delphi Method, II; Structure of Experiments.* Report no. RM–5957–PR. Santa Monica, Calif.: The Rand Corporation, 1969.

Brown, George W.; Miller, James G.; and Kennan, Thomas A. *EDUNET.* New York: Wiley and Sons, 1967.

Butler, Pierce. *An Introduction to Library Science.* Chicago: University of Chicago Press, 1933.

Campbell, Robert Moore. *A Methodological Study of the Utilization of Experts in Business Forecasting.* Ph.D. dissertation, University of California Graduate School of Business Administration, 1966.

Dalkey, Norman C. *The Delphi Method: An Experimental Study of Group Opinion.* Report no. RM–6118–PR. Santa Monica, Calif.: The Rand Corporation, 1970.

Dalkey, Norman C.; Brown, Bernice B.; and Cochran, Samuel. *The Delphi Method III: Use of Self-Ratings to Improve Group Estimates.* Report no. RM–6115–PR. Santa Monica, Calif.: The Rand Corporation, 1969.

———. *The Delphi Method, IV: Effect of Percentile Feedback and Feed-in of Relevant Facts.* Memorandum no. RM–6118–PR. Santa Monica, Calif.: The Rand Corporation, 1970.

Fine, John V. A. "Delphi," *Encyclopedia Americana,* vol. 8, 1970.

Helmer, Olaf. *The Future of Science.* Report no. 3607. Santa Monica, Calif.: The Rand Corporation, 1967.

———. *Prospects of Technological Progress.* Report no. 3643. Santa Monica, Calif.: The Rand Corporation, 1957.

———. *Social Technology.* New York: Basic Books, Inc., 1966.

———. *The Use of the Delphi Technique in Problems of Educational Innovation.* Publication no. 3499. Santa Monica, Calif.: The Rand Corporation, 1966.

Helmer, Olaf, and Rescher, Nicholas. "On the Epistemology of the Inexact Sciences." *Management Sciences* 6:25–52 (Oct. 1959).

Reilly, Kevin D. Review of Bjerrum, Chresten A. *Forecast . . . Journal of Educational Data Processing* 6:323–24 (1969).

Wilson, John H. *Modular Man-Packaged Information.* Report UCRL–19806. Preprint of a paper presented at the Seventh National Colloquim on Information Retrieval, 7–8 May 1970, at Philadelphia. Berkley, Calif.: University of California Lawrence Radiation Laboratory (n.d.).

Harold Borko

Predicting Research Needs In
Library Science Education

In the preceding essay, Kevin Reilly has described the background and methodology of the Delphi Technique. Additionally, it is important and useful to describe in detail the application of the Delphi method to the determination of the priority needs for research in library science education. The task undertaken by the investigators was to predict the relative importance and probable impact that proposed research projects would have in improving library science education. Since the impact of the research would not be felt until sometime in the future, the task was formulated as a problem in prediction, and the Delphi Technique was used to obtain accurate measures of the group opinion on the relative importance of the various research projects which had been proposed in the field of library and information science education.

Development of the questionnaire

As has been noted in Reilly's paper, a typical Delphi study begins with a survey of alternative courses of action. In the present study, possible research projects of importance to library science education were obtained by having educators review the literature, identify problems, and suggest research which, if undertaken, could contribute toward the solution of these problems. Approximately eighty non-independent projects were suggested.

The proposal statements went through several stages of review. The project staff met with senior members of the UCLA Survey Research

Center and debated the form and substance of each item. To make the survey as simple and as painless as possible for the respondents, it was agreed to reduce the number of items to about half. Furthermore, some of the originally suggested projects overlapped, and so it was possible to pare the list down by eliminating duplicates and combining related projects. The latter task was not simple, and one of the critically debated issues was whether the value of certain projects was diluted or made less practical by a proposed combination. Another, perhaps less crucial debate, concerned the issue of whether it was "research" to organize a conference. It was decided that, since conferences had been suggested as projects, they should be accepted as such. When it was agreed that a proposed topic should be included in the questionnaire, the item was cast in a canonical form, beginning with the phrase: "It is proposed that a research project be undertaken to. . . ." Then the wording of each item was carefully studied to eliminate possible ambiguities.

After these internal reviews, a preliminary form of the questionnaire was prepared, and the format and content of the items were discussed with and approved by the project advisors. Finally, the preliminary form was pretested by being administered to about three dozen subjects who, after completing the questionnaire, were asked to comment on any difficulties they might have had in scoring the items. Even at this stage, some changes were made.

The object of all this debate, advice, and pretesting was to provide the respondents of the questionnaire with a wide range of reasonable alternative research proposals which, when ranked, would result in meaningful information on the relative importance of different types of projects. When all the reviews were completed, the printed questionnaire was prepared. The final choice of the projects included in the questionnaire was the responsibility of the principal investigator. The questionnaire contained thirty-six items covering the entire range of topics that had been proposed for research to improve library education. Couched in broad categories, the list included the objectives of library education, curricula, methods and techniques of instruction, continuing education, administration, library skill requirements, etc. Respondents were asked to assign a single "importance" score for each proposal. The cover letter accompanying the questionnaire defined "importance" in terms of "how educators and administrators need the kinds of data that the suggested research projects would provide and . . . the probable impact that the anticipated research results would have on library education and practice." Every proposal in the questionnaire was to be rated on a scale from 0 to 100. Each 20-point mark on the scale was assigned to a descriptive phrase; e.g., "20" signifies "of very little importance," and "100" indicates "of very great importance." Considering the types of proposals included in the study, it is interesting to note that the range of responses in practically every item varied from 0 to 100; that is, at least one person thought the project to be almost useless, and at least one other considered it to be of very great importance. The diversity of response was convincing evidence that the items selected were capable of providing meaningful and varied opinions. (A copy of the questionnaire follows this section.)

Selection of respondents

The choice of respondents in a Delphi study is generally designed to provide a fairly broad range of representation from competent and interested individuals in the areas under investigation. The present study, with its primary focus on library education, utilized a sample drawn from all over the United States and Canada made up of teachers, librarians, researchers, government officials, and workers in industry. This was not a random sample but rather a highly selected sample composed of people who had a stake in library education and who were competent to evaluate the probable effectiveness of proposed research. The specific names of the respondents were suggested by the project advisors. The largest single group of subjects was associated with library schools (55 percent), but many other groups were represented in sufficient numbers to justify a separate Delphi analysis. The original list, to whom the first questionnaire was sent, consisted of 160 individuals. This number was selected to allow for attrition in the hope that at least 100 people would respond to both questionnaires. The final total of completed questionnaires returned for both rounds was 104!

Delphi study: Round I results

Two weeks after the questionnaire was mailed to the 160 respondents, a follow-up letter and questionnaire were sent to those subjects whose responses had not been received. One month after the original mailing, 129 questionnaires had been returned. This is a phenomenal 83 percent response and is indicative of the high interest and excellent cooperation with which this project was received.

A number of preliminary analyses were performed on the data. First of all, each returned envelope and form were examined for comments. Although no great effort was made to solicit comments, approximately 20 percent of the respondents felt moved to make some remarks. These were all read carefully, obviously because we were interested in the comments, but also to determine whether any of the items would have to be reformulated. For the most part, the comments were of a rather general nature, and there was no focused criticism of any of the individual questionnaire items. Consequently, no revisions were made for the second round of the Delphi study.

Other aspects of the analysis consisted of calculating various statistical elements useful in describing the data. All of the questionnaire responses were keypunched and the analyses completed on the computer by means of standard statistical programs. Each questionnaire item was treated as a separate distribution with an N of 129, and the following statistics were computed: median, mean, standard error of the mean, standard deviation, skewness, and kurtosis.

The minimum results we wished to obtain from this first analysis were the median score and the semi-inter-quartile range for the distribution of scores for all thirty-six items. In keeping with the traditions of the Delphi Technique, feedback by means of a second questionnaire was provided in the form of a diagram in which the median and the semi-inter-quartile range would be shown on each scale as illustrated.

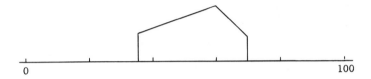

Although the median was used for feedback purposes, the statistical analysis of the data was based upon the mean and standard deviation; so, of course, these scores were calculated. It was also necessary to gain an understanding of the shape of each distribution and the degree to which it deviates from the normal distribution curve, e.g., the degree of skewness and kurtosis. Our basic hypothesis was that, although the mean score of each questionnaire item may not shift substantially from the first to the second round, the standard deviation should decrease and the shape of the distribution should become more leptokurtic or peaked. Should this occur, the rank order position of each item would become more significant, even though the ranking had not changed.

Table 1 is a rank order of the questionnaire items by mean score. Also included on this table are the standard deviation and median scores. For simplicity, skewness and kurtosis scores are not included. It is important to note that, although the ranking by mean and by median are highly correlated, there are some inversions. Specifically, item number 24 would be ranked 1 by median and 5 by mean. Clearly, it would be necessary to observe the stability of item 24 in the next round.

A frequency distribution of the mean scores was plotted for the thirty-six questionnaire items (Table 2). The shape of the distribution is clearly not normal. The total range of the distribution is quite narrow, varying from a score of 40 to one of 70. This was an unwelcome finding, for it gave warning that the range of the Round II scores could not possibly be much less.

Another item of interest clearly visible on this distribution was the fact that more than half of the items ranked below 60, indicating that the majority of the respondents considered most items to be of less than "moderate importance."

TABLE 1. RANK ORDER LISTING BY MEANS: ROUND I
(N = 129)

RANK	ITEM	MEAN	STANDARD DEVIATION	MEDIAN
1	9	69.06	25.21	73.75
2	35	68.27	24.50	71.56
3	19	67.05	27.05	69.06
4	17	65.39	26.05	70.91
5	24	65.31	28.92	75.00
6	34	62.05	24.80	66.59
7	2	61.75	24.56	63.40
8	10	61.02	26.02	62.50
9	1	60.87	25.07	63.54
10	27	60.79	25.12	60.87
11	14	60.62	27.34	66.11
12	26	60.23	27.31	63.82
13	30	60.00	28.12	63.85
14	36	59.84	28.23	66.39
15	4	59.77	26.99	61.67
16	23	56.80	27.83	60.00
17	29	56.77	27.80	62.00
18	8	56.69	26.91	59.57
19	12	56.41	26.97	58.53
20	31	56.19	28.45	58.50
21	16	54.65	28.17	57.83
22	25	53.75	28.42	58.33
23	32	53.49	25.94	56.90
24	33	52.95	27.74	58.52
25	22	52.76	27.85	56.32
26	6	52.20	25.04	57.50
27	20	51.43	27.39	56.00
28	15	51.36	27.34	51.94
29	11	51.18	26.11	53.33
30	18	51.17	27.14	55.87
31	13	50.24	27.81	51.87
32	7	48.37	30.49	52.31
33	28	47.56	24.42	48.46
34	21	42.29	27.18	49.09
35	5	43.18	27.64	40.00
36	3	41.98	25.46	38.89

TABLE 2. FREQUENCY DISTRIBUTION OF THE MEAN SCORES FOR THE
36 QUESTIONNAIRE ITEMS: ROUND I
(N = 129)

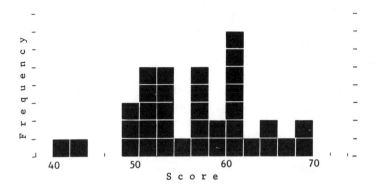

The preliminary analysis provided the following results:
1. There were no "bad" items, and the respondents were able to score each proposal for importance.
2. The initial rank-order listing of the items provided the investigators with some preliminary indications of the rated importance for each proposed research project.
3. The mean scores of the thirty-six distributions tended to be bunched fairly close together.
4. Most items on this first questionnaire were regarded as being of less than moderate importance.

Delphi study: Round II results

While the preliminary analysis was taking place, a second questionnaire was being prepared. This was identical to the first one except for a change in the cover letter and the addition of the Delphi type "houses" on each scale to indicate the median score and the semi-inter-quartile range. This new form was sent to each of the 129 respondents who had returned the first questionnaire. Also, as indicated in the original cover letter, the initial rating scores were copied on the new form, and a circle was drawn around each item number for which the respondent's score fell outside the mid-range.

Essentially, the Delphi study attempts to increase the reliability of predictions by providing each respondent with feedback knowledge of group interaction. Generally, one does not expect a radical revision in the ranking of survey items from one round to the next, although some changes are likely. The statistical variable that is expected to change with feedback is the range of the responses. Specifically, it was hypothesized that the range of the distribution would decrease and that the shape of the distribution would become more peaked or leptokurtic. Such a change would increase the reliability of the rankings as well as increase the degree of confidence one can place in the predictions.

In this particular study, as has been pointed out, the range of the mean scores for the first round was already narrow, so the second-round scores were not expected to show a statistically significant decrease in the standard deviations. Nevertheless, it was assumed that the group feedback would improve the over-all reliability of the predictions and that this could be demonstrated statistically. Also, many other statistical comparisons could be made.

The resulting rank-order distribution of mean scores for Round II is shown in Table 3. Note that the number of respondents for Round II is 104, whereas for Round I, it was 129.

A frequency distribution of mean scores for Round II was plotted (Table 4). Although somewhat similar to the Round I plot, there are some important differences. First, there was a slight shift in the distribution to the upper range of the scale, and the total range of the distribution was extended slightly. There was also a slight decrease in the average separation. Of particular significance was the clear separation of the items into four groups, which improved the interpretability of the data.

The shift in the rank order of the items from Round I to Round II can be seen in Table 5. Note that this table is calculated on the basis of the 104 respondents who answered both Round I and Round II questionnaires. There is, therefore, a slight difference in the Round I scores on this table as compared with results recorded in Table 1.

In interpreting Table 5, note also that the rank-order distribution divides itself into five reasonably distinct groups, and, although there are inversions of items within the groups, the groupings remain remarkably stable. There may be some question as to whether item 19 should be considered the most important research project, but it is quite clear that the consensus reached by the respondents considers items 19, 9, and 35 to have greater significance than items 24, 17, and 2.

It has been mentioned that the distribution of scores in item 24 was quite skewed, and that, if the ranking had been done by median scores, item 24 would have ranked first in Round I. In Round II, the degree of skewness decreases somewhat; the mean rank is raised from 5 to 4; and, by median, it drops from position 1 to 2, thus indicating that increased stability is achieved by the Delphi method of providing feedback.

TABLE 3. RANK ORDER LISTING BY MEANS: ROUND II
(N = 104)

RANK	ITEM	MEAN	STANDARD DEVIATION	MEDIAN
1	19	72.60	23.02	73.89
2	9	72.21	22.98	76.92
3	35	70.39	23.64	73.21
4	24	66.63	26.75	74.37
5	17	66.06	25.52	71.00
6	2	65.39	21.83	65.00
7	26	63.75	25.55	66.87
8	34	62.33	23.36	64.42
9	10	62.31	24.58	63.00
10	1	62.04	24.31	64.77
11	4	61.92	26.62	62.83
12	27	61.84	24.60	62.11
13	36	61.27	27.02	67.94
14	14	60.77	26.90	64.50
15	30	60.67	26.92	64.17
16	12	60.10	26.29	62.19
17	31	59.71	26.73	60.77
18	23	59.03	26.59	61.07
19	16	58.65	25.66	59.76
20	8	58.37	25.35	60.65
21	29	56.92	27.27	62.86
22	6	55.78	22.62	58.91
23	25	55.15	26.45	60.00
24	22	55.05	26.27	57.65
25	11	53.75	24.34	57.61
26	18	53.20	26.05	56.67
27	32	53.17	23.37	55.80
28	33	52.69	26.96	56.00
29	15	52.43	25.26	52.81
30	13	50.88	26.96	51.25
31	20	50.68	25.87	55.23
32	7	49.52	31.11	55.00
33	28	49.23	23.68	51.00
34	21	45.48	25.39	46.25
35	5	42.50	27.44	36.68
36	3	41.55	25.20	38.21

In this study of research needs, only two rounds of questionnaires were used. The primary objective was to obtain a stable rank-order listing of the thirty-six research proposals. This has been achieved and the results interpreted here and in the introduction. However, some additional analyses were performed, and these will also be described and interpreted.

TABLE 4. FREQUENCY DISTRIBUTION OF THE MEAN SCORES FOR THE
36 QUESTIONNAIRE ITEMS: ROUND II
  (N = 104)

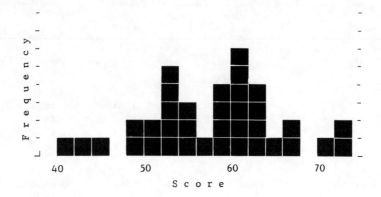

Additional Delphi analyses

The additional analyses were performed to shed light on the changes that occurred between the first and second rounds of the Delphi study. The second round provided each respondent with feedback information on how he rated each questionnaire item in comparison with how the group as a whole rated each item. What effect, if any, did this feedback have on the behavior of the respondent in scoring Round II?

Analysis of changes: total group

One hundred and four (104) respondents answered both questionnaires; there were thirty-six (36) items on the questionnaire. Thus there is a theoretical possibility of having 3744 changes.

What percentage of responses were actually changed?

$$511 \div 3744 = 13.6\%$$

Of the changes that occurred, how many modified their Round II scores toward the group median?

$$322 \div 511 = 65.0\%$$

How many moved away from the median?

$$179 \div 511 = 35.0\%$$

Interpretation. Only slightly more than 10 percent of the ratings were changed between Round I and Round II. These results indicate that respondents, who were selected on the basis of their expert knowledge, were secure in their opinions and that these opinions were reasonably stable. When changes did occur, such changes were influenced by the

TABLE 5. Rank Order Listing by Means: Rounds I and II
(N = 104)

| | ROUND I | | ROUND II | |
RANK	ITEM	MEAN	ITEM	MEAN
1	9	70.29	19	72.60
2	35	69.61	9	72.21
3	19	69.13	35	70.39
4	17	65.73	24	66.63
5	24	65.05	17	66.06
6	2	64.50	2	65.39
7	26	62.60	26	63.75
8	34	62.16	34	62.33
9	10	61.76	10	62.31
10	4	61.75	1	62.04
11	27	61.08	4	61.92
12	14	60.98	27	61.84
13	36	60.88	36	61.27
14	30	60.67	14	60.77
15	1	60.59	30	60.67
16	31	59.21	12	60.10
17	12	58.82	31	59.71
18	23	58.04	23	59.03
19	8	57.82	16	58.65
20	16	57.09	8	58.37
21	6	56.37	29	56.92
22	29	55.49	6	55.78
23	22	54.71	25	55.15
24	25	54.37	22	55.05
25	18	53.43	11	53.75
26	33	52.98	18	53.20
27	32	52.33	32	53.17
28	15	51.76	33	52.69
29	20	51.67	15	52.43
30	11	51.58	13	50.88
31	13	51.50	20	50.68
32	7	49.90	7	49.52
33	28	48.92	28	49.23
34	21	46.83	21	45.48
35	5	43.37	5	42.50
36	3	42.18	3	41.35

group consensus, for the modifications were almost twice as likely to be in the direction of the group median than away from it. The move toward the median resulted in a slight narrowing of the standard deviation of the distribution and contributed toward the increased reliability of the second-round results.

Continuing the analysis of the total population, let us examine the behavior of those individuals whose Round I scores were outside the semi-inter-quartile range, and who were therefore asked to consider their ratings on these questions carefully.

The semi-inter-quartile range, by definition, includes 50 percent of the ratings or 1872 of the possible responses. Because of rounding errors and borderline scores, only 1746 ratings (46.6 percent) were considered to be outside the mid-range.

What percentage of these extreme ratings were changed?

$$292 \div 1746 = 16.7\%$$

Of those ratings that were changed, what percentage of them moved into the mid-range?

$$184 \div 292 = 63.0\%$$

Since it is possible to move toward the median, but not into the inter-quartile range, what percentage of the changes followed this course of action?

$$14 \div 292 = 4.8\%$$

What percentage of the ratings moved still further away from the median?

$$94 \div 292 = 32.2\%$$

Interpretation. Although one may well expect that the extreme scores would be those with the greatest tendency to move toward the median, this was not the case. In actual fact, only 67.8 percent of these extreme scores, compared with 65 percent of all scores, were modified in the direction of the group norm, and, of these, only 63 percent were modified sufficiently to bring them into the mid-range. These slight differences are not statistically significant. What is significant interpretively is that 32 percent of the extreme ratings moved further away from the median! This result was not anticipated in advance. It may be interpreted from a psychological point of view to mean that those experts, when confronted with a mass opinion, tended to become even more firmly committed to their own opinions. This tentative conclusion, although interesting, will need further investigation before it can be substantiated.

Analysis by sub-groups: rank-order ratings

Not only were the data of the total population of 104 analyzed as a unit, but separate analyses were performed based upon the rating scores obtained from educators and non-educators and from males and females. Table 6 contains the rank-order ratings of the thirty-six questionnaire items for the total population and the four sub-groups based on the

Round II scores. As expected, there is a great deal of similarity, but it is the differences which occurred that deserve attention and study.

Comparison of educator and non-educator ratings

Educators and non-educators were divided into groups on the basis of their place of employment. Essentially, if their address was at a library school, they were considered to be library school educators. All others, including those who gave their address as a university library, were counted as non-educators. Some modifications were made as a result of personal knowledge, but place of employment was the essential criterion. Obviously, it is an imperfect criterion, for many librarians teach, and many teachers work in libraries or are primarily researchers. However, for the purposes of this study, a rough division was all that was required, since the aim was to determine whether, *in general*, practitioners differed from teachers in rating the importance of proposed research projects.

Indeed, there are some interesting differences in the ratings, quite obviously based on differing viewpoints and organizational problems. All agree that items 19, 9, and 35 are the most pressing problems. Then agreement ends.

Practitioners place item 30 in rank #4, while the educators relegate this item to rank #27. Item 30 states: "It is proposed that a research project be undertaken to investigate methods and techniques of developing close reciprocal relationships between professors of library science and practicing library administrators in order to enhance the relevance of library school education." Educators do not believe this to be an important problem, while practicing librarians and administrators do. The difference in ratings for this one item clearly demonstrates the extent of the gap that exists between educators and non-educators and the lack of perceptual congruence in their views of librarianship as well as the problems faced by the profession.

Items 26 and 12 deal with practical problems of the use of the library by the community and the library's role in improving race relations and providing services to the culturally disadvantaged. Again, educators did not give these topics as high a priority as did non-educators.

In contrast, educators rated item 8, which deals with standards for evaluating library schools, as a high-priority item (rank #7), while non-educators do not find this of vital concern and relegate it to rank #28.

Comparisons of male and female ratings

Although there may have been some difficulty in distinguishing between educators and non-educators, it can be said with a great deal of

TABLE 6. RANK-ORDER RATINGS OF THE DIFFERENT SUB-GROUPS: ROUND II

RANK ORDER	TOTAL POPULATION ITEM	EDUCATORS (62) ITEM	NON-EDUCATORS (42) ITEM	MALES (79) ITEM	FEMALES (25) ITEM
1	19	19	9	19	9
2	9	9	19	9	35
3	35	35	35	35	10
4	24	24	30	24	19
5	17	17	26	2	17
6	2	2	2	17	26
7	26	8	12	4	27
8	34	4	36	1	30
9	10	1	24	26	34
10	1	27	17	36	2
11	4	23	16	34	24
12	27	10	34	14	16
13	36	34	14	12	8
14	14	31	10	23	1
15	30	26	27	27	36
16	12	14	1	10	31
17	31	25	4	31	11
18	23	18	29	30	6
19	16	36	31	29	4
20	8	6	32	16	32
21	29	33	22	8	14
22	6	29	23	25	22
23	25	12	28	22	25
24	22	16	11	6	20
25	11	22	6	18	33
26	18	11	15	15	12
27	32	30	13	33	13
28	33	20	8	11	15
29	15	15	25	32	29
30	13	32	7	28	23
31	20	13	20	7	18
32	7	7	33	13	7
33	28	21	18	20	28
34	21	28	21	21	3
35	5	3	5	5	5
36	3	5	3	3	21

confidence that there were 79 males and 25 females among the respondents. There are also some significant differences in their views of the important problems needing study in library education and librarianship.

Women rate item 10, which suggests that research be undertaken to, "Develop an instrument to be used in periodic national surveys to:

(a) determine the self-perceived educational needs of professional librarians, their job functions, and personal characteristics; and (b) recommend content and methods of providing continuing education" as deserving one of the top three priorities. Males rank this as #16. One can interpret this difference as indicating a lack of complacency that women feel in their roles as professional librarians and their desire to upgrade their status by continuing education. Apparently, the male members of the profession feel more secure or at least experience a lesser need for self-examination and study.

Men rate item 4, which deals with the recruitment, selection, and education of minority group students, as a high-priority problem, while women consider it less important and rank it #19. Since recruitment is largely a problem faced by library school administrators, one wonders whether this difference (which also occurs between educators and non-educators) is a reflection of the fact that relatively few women are in administrative positions such as deans of library schools.

In considering the differences in the ratings by sub-groups, it should be noted that there was a near unanimity of opinion on the items rated low in the hierarchy; there were no sub-group differences.

Analysis by sub-groups: comparison of score changes

The questions to be considered in this section are whether educators tended to be more changeable than non-educators and whether women changed scores more frequently than men. Table 7 provides a summary of all categories of changes that occurred between Rounds I and II for the various sub-groups.

Interpretation. There were differences in the percentage of scores changed between the groups of educators and non-educators in this sample of respondents, but the explanation of the differences can only be tentative. In most instances, the magnitude of the differences was not statistically significant. Furthermore, the differences that did occur could be specific to this sample of respondents which may or may not be a representative one. Finally, since all interpretations are necessarily subjective, the reader is cautioned to consider these remarks as opinions only. At best, these interpretative remarks can be used as a source of ideas and hypotheses for future research but not as conclusions. This disclaimer, if it may be called that, is especially important, because the investigators had no hypothesis in mind as to the expected differences in rating performances between educators and non-educators. From previous Delphi studies, we did entertain a hypothesis regarding differences in score changes between men and women. Even so, this aspect of the project should be regarded as a search for ideas rather than as research to test hypotheses.

From the results given in Table 7, it can be seen that the non-educator group was somewhat less likely to change scores than were the educators. However, when they did change scores, they were much more likely to be influenced by the group norms and to change in the direction of the median score. This tendency is seen again on the last line of the table, which indicates that, when non-educators changed scores that were outside the inter-quartile range, they were less likely to move away from the median (29.1 percent vs. 33.9 percent). This explanation is consistent with the interpretative comments about the behavior of experts made previously—that is, it is consistent, if one believes that experts are more likely to be educators (or that educators are more likely to consider themselves experts) than otherwise. Some doubt is cast on this explanation by the fact that fewer scores outside the inter-quartile range made by non-educators (13.7 percent vs. 19.0 percent) were changed. Could this be due to less interest or motivation to review their questionnaire results and make changes?. Possibly, since 15.9 percent of educators' scores were changed vs. 10.3 percent for non-educators.

Turning to the male and female dichotomy, we find small but con-

TABLE 7. COMPARISON OF SCORES CHANGED BETWEEN ROUNDS I AND II
BY SUB-GROUPS
    (In Percent)

TYPE OF CHANGE	EDUCATORS	NON-EDUCATORS	MALES	FEMALES
Respondents who changed scores	15.9	10.3	13.3	14.7
Changes toward the median	61.5	72.9	64.1	67.4
Changes away from the median	38.5	27.1	35.9	32.6
Scores that were outside inter-quartile range	42.9	49.7	46.4	47.2
Scores outside the range that were changed	19.0	13.7	16.7	16.7
Changes that moved inside the range	62.4	64.1	62.0	66.2
Changes that moved toward median but not into the range	3.7	6.8	4.1	7.0
Changes that moved away from the median	33.9	29.1	33.9	26.8

sistent differences which indicate that women are more likely to change their scores than are men, and that they are more likely to be influenced by the feedback provided in the form of group norms. Does this finding also mean that they are less expert than men or more highly motivated to introspect and review previously held opinions? This variable was not controlled experimentally and cannot be answered by the present study. However, it should be pointed out that the results—namely that women are more likely to change their scores than are men—are consistent with the findings of previous Delphi studies.

Let us now examine not just the numerical ratings but the kinds of research the respondents deemed to be important or unimportant and to propose a program of research in librarianship. The many suggestions made by the ten consultants were compacted into thirty-six proposed research projects, and these were rated using the Delphi technique by over one hundred carefully selected respondents. The results of the survey were tabulated in Table 5.

All thirty-six items were assigned positions in a rank-order scale. Thus, in one sense, we have a research priority order ranging from one to thirty-six. But this simple manner of interpreting the results is not quite accurate. A rank-order scale is not an equal interval or a ratio scale. If we were to arrange all thirty-six ratings on a linear scale according to their mean scores, some items would bunch together and some would be separated. The inequalities can be seen by examining the last column in Table 5, which lists the mean scores. Note that the difference, the linear spatial distance, between ranks #9 and #8 is 0.02; between #8 and #7 it is 1.42; and between #4 and #3 it is 3.76. These differences must be considered in interpreting the importance of the projects and in assigning research priorities. The fact is that not all of the rank positions are equally reliable statistically; some, but certainly not all, of the assignments may be accidents of sampling and should not be used as a basis for assigning priorities.

By way of illustrating this concept, let us re-examine the data in this table. In Round I, item #14 is ranked higher than item #36; the mean difference is 0.10. In Round II, item #36 is ranked higher than item #14; the mean difference is 0.50. Both of these differences are within sampling errors. For all practical purposes, the ranks of these items are interchangeable, and it cannot be said with any degree of confidence that one deserves a higher priority than the other. This does not mean that we cannot establish any priorities, but it does mean that we cannot establish thirty-six individual priorities. The projects must be grouped, and we can establish five statistically determined priority groupings. These groupings are illustrated in Table 5 and are the basis for the interpretations that follow.

Based upon the results of the Delphi ratings, five groups were established and assigned the following significance:

Priority Group I—of very great importance
Priority Group II—of great importance
Priority Group III—of moderate importance
Priority Group IV—of lesser importance
Priority Group V—of least importance

These groups were formed at the natural breaking points in the continuum and are relatively stable with the possible exception of some of the border items. By working with groups of items, rather than individual items, a more meaningful interpretation of the data is possible.

Priority group I—Projects of very great importance:
Improving and updating the skills
of professional librarians.

Items 9, 19, and 35 have been rated consistently as being of the greatest importance. All three of these items deal with the need of practicing librarians to acquire and continually update their skills to provide improved library services.
Separate but related research projects were proposed:

1. To investigate current library school education and its relationship to the knowledge and skills required by librarians during their first five years on the job (9)
2. To study alternative methods of providing continuing education and the feasibility of a national program (19)
3. To develop packaged programs, for individual and home use, by which critically needed skills could be learned (35).

In essence, the consensus of informed opinion is that the most critically needed task is to engage in research that would provide the librarian with an efficient means for continually updating his knowledge and skills.

Priority group II—Projects of great importance:
Library school educational planning and relevance

Whereas Priority group I dealt with the educational problems of librarians after graduation, the items in the second priority group concern graduate school education. Projects that will improve the quality and relevance of the graduate library school are rated as of great importance. It is suggested that research be undertaken:

1. To estimate the future impact of technology on libraries of various types and sizes so that needed innovations could be included in the curricula (2)
2. To investigate factors influencing the selection and retention of students and the relationship between academic performance and job success (17)
3. To investigate and clarify the different educational and job requirements of the MLS graduate and those of the library technician (24).

These Priority group II projects did not deal with the pros and cons of specific courses in library schools but probed the underlying concepts on which library education is based. What factors influence the selection of students? Are we training technicians or professionals? Are we teaching computer technology because it is the "in thing" or because these skills will soon be needed by librarians? These are the questions the respondents felt were of great importance and needed investigation immediately.

Priority group III: Projects of moderate importance:
Administration of the library school and library with regard to specific courses, skills, and programs.

A conglomeration of projects was rated as being of moderate importance. Because this is a conglomeration, it is difficult to classify the topics into a manageable set of categories. Each research project should be considered individually. Yet, because it is impossible to cope with fourteen individual topics simultaneously, we have attempted to impose some organization by suggesting groupings of projects into four rough categories, as follows:

A. Projects related to the administrative aspects of library schools
B. Projects related to educational content
C. Projects related to the culturally disadvantaged
D. Projects related to library administration and library utilization.

A. Projects related to the administrative aspects of library schools:

1. To investigate problems relating to library school organization, faculty, curriculum planning, and innovative teaching (27)
2. To investigate the effects of establishing research centers in library schools (31)
3. To investigate and evaluate the standards, procedures, and costs of accrediting library schools (8)

4. To investigate methods and techniques of developing close reciprocal relationships between professors of library science and practicing library administrators (30)
5. To investigate ways to achieve close coordination of library school activities with the programs of the university library, the university in general, and the community (16).

B. Projects related to educational content:

1. To investigate, compare, and evaluate the effectiveness of MLS educational programs that emphasize more core curricula and less specialization vs. those that minimize the core program in favor of specialization (14)
2. To investigate the relative merits of providing courses in information science and library automation as part of the regular curricula or otherwise (34)
3. To develop an instrument to be used in periodic national surveys to determine the educational needs of professional librarians and to recommend content and methods for providing continuing education (10).

C. Projects related to the culturally disadvantaged:

1. To investigate the possible roles that libraries and library schools could play in improving race relations and providing library services to minority and culturally disadvantaged groups (12)
2. To investigate the special problems involved in the recruitment, selection, and education of minority group students and others who require special attention (4).

D. Projects related to library administration and library utilization:

1. To develop a set of job analyses for library positions that concentrate on the knowledge required rather than on the operations performed (1)
2. To develop measures of professional proficiency in library service functions at different levels and skills (36)
3. To investigate the "sociology of reading" to determine relationships between the effects of reading, television, and paperbacks on library use (23)
4. To study current library use patterns to identify and relate elements in the library system and in the community that influence the nature of library use by various individuals and groups (26).

Priority group IV: Projects of lesser importance:
Forms of instruction and supportive facilities for maintaining
instruction.

Although the items comprising Priority group IV are listed as being "of lesser importance," the term is a relative one. All of the projects selected for inclusion in the questionnaire are worthwhile projects. The respondents had the difficult task of selecting the best from among the good. The projects in this group are of lesser importance only when compared with the other projects from which the selection was made.

Like the preceding grouping, the projects in Priority group IV cover a conglomeration of topics on which an *ex post facto* classification into broad categories has been imposed. These categories deal with:

A. Administrative aspects of library schools
B. Innovative teaching and newer media
C. Continuing education

A. Projects related to administrative aspects of library schools:

1. To investigate factors that influence recruitment of library school faculty (29)
2. To investigate problems relating to library school financing and sources of funds (15)
3. To study and compare the effects that different accreditation procedures would have on library education (18)
4. To study the trend toward specialization in library education as compared with that of other professional schools (33)
5. To construct a model that can be used by educators and administrators to predict library personnel needs (25)
6. To investigate the need for, and the function of, the doctorate degree in librarianship (7).

B. Projects related to innovative teaching and newer media:

1. To organize regional conferences to encourage wider utilization of the newer media and innovative techniques such as tele-lecture, television, and videotape for library school education (6)
2. To organize regional conferences to demonstrate the methodology and effectiveness of the seminar, case study, and field work methods in library education (13)
3. To evaluate pre-service and in-service laboratory experience in bibliography, reference, cataloging, and information storage and retrieval (20)

4. To survey and disseminate information about the activities and program concerned with the organization and control of newer media materials (28).

C. Projects related to continuing education:

1. To study the motivational factors related to participation in continuing activities (22)
2. To evaluate the effectiveness of postgraduate supervised training programs and to study the desirability and practicality of utilizing practicum training in continuing education programs (11)
3. To explore possible roles that a library school could perform in developing educational materials for in-service training programs (32).

Priority group V: Projects of least importance:
The role of professional associations and communication
among librarians.

As is true of all rating scales, some items must be placed on the bottom of the list. Which were the projects rated of least importance by the majority of the respondents? The three items in Priority group V deal with different subjects and provide an indication of the kinds of projects in which the library profession is uninterested at this time.

The low-rated projects are:

1. To study patterns of communication and information exchange among library scientists and to compare these patterns with those of other professional groups (21)
2. To investigate the programs and activities of the several professional library associations and determine the degree of duplication (5)
3. To investigate the validity of generally held ideas and practices concerning the physical facilities, equipment, and space needed by library schools (3).

With completion and publication of the research to establish priorities, the work of the editor is concluded. If, however, there is no implementation, the purpose of his effort and that of the contributors will not become realized. This is because a responsible analysis of research needs has three components:

1. A survey of alternatives, that is, an exploration and description of the major possible courses of action—the various useful research projects—that might be undertaken

2. An analysis of preferences, that is, a prediction of the desirability of each research project in accordance with the criterion of importance by which the possible consequences are to be judged
3. Implementation, that is, the construction of a policy for carrying out preferred alternatives and thus increasing the probability of achieving a more desirable future—more effective and relevant library education—as a result of planned action.

Only the first two components have been completed. We now have a better idea of what research is required to improve educational practices. Suggestions have been made and priorities established. Now the plans must be implemented. It is up to the concerned professionals in library science education to propose, plan, and execute the specific research projects that would provide information and then to convert our knowledge into a program for improving library education. Without implementation, research planning is a useless exercise. The proposed research must be undertaken and the results transferred into improved curricula for the education of librarians.

Appendix

A STUDY OF THE NEEDS FOR RESEARCH IN
LIBRARY AND INFORMATION SCIENCE EDUCATION

Los Angeles, California
February 4, 1970

Dear Colleague:

The Association of American Library Schools, with the support of the Library Sciences Research Branch of the U.S. Office of Education, has undertaken a project to study what research is needed to improve the effectiveness of library school education. In the course of this study, the organization, structure and content of library schools has been analyzed and a number of research projects have been proposed to gather the information needed for improving library education. The amount of money available to support such research is not adequate to undertake *all* worthwhile projects. Your help is needed to determine the importance of the proposed projects and to establish priorities.

Your name has been selected as part of a controlled sample of only 100 educators and researchers, because we need *your* opinions.

In the following pages, thirty-six possible research projects have been briefly described. You are asked to rate each of these projects by placing a "/" crossing a point on the accompanying 100 point scale which best reflects your professional judgement of its potential importance. Importance can be judged on the basis of how desperately library school educators and library administrators need the kinds of data that the suggested research projects would provide and by estimating the probable impact that the anticipated research results would have on library education and practice.

When you have completed the ratings, please return the questionnaire in the self-addressed, stamped envelope. Your name will in no way be connected with your replies in the analysis of this study. You will, however, be informed of the results of all the ratings as soon as these are available. You will also be provided with an opportunity to re-evaluate and modify your own rating in light of these averaged results.

These ratings will have significant impact on future library school education and research. Your opinions therefore are important in this critical study concerning our profession.

Sincerely yours,

Harold Borko

HAROLD BORKO
Project Director

The Scale   ID

In all cases the reference points on the scales have the following meanings:

0 = of no importance
20 = of very little importance
40 = of slight importance
60 = of moderate importance
80 = of great importance
100 = of very great importance

It is proposed that a research project be undertaken to:

01. Develop a set of job analyses for library positions that concentrates on the knowledge required rather than on the operations performed for specialized education in library practice.

0 └─────┴─────┴─────┴─────┘ 100

02. Estimate, for purposes of library school curricula planning, the future impact of technology on various types and sizes of libraries with particular reference to when these libraries will be able to afford and use automated information processing techniques in their normal operations.

0 └─────┴─────┴─────┴─────┘ 100

03. Investigate the validity of generally held ideas and practices concerning the physical facilities, equipment and space needed by library schools to make teaching, studying and research more effective.

0 └─────┴─────┴─────┴─────┘ 100

04. Investigate the special problems involved in the recruitment, selection and education of minority group students and others that require special attention.

0 └─────┴─────┴─────┴─────┘ 100

05. Determine the degree of duplication and coordination in the programs and activities of the several professional associations or units concerned with education for librarianship and related fields.

0 └─────┴─────┴─────┴─────┘ 100

06. Organize conferences on a regional basis to encourage wider utilization of newer media and materials demonstrating and evaluating some recently completed experiments on the applications of innovative procedures to library school education, e.g.,
a) cataloguing as taught by computer-assisted instruction and by tele-lecture,
b) children's literature and storytelling by television,
c) library automation by videotape.

0 └─────┴─────┴─────┴─────┘ 100

07. Investigate the need for and the function of the doctorate degree in librarianship as well as the desirability of having another type of advanced degree that is service rather than research oriented, e.g., a Doctor of Librarianship.

0 └─────┴─────┴─────┴─────┘ 100

08. Evaluate the standards, procedures and costs in accrediting library schools including the extent to which quantitative data can be used as an index to the quality of a library school.

0 └─────┴─────┴─────┴─────┘ 100

09. Investigate (a) the administrative and management roles that librarians are likely to fill, during their first five years on the job, in such

areas as planning, cost and production control, personnel, systems analysis, etc., (b) the knowledge and skills required to properly carry out these functions, and (c) whether current library school curricula are providing adequate preparation.

0 ⌞_____,_____,_____,_____⌟ 100

10. Develop an instrument to be used in periodic national surveys to:
    a) determine the self-perceived educational needs of professional librarians and their job functions and personal characteristics,
    b) recommend content and methods of providing continuing education.

0 ⌞_____,_____,_____,_____⌟ 100

11. Evaluate the effectiveness of postgraduate supervised training programs and to study the desirability and practicality of utilizing a practicum training in continuing education programs.

0 ⌞_____,_____,_____,_____⌟ 100

12. Investigate the possible roles that libraries and library schools could fulfill, and the methods they could use, in improving race relations and in providing library services to minority and culturally disadvantaged groups.

0 ⌞_____,_____,_____,_____⌟ 100

13. Organize conferences on a regional basis to demonstrate the methodology and effectiveness of innovated teaching techniques in library education, e.g.,
    a) seminar method,
    b) case study method,
    c) field work on supervised internship.

0 ⌞_____,_____,_____,_____⌟ 100

14. Compare and evaluate the effectiveness of MLS educational programs that emphasize more core curricula and less specialization, vs. those that minimize the core program in favor of specialization.

0 ⌞_____,_____,_____,_____⌟ 100

15. Investigate problems relating to library school financing, including such matters as basic budgets and sources of funds (federal, foundation, etc.) for additional library activities and projects, e.g., student aid.

0 ⌞_____,_____,_____,_____⌟ 100

16. Investigate ways to achieve close coordination of library school activities with the programs of the university library, the university in general, and the community.

0 ⌞_____,_____,_____,_____⌟ 100

17. Investigate factors influencing the selection and retention of students, including:
    a) educational background and work experience,
    b) personality, attitudes and goals,
    c) performance measures,
    and the relationship between academic performance and job success.

0 ⌞_____,_____,_____,_____⌟ 100

18. Study and compare the effects that different accreditation procedures and the organizational level of the accrediting bodies (e.g., national, statewide, professional association, etc.), have no professional education in librarianship and other fields.

0 ⌞_____,_____,_____,_____⌟ 100

19. Study the feasibility of a national program of continuing education for librarians and evaluate this and

alternative ways of providing continuing education through the effective utilization of library schools, libraries and professional associations.

0⊢————————————⊣100

20. Evaluate pre-service and in-service laboratory experience in:
a) bibliography and reference work
b) catalog practice
c) information storage and retrieval,
and support faculty visits to these demonstration laboratories.

0⊢————————————⊣100

21. Study the patterns of communication and information exchange among library scientists and compare these patterns with those of other professionals as identified in the study of the American Psychological Association.

0⊢————————————⊣100

22. Study the motivational factors related to levels of participation in continuing education activities, including the attitudes and support of top library management to such programs, and the correlation between an involvement in community affairs and personal professional growth.

0⊢————————————⊣100

23. Investigate the "sociology of reading" in order to determine relationships between
a) the effect of reading on scholarship interest patterns, prejudices, likes and animosities;
b) the effect of television, or other distractions on reading;
c) the effect of paperbacks on library use, etc.

0⊢————————————⊣100

24. Investigate the extent to which the duties required of an MLS graduate in his first professional position are those that could be performed by library technicians.

0⊢————————————⊣100

25. Construct a model, based upon an adequate sample of libraries, which can be used to provide educators and administrators with information on actual and anticipated personnel needs by geographic area, by size and type of library, by function, by skill level, etc.

0⊢————————————⊣100

26. Study current library use patterns in order to identify and relate elements in the library system and in the community that influence the nature of library use by various individuals and groups.

0⊢————————————⊣100

27. Investigate problems relating to library school organization, including:
a) the role of faculty and students in decision-making and curricula planning,
b) the size and stability of the faculty,
c) the desirability of using non-library specialists for teaching,
d) the means of encouraging innovative teaching and creative research by faculty.

0⊢————————————⊣100

28. Survey and disseminate information about the activities and programs concerned with the organization and bibliographic control of the newer media and the extent of in-house and local production of such materials for use in library education.

0⊢————————————⊣100

29. Investigate factors that influence recruitment and selection of faculty, including:
    a) education and preparation,
    b) research and publications,
    c) use of specialists and part-time faculty,
    d) factors that contribute to excellence in teaching.

    0 ∟_____⌐ 100

30. Investigate methods and techniques of developing close reciprocal relationships between professors of library science and practicing library administrators in order to enhance the relevance of library school education.

    0 ∟_____⌐ 100

31. Investigate the effect of establishing research centers in library schools on the school's curricula, publications and research activities.

    0 ∟_____⌐ 100

32. Explore possible roles that a graduate library school could perform in developing educational materials for in-service training programs.

    0 ∟_____⌐ 100

33. Study the trend toward specialization in library education and compare with that of other professional schools, e.g., engineering and social work.

    0 ∟_____⌐ 100

34. Investigate the relative merits of providing courses in information science and library automation
    a) as part of the regular library curricula,
    b) as specialized post-MLS training,
    c) as special short-term courses (credit and/or non-credit).

    0 ∟_____⌐ 100

35. Develop model packaged programs of study in areas pertinent to the needs of librarians for updating and expanding their knowledge. Such programs could include programmed budgeting, automation, library insurance, MARC II tapes, etc.

    0 ∟_____⌐ 100

36. Develop measures of professional proficiency in library service functions at different levels and skills, so that these may be used in evaluating the education and training provided.

    0 ∟_____⌐ 100

Subject Index

AASL (*see* American Association of School Librarians)

ALA (*see* American Library Association)

Accreditation standards (1951), 103, 126
  (*see also* American Library Association)

Administrative organization, 88
  internal, 89

Allerton Park Conferences, 24, 41, 97

American Association of Colleges for Teacher Education
  accreditation responsibilities, 120

American Association of School Librarians
  School Library Manpower Project, 135, 138, 149

American Documentation Institute, 120
  (*see also* American Society for Information Science)

American Library Association, 117, 120, 121, 123
  A-V Task Force Survey, 80
  accreditation, 87, 90, 119, 122, 124
  Board of Education for Librarianship, 14, 16, 87, 117, 118, 119
  certification of librarians, 122
  Committee on Accreditation, 120, 122
  Congress for Change, 101, 121, 122, 123

Criteria for Programs to Prepare Library Technical Assistants (1969), 134–35

Guidelines for the Education of Library Technicians (1968), 140

Library Education Division, 98, 118, 120, 121, 134

national plan for library education, 18

Office for Library Education, 18, 22, 121

Office for Recruitment, 123

Professional Training Round Table, 118

Standards for Accreditation, 126

Standards for School Library Programs, 131

American Society for Engineering Education, 44

American Society for Information Science, 120, 122

Association of American Library Schools, 99, 117, 118, 120, 121, 122, 123
  certification of librarians, 122, 128

Association of Higher Education, 79

Bibliographic control of media, 72, 80, 81
  (*see also* Instructional media)

Bookmobiles
  degree of effectiveness, 176

229

California, University of
  Center for the Study of Higher
    Education, 80
  Institute of Library Research, 79
  UCLA Survey Research Center,
    200–201
Carnegie Commission on Higher
  Education, 80
Carnegie Corporation of New York,
  11, 12, 15, 16, 17, 22, 87, 105,
  117, 118
Case Western Reserve University, 120
  foundations course, 18
Certification (*see* Librarians)
Chicago, University of, Graduate
  Library School
  establishment, 12–13
  publications programs, 13
  research areas, 13
Chicago Conferences on librarianship,
  36, 97, 100
College Librarians
  continuing education needs, 149
  (*see also* Continuing education for
    librarians)
Columbia University, School of
  Library Economy, 87
Commission on a National Plan for
  Library Education
  Joint Committee on Library Educa-
    tion, 120
Congress for Change, 101, 121, 122,
  123,
Continuing education for librarians,
  145–61
  Historical review, 147–50
  media centers, 149
  need for, 145–47
  practices of other disciplines, 146,
    147, 148
  research needs and proposals,
    151–61
    educational needs for professional
      librarians, 146, 148, 151–53
    evaluation of internship and
      trainee programs, 160–61
    improving library school/ prac-
      ticing librarian relationships,
      159–60
    information exchange, 156–57
    librarians' part in community,
      161–62
    model programs, 154–56, 157–58
    motivational factors, 153–54
    use of media, 158–59
*Continuing Education for Librarians—
  Conferences, Workshops, and Short
  Courses,* 148

Core curriculum (*see* Library schools)
Council of Library and Information
  Work Education, 122
Council of National Library Associa-
  tions, 118
Council on Social Work Education, 44
Curriculum planning (*see* Library
  schools)

Delphi Technique, 187–99, 200–21
  early studies, 190
  educational studies, 197–98
  error reduction techniques, 194–97
    (*see also* experimental studies of
      methodology)
    feedback, 195
    self ratings, 196
  evaluation studies, 192
  experimental studies of methodology,
    192–97
    convergence patterns, 193
    reliability, 193
    response distribution form, 193
    sex differences, 193
  feedback (*see* error reduction
    techniques, methodology)
  goals, 188
  library and information science
    studies, 197–98
  methodology, 188–90
    bandwagon effect, avoidance, 189
    feedback, 189, 190
    questionnaire, 189
    researchers, 188, 189
    respondents, 188, 189
    statistics, 189
    survey research, 190
  respondents, 188, 189, 202
  social technology, 190, 191
  technology prediction studies, 198
  time prediction studies, 191

Education
  general vs. specialized, 31–48, 87, 95
  studies on, 35–37
*Education and Manpower for Librar-
  ianship* (1968), 134, 140
Education reform
  "Great Man" theory, 13
Educational theory
  contributions, 25
*Empirical Test of The Validity of the
  Core Concept in Preparation of
  University Librarians* (1967), 31
Enoch Pratt Free Library, 19

Federal librarians
  continuing education needs, 149

High John project, 175–76
Higher Education Media Study, 65, 66
    purposes, 75

Illinois Library Conference, 107
Information science
    (*see also* Library automation)
    computers, 51, 52
    curricula, 51, 53, 55, 57–81, 59
        choice of alternatives, 59–60
    definition, 49–50
    education for, 32, 34, 40
    in relation to librarianship, 51–53
    research projects
        behavioral objectives, 62
        indexing and indexes, 60–62
        teaching aids, 63
        teaching techniques, 62
    students
        essential background knowledge, 54–55
    systems analysis, 52
    teachers
        essential background knowledge, 55
    teaching methods, 54, 56, 58
Institute for Library School Administrators, 103
International Conference on Education for Scientific Information Work (1967), 34
Instructional media, 65–83
    audio tapes, 68
    computer-assisted instruction, 69–70, 79
    higher education, 75
    library education, 71–72, 76–78
        experimental instruction, 78–79
    motion picture films, 67–68
    multi-media facilities, 70
    need for administrative support, 72–73, 78, 81
    non-print materials, 75
    overhead projection transparencies, 70
    programmed instruction, 68
    research proposals, 82, 83
    simulation, 72
    teaching, 65–66, 78
    tele-lectures, 71
    television, 66–67
Isabel Nichol Lectures, 97

Job analysis (*see* Librarians)
Joint Committee on Library Work as a Career, 119

Journal of Education for Librarianship, 90

LEEP (*see* Library Education Experimental Project)
Learning systems, 66
    (*see also* Instructional media)
Librarians
    certification, 117, 118, 119, 120, 122, 126
        need for national board, 117
        practices in other professions, 128
        relationship to accreditation of library schools, 124
        state responsibility, 119
    duties and responsibilities, 112, 131–32, 135–36
    education, 133–34
        clerical vs. professional training, 133
        methods, 137
        on the job, 33, 133
    job analysis, 11–12, 35, 36–37
    job satisfaction, 132
    job success, 107, 110
    manpower problems, 148
    need for new skills, 130, 134, 136, 152–53
    recruitment, 119, 121, 123
        evaluation of techniques of professional associations, 127
        from minority groups, 121
        needs, 125, 127
    salaries, 132–33
Librarianship
    careers, 123
    historical review, 87
    professional leadership, 109
Libraries
    as recruiting agencies, 118
    community use, 175–79
        by children, 178–79
        by students, 177
        by underprivileged, 175–76
        non-user problems, 174
    cost of services, 180
    staffing problems, 130–44
        manpower needs, 131, 133, 135–36, 140–42
        research needs and proposals, 138–42
        training for management, 138–39
        training for supervision, 138–39
Library automation, 49
Library consultants, state, 36
Library education
    doctoral degree, 19–20, 41
    faculty-student ratio, 81

history, 12
influence of media, 72
in-service training
    media, 72, 78
master's degree, 15
national plan, 18, 120
objectives, 9, 14–15
quality, 22
related to other disciplines, 26
research, 2, 3, 9
sixth-year program, 21, 33, 36, 78, 149
Library Education Experimental
    Project (LEEP), 54, 79
Library role in the community, 173–84
    research methods, 182–83
    research needs and proposals
        service to adults, 177
        service to central city, 180
        service to children, 178–79
        service to the community, 174
        service to industry, 177
        service to the non-user, 174
        service priorities and cost effectiveness, 175, 181
        service to the underprivileged, 175–76
Library school administration research
    needs, 86
    administrative organization, 88
    curriculum planning, 95
    facilities, 92
    faculty preparation, 93
    faculty recruitment, 93
    faculty research stimulation, 97
    financial assistance, 95
    foreign students, problems, 95
    funding, 98
    placement services, 95
    predicting student success, 95
    publications of library schools,
        nature and quality, 98
    research center programs, 96
    student activism, 89
Library school faculties, 100–15
    academic background, 103
    accreditation of school, 104
    evaluation, 111
    historical review, 102–105
    leadership, 109
    part-time, 103, 108
    recruitment, 92–93, 102–103, 108,
        111, 117
    research needs and proposals, 112–13
    status and privileges, 109

student evaluation, 105
training in teaching, 104
Library school libraries, 91
Library school students, 100–15
    career choice, 106
    characteristics, 106, 107–108
    composite description, 105
    evaluation, 107, 111
    library experience, 109
    library school achievement, 105
    minority groups, 109
    part-time, 109
    participation in decision-making, 89,
        101, 104
    professional preparation and jobs,
        107
    recruitment and admission, 26,
        93–94, 109–10, 117
    research needs and proposals, 112–13
    research sensitivity, 107
Library schools
    accreditation, 117, 118, 119, 122,
        124
        evaluation methods, 111
        standards, 103
    administrative performance, 23
    autonomy, 88–89
    coordinated research program, 23
    core curriculum, 17–18, 31, 32, 34,
        36, 39, 42
    curricula
        electives, 34, 39, 107
        inclusion of instructional media,
            71–72
        innovative courses, 73–75
        planning, 95
        relation to education efficiency, 74
        relation to educational quality, 74,
            77
        relation to individualization, 74–75
        relation to interdisciplinary
            studies, 74
        relation to social change, 74
        studies, 13–14, 16, 19, 21, 31,
            37–38
    facility needs, 23, 90–92
    faculty
        qualifications, 26, 72
        size, 23
    funds, 98
    in-service training responsibilities,
        142
    placement services, 93, 94–95
    programmed learning, 137
    publications, 97–98

recruitment of faculty and students, 26, 117
relationship to certification of librarians, 119, 124
relevance of programs to community needs, 174–75
research on scope and organization, 127
standards, 117–18, 120, 121
teaching methods
  "donkey" courses (excessive detail), 73
  "elephant" courses (large classes), 73
training for supervision and management, 138–40
use of media, 71–72, 76–77
  (*See also* Instructional media)
Library technicians, 131, 133, 134–35, 136–37, 140–42
as reference librarians, 136
Library's Public, The, 175

Manpower Project, University of Maryland, 22, 113, 135–36, 138, 148
Maryland, University of, School of Librarianship and Information Science
manpower requirements project, 22, 113, 135–36, 138, 148
Medical Library Association, 119, 122
certification of librarians, 128

National Advisory Commission on Libraries, 182, 183–84
National Education Association (NEA)
Department of Audio-Visual Instruction, 75
National Medical Audio-Visual Center, 76
Nelson Associates study (1969), 180

Planning Academic and Research Library Building, 90
Post-master's degree (*see* Sixth-year program)
Princeton Conference (1948), 118, 123
Professional associations, 122
attitudes toward library education problems, 122
program coordination, 127
recruitment programs, 125
relations with each other, 116–17
relations with library schools, 116–17
research needs and proposals:
  accreditation of schools, 127, 128

certification of librarians, 128
duplication of programs, 127
personnel needs in libraries, 127
recruitment, 127
roles in library education, 124
Public librarians
skills needed, 136
Public libraries
effectiveness, 174–78, 180–81, 182
Public Library Inquiry, 15, 16, 102, 119
Publications of library schools, 97–98

Race relations
public library's role, 181
Reference librarians
training in relation to successful techniques, 136
Research centers, 96–97
Research in library education, 35, 39–44
generals vs. specialized library education
  curriculum structure, 39, 42
  definition of terms, 39
  interdisciplinary studies, 42
  internship, 42
  leadership development, 43
  levels of specialization, 41
  manpower studies, 43
  methods, 44
  mobility and change, 43
  role of electives, 40
  standards development, 40, 41
Research needs, prediction procedures
Delphi questionnaire
  development, 200–202
  subjects, 202
  Round I, 202–205
  Round II, 205–208
  statistical analyses, 204, 205, 207, 208, 209, 212, 214
Research needs, prediction results
  Priority I, 216
  Priority II, 216–17
  Priority III, 217
  Priority IV, 219–20
  Priority V, 220–21

School librarians, 32, 135
continuing education needs, 149
research programs, 38, 40
state certification, 38
School libraries
effectiveness, 179
Sixth-year program, 21, 33, 36, 78, 149
Special Libraries Association, 119, 120, 122

Specialization
  (*see also* Library education)
  areas, 33–34
  definitions, 39
  point in program, 34
  type of library or type of clientele,
    34, 38
State Library Consultant at Work
  (1965), 36
System Development Corporation, 137

Television
  (*see also* Instructional media)
  effect on reading, 178
Training
  (*see also* Library education)
  on the job, 33, 133

Training and Development Handbook
  (1967), 137
*Training Needs for Librarians Doing
  Adult Education Work* (1955), 41

Undergraduate preparation, 38, 40
U.S. Office of Education, 120
  Bureau of Higher Education, 65
  grants to library schools, 96
  statistical survey, 99

Western Reserve University, 120
  foundation course, 18
Williamson report (1923), 11, 87, 102,
  105
Wilson (H.W.) Foundation, 18
Windsor Lectures in Librarianship, 97
Women in librarianship, 133

Index of Names

Aceto, V. 113
Adelson, M. 162 *ref.*
Alderman, E. 165 *ref.*
Allen, L. A. 160 *ref.*
Alvarez, R. S. 147, 148, 162 *ref.*
Anderson, F. 154, 162 *ref.*
Andrews, K. R. 156, 162 *ref.*
Armsby, H. H. 44, 45 *ref.*
Asheim, L. E. xi, 17, 18, 27 *ref.*, 34, 36, 39, 41, 43, 45 *ref.*, 50, 51, 53, 63 *ref.*, 116, 121, 123, 124, 125, 128, 128 *ref.*, 134, 138, 140, 142 *ref.*, 162 *ref.*
Ayers, S. F. 161, 162 *ref.*

Baechtold, M. 78, 83 *ref.*
Baillie, G. S. 107, 113 *ref.*
Banfield, E. C. 181–82
Baskin, S. 80, 83 *ref.*
Batty, C. D. 54, 63 *ref.*
Beals, R. A. 10, 17, 27 *ref.*
Bentley, B. 161, 162 *ref.*
Berelson, B. R. 15, 17, 22, 27 *ref.*, 45 *ref.*, 47 *ref.*, 114 *ref.*, 174, 175, 184 *ref.*
Bishop, W. W. 89
Bittel, L. R. 143 *ref.*
Bjerrum, C. A. 197, 198, 199 *ref.*
Bloom, B. S. 25, 27 *ref.*
Blough, L. E. 45 *ref.*
Boag, W. R. 163 *ref.*
Boaz, M. 107, 114 *ref.*, 148, 163 *ref.*
Boehm, W. W. 44, 45 *ref.*

Boelke, J. H. 140, 143 *ref.*
Bone, L. E. 28 *ref.*, 29 *ref.*, 99 *ref.*, 104, 114 *ref.*, 129 *ref.*
Bradshaw, F. R. 174, 184 *ref.*
Brault, N. xiv
Briggs, L. J. 159, 163 *ref.*
Brodman, E. 161, 163 *ref.*
Brown, B. B. 193, 199 *ref.*
Brown, C. A. 143 *ref.*, 148, 149, 165 *ref.*
Brown, G. W. 189, 199 *ref.*
Brown, J. W. 75, 83 *ref.*, 172 *ref.*
Bruner, J. S. 25, 27 *ref.*
Brunner, E. DeS. 163 *ref.*
Bryan, A. I. 28 *ref.*, 46 *ref.*, 102, 114 *ref.*, 119, 128 *ref.*
Bundy, M. L. xi, 122, 128 *ref.*, 144 *ref.*, 148, 163 *ref.*, 172 *ref.*
Bunge, C. A. 35, 45 *ref.*, 136, 143 *ref.*
Burchard, J. E. 182
Butler, G. E. 38, 45 *ref.*
Butler, P. 190, 199 *ref.*

Campbell, R. M. 196, 199 *ref.*
Carl, H. A. xi
Carmichael, O. C. 22, 27 *ref.*
Carnovsky, L. xi, 37, 41, 45 *ref.*, 104, 114 *ref.*, 121, 128, 128 *ref.*, 180, 183, 184 *ref.*
Carpenter, D. R. 74, 83 *ref.*
Carter, L. F. 74, 83 *ref.*
Case, R. N. 135, 140, 143 *ref.*, 149, 163 *ref.*
Casswell, H. 31 *ref.*

Charters, W. W. 12, 17, 19, 28 *ref.*, 35, 45 *ref.*
Clapp, V. W. viii
Clayton, H. 107, 114 *ref.*
Clegg, D. O. 154, 163 *ref.*
Coates, R. H. 168 *ref.*
Cochran, S. 199 *ref.*
Cohen, D. 163 *ref.*
Cohen, L. 34, 45 *ref.*
Cohen, M. L. 34, 45 *ref.*
Conant, R. W. 182, 184 *ref.*
Cook, D. L. 163 *ref.*
Cooper, R. M. 73, 83 *ref.*
Corson, J. J. 152, 164 *ref.*
Coughlin, V. L. 65, 77, 83 *ref.*, 104, 114 *ref.*
Craig, R. L. 143 *ref.*
Craven, K. 34, 45 *ref.*
Cross, K. P. 164 *ref.*
Cuadra, C. A. 164 *ref.*
Culbertson, J. A. 164 *ref.*
Cummings, R. J. 164 *ref.*
Cylke, F. K. xiv, 2

Dalkey, M. C. 193, 194, 199 *ref.*
Dalton, J. xiii
Daniel, E. xii *ref.*
Danton, J. P. 20, 28 *ref.*, 33, 40, 45 *ref.*, 100, 102, 105, 114 *ref.*, 118, 126, 128 *ref.*, 133, 134, 140, 143 *ref.*, 148, 164 *ref.*
Darling, R. L. 34, 45 *ref.*, 131, 143 *ref.*
Davies, D. 164 *ref.*
Davis, R. A. 20, 28 *ref.*, 164 *ref.*
Dearing, G. B. 103–104, 114 *ref.*
Dewey, J. 26
Dewey, M. 16, 87
Dietrich, J. E. 74, 83 *ref.*
Dill, W. R. 164 *ref.*
Dillman, B. R. 162, 164 *ref.*
Donaldson, M. J. 104, 114 *ref.*
Douglass, R. R. 106, 114 *ref.*, 147, 164 *ref.*
Downs, R. B. 99 *ref.*
Drennan, H. T. 131, 132, 138, 140, 143 *ref.*, 147, 164 *ref.*
Dryer, B. V. 151, 164 *ref.*
Dubin, S. S. 151, 153, 154, 163 *ref.*, 164 *ref.*, 165 *ref.*
Duncan, M. 148, 165 *ref.*
Dunkin, P. S. 73, 83 *ref.*, 104, 114 *ref.*

Egan, M. E. 17, 18, 28 *ref.*
Eliot, C. W. 13, 26
Ennis, P. H. 10, 28 *ref.*
Ersted, R. 38, 45 *ref.*
Evans, R. K. 165 *ref.*

Faegre, C. L. 159, 165 *ref.*
Fargo, L. 12
Fenwick, S. I. 38, 46 *ref.*
Filderman, M. 115 *ref.*
Fine, J. V. A. 188, 199 *ref.*
Fitch, V. E. 165 *ref.*
Flexner, J. M. 12
Focke, H. N. xi, 18, 28 *ref.*
Fox, A. M. 78
Frarey, C. J. 132, 143 *ref.*
Frenckner, T. P. 165 *ref.*
Fryden, F. N. 21, 28 *ref.*, 33, 40, 46 *ref.*, 148, 165 *ref.*, 175, 184 *ref.*

Gagne, R. M. 159, 165 *ref.*
Galvin, T. J. 18, 28 *ref.*, 122, 129 *ref.*
Gardner, J. W. 145, 165 *ref.*
Garrison, G. G. xiii, 48 *ref.*
Garrison, L. N. 154, 165 *ref.*
Gaver, M. 165 *ref.*
Ginsburg, E. 133, 143 *ref.*, 148, 149, 165 *ref.*
Goheen, R. F. 165 *ref.*
Goldstein, H. 71, 76, 83 *ref.*, 107, 114 *ref.*, 115 *ref.*, 166 *ref.*
Gomersall, E. R. 166 *ref.*
Graves, J. xiv
Gull, C. D. 54, 55, 56, 63 *ref.*

Hall, A. C. 19, 28 *ref.*, 35, 37, 44, 46 *ref.*, 136, 140, 143 *ref.*
Hamreus, D. G. 159, 166 *ref.*
Hanyas, B. 166 *ref.*
Harlow, N. 20, 28 *ref.*, 140, 143 *ref.*
Harmon, G. 107, 114 *ref.*
Harrison, J. C. 20, 28 *ref.*
Harvey, J. F. 104, 114 *ref.*, 147, 166 *ref.*
Hatch, L. 34, 46 *ref.*
Hayes, R. M. xiv, 51, 52, 54, 55, 63 *ref.*
Heckman, D. M. 80, 84 *ref.*
Heilprin, L. B. 28 *ref.*, 29 *ref.*, 34, 46 *ref.*
Helmer, O. 189, 190, 191, 197, 198, 199 *ref.*
Henderson, A. 101, 114 *ref.*
Henne, F. 34, 46 *ref.*
Herrick, V. E. 25, 28 *ref.*
Herzberg, F. 154, 166 *ref.*
Hewitt, G. B. 151, 166 *ref.*
Himmelweit, H. T. 178, 184 *ref.*
Hines, T. C. 53, 63 *ref.*
Hintz, C. 121, 129 *ref.*
Holton, G. 166 *ref.*
Holzbauer, H. 166 *ref.*
Honey, J. C. 166 *ref.*
Honley, P. xiv

Horn, A. H. xiv
Horn, F. H. 166 *ref.*
Hoselitz, B. F. 17, 28 *ref.*
Houle, C. O. 148, 166 *ref.*
Howe, H. E. 105, 114 *ref.*
Humphrey, A. J. 79
Hunt, D. H. 121, 129 *ref.*
Hutchins, R. M. 13, 26

Isbell, M. D. xi

Jackson, E. 32, 34, 46 *ref.*
Janke, L. H. 34, 46 *ref.*
Jencks, C. 23, 25, 26, 28 *ref.*
Jerkedal, A. 154, 166 *ref.*
Jesse, W. H. 148, 166 *ref.*
Johnson, A. S. 11

Kaplan, A. 23–24, 28 *ref.*
Katz, S. M. 166 *ref.*
Kauffman, J. F. 115 *ref.*
Kennan, T. A. 199 *ref.*
Kennedy, M. 148, 167 *ref.*
Kenny, L. A. 161, 167 *ref.*
Kerr, C. 26
King, M. xiv
Klassen, R. 167 *ref.*
Klempner, I. M. xiii, 146, 167 *ref.*
Knapp, P. B. xii
Knezevich, S. J. 167 *ref.*
Knox, A. B. 167 *ref.*, 168 *ref.*
Knox, M. E. 167 *ref.*
Kochen, M. 19, 28 *ref.*
Kortendick, J. J. xiii, 2, 148, 149,
   167 *ref.*
Krathwell, D. R. 25, 28 *ref.*
Kroll, N. 45 *ref.*
Kurmey, W. J. 52, 63 *ref.*

Lancour, A. H. xi, 116, 118, 119, 123,
   129 *ref.*
Land, R. B. 91, 99 *ref.*
Lazarus, C. Y. 162, 167 *ref.*
Leigh, R. D. viii, xi, 15, 16, 19, 28 *ref.*,
   34, 35, 46 *ref.*, 102–103, 106, 115 *ref.*,
   119, 129 *ref.*
Leppman, K. 165 *ref.*
Levy, M. J. 25, 28 *ref.*
Libbey, M. H. 122, 129 *ref.*
Lieberman, I. 34, 46 *ref.*, 81, 84 *ref.*
Liesener, J. W. 36–37, 46 *ref.*
Likert, R. 153, 168 *ref.*
Long, M. A. 35, 36, 46 *ref.*, 109,
   115 *ref.*
Lorenz, J. G. xi, 146, 168 *ref.*
Lowrey, A. M. 143 *ref.*
Lowrie, J. E. 33, 41, 46–47 *ref.*

McConnell, T. R. 168 *ref.*
McCreedy, *Sr.*, L. 106, 115 *ref.*
McCrossan, J. A. 35, 47 *ref.*, 115 *ref.*,
   136, 143 *ref.*
Machlup, S. 27, 28 *ref.*
McJenkin, V. 148, 168 *ref.*
McKeachie, W. J. 153, 168 *ref.*
McMahon, E. E. 151, 168 *ref.*
Mager, R. F. 168 *ref.*
Mahar, M. H. 46 *ref.*
Mann, M. 12
Marlow, H. L. 165 *ref.*
Maron, M. E. 79, 84 *ref.*
Martin, L. A. x–xi, xii *ref.*, 34–35,
   47 *ref.*, 177, 184 *ref.*
Mausner, B. 166 *ref.*
Mayhew, L. B. 79, 84 *ref.*
Mee, J. 168 *ref.*, 182
Meredith, J. C. 79
Merrell, V. D. 168 *ref.*
Merritt, LeR. 105, 114 *ref.*
Metcalf, K. D. 14, 28 *ref.*, 90, 99 *ref.*
Meyerson, M. 26
Milam, C. 12
Miller, J. G. 199 *ref.*
Miller, R. I. 168 *ref.*
Mitchell, A. E. 166 *ref.*
Mohrhardt, F. 2
Monroe, M. E. 47 *ref.*, 146, 168 *ref.*
Moon, E. E. 168 *ref.*, 175, 184 *ref.*
Morrison, P. D. 147, 168 *ref.*
Morton, F. F. 103, 115 *ref.*
Mosher, F. 159, 168 *ref.*
Mowrer, O. H. 25, 29 *ref.*
Mullen, E. D. xi
Muller, R. 34, 47 *ref.*
Munn, R. 14, 20, 29 *ref.*, 34, 47 *ref.*,
   105, 115 *ref.*, 117, 129 *ref.*
Munthe, W. 14, 29 *ref.*
Myer, R. S. 166 *ref.*

Nakata, Y. I. 169 *ref.*
Newman, J. H. 26
Nichol, I. 35, 47 *ref.*
Noonan, F. S. 169 *ref.*

O'Connor, J. 54, 64 *ref.*
Odiorne, G. S. 154, 169 *ref.*
O'Donnell, C. J. 169 *ref.*
Ofiesch, G. D. 159, 169 *ref.*
Ortega y Gasset, J. 26
Osborn, A. D. 14, 20, 28 *ref.*, 29 *ref.*

Papier, L. S. xiv
Parr, M. Y. 115 *ref.*
Paul, R. S. 164 *ref.*
Pfeiffer, J. 169 *ref.*

Pierce, H. F. 14, 29 *ref.*
Poorman, L. E. 169 *ref.*
Porter, E. H. 169 *ref.*
Postell, W. D. 161, 169 *ref.*
Proctor, V. 122, 129 *ref.*

Randall, M. H. 104–105, 115 *ref.*
Randall, R. L. 169 *ref.*
Ranta, R. R. 169 *ref.*
Rawski, C. H. 23, 29 *ref.*
Reagan, A. L. 23, 29 *ref.*, 106, 115 *ref.*
Reece, E. J. 13–14, 29 *ref.*, 33, 34–35,
    47 *ref.*, 134, 136, 140, 143 *ref.*
Reed, S. R. 30 *ref.*, 47 *ref.*, 76, 114 *ref.*,
    115 *ref.*, 116, 117 *ref.*, 129 *ref.*, 131,
    143 *ref.*, 148, 169 *ref.*
Rees, A. M. xiii, 21–26, 53, 54, 64 *ref.*,
    170 *ref.*
Reilly, K. D. xiv, 187, 198, 199 *ref.*,
    200
Reisman, A. 170 *ref.*
Rescher, N. 199 *ref.*
Riesman, D. 23, 25, 26, 28 *ref.*
Ripley, K. J. 170 *ref.*
Robert, H. 168 *ref.*
Roberts, T. J. 170 *ref.*
Rockwood, R. 106–107, 115 *ref.*
Rogers, E. M. 74, 84 *ref.*
Rosenstein, R. S. 143 *ref.*
Rosenthal, J. A. 136, 143 *ref.*
Rothstein, S. 32, 46 *ref.*, 92, 99 *ref.*,
    104, 115 *ref.*, 121, 129 *ref.*, 146,
    170 *ref.*
Russell, J. D. 14, 28 *ref.*
Rutherford, F. J. 166 *ref.*
Ryan, D. E. 35, 47 *ref.*
Ryans, D. G. 170 *ref.*

Saracevic, T. 54, 64 *ref.*
Schick, F. L. xi, xii, xii *ref.*, 23, 29 *ref.*,
    52, 64 *ref.*, 98, 99 *ref.*, 120, 129 *ref.*
Schiller, A. R. 132, 138, 140, 143 *ref.*,
    147, 170 *ref.*
Schramm, W. 170 *ref.*
Shaffer, K. R. 18, 29 *ref.*
Shank, R. 148, 170 *ref.*
Shera, J. H. 9, 17, 18, 24, 26, 28 *ref.*,
    29 *ref.*, 33, 47 *ref.*
Shores, L. 107–108, 115 *ref.*
Simpson, D. W. 169 *ref.*
Simpson, R. H. 107, 115 *ref.*
Slamecka, V. xiii
Slavens, T. P. 54, 64 *ref.*
Sloane, M. N. 170 *ref.*
Smith, R. G. 154, 171 *ref.*
Soffen, J. 115 *ref.*

Stallman, E. L. 121, 129 *ref.*, 171 *ref.*
Stephens, I. R. 183, 184 *ref.*
Stevenson, G. T. 148, 171 *ref.*
Stolurow, L. M. 171 *ref.*
Stone, C. W. 149, 171 *ref.*
Stone, E. W. 148, 151, 154, 171 *ref.*
Stone, M. H. 161, 171 *ref.*
Stuart, W. J. 19, 29 *ref.*
Suppes, P. 171 *ref.*
Swank, R. C. 21, 30 *ref.*, 32–33, 41,
    47 *ref.*, 53, 64 *ref.*, 171 *ref.*
Swanson, H. B. 154, 171 *ref.*
Synderman, B. 166 *ref.*

Taba, H. 25, 30 *ref.*
Tauber, M. F. viii, x, xii *ref.*, 13,
    30 *ref.*, 183, 184 *ref.*
Taylor, E. B. 151, 171 *ref.*
Taylor, R. S. 34, 47, 51, 64 *ref.*
Thornton, J. W. 65, 66, 69, 75, 84 *ref.*,
    171 *ref.*
Tishler, M. 26, 30 *ref.*
Totter, H. L. 72, 76–77, 84 *ref.*
Tough, A. M. 171 *ref.*
Trow, W. C. 171 *ref.*
Truman, D. B. 40, 47 *ref.*
Tyler, R. W. 25, 30 *ref.*

Vainstein, R. 33, 48 *ref.*
Vann, S. K. 11, 30 *ref.*

Walker, R. D. 20, 30 *ref.*, 137, 143,
    171 *ref.*
Wallace, E. M. 137, 143 *ref.*, 158,
    171 *ref.*
Walrath, D. C. 171 *ref.*
Waples, D. 27 *ref.*, 174, 184 *ref.*
Warncke, R. 120, 129 *ref.*
Wasserman, P. ix–x, xii *ref.*, 19,
    144 *ref.*
Watson, F. G. 166 *ref.*
Welch, W. W. 172 *ref.*
Wheeler, J. L. 15–16, 30 *ref.*, 102, 105,
    115 *ref.*, 118, 129 *ref.*
White, A. D. 13
White, C. M. 14, 32, 43 *ref.*
White, R. 22, 113
Whitehead, A. N. 26
Wight, E. A. 35, 48 *ref.*, 122, 129 *ref.*
Williamson, C. C. 11, 30 *ref.*, 33, 35,
    48 *ref.*, 87, 99 *ref.*, 102, 105, 115 *ref.*,
    116, 117, 123, 129 *ref.*, 133, 140,
    144 *ref.*
Wilson, C. I. 161, 171 *ref.*
Wilson, E. H. 102, 105, 115 *ref.*
Wilson, J. H. 187, 199 *ref.*

Wilson, L. R. 13, 14, 15, 30 *ref.*
Winger, H. W. 34, 48 *ref.*
Winthrop, H. 31 *ref.*

Woodworth, M. L. 149, 171 *ref.*
Works, G. A. 12
Wriston, H. M. 26

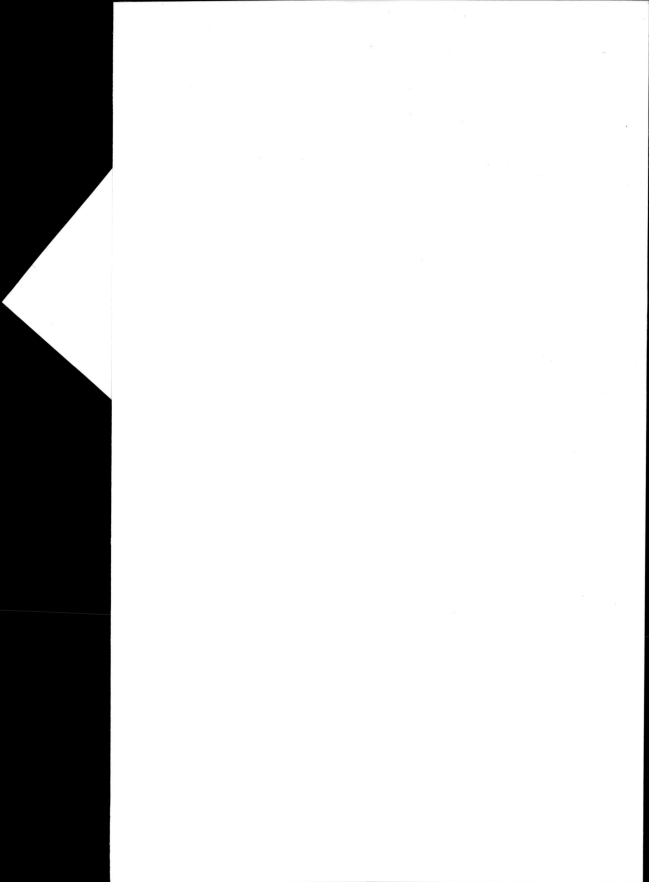

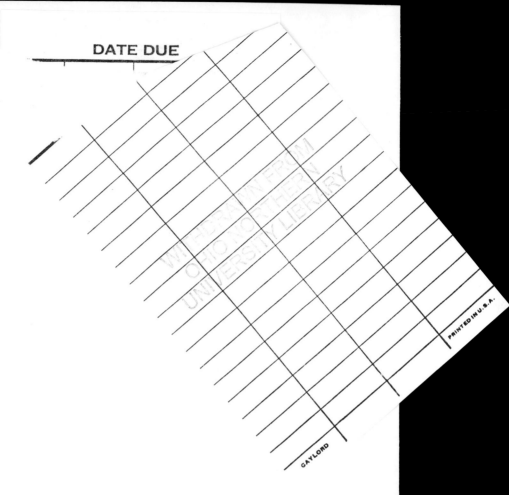